To my mother, Lillian Kumock Cohen.
    RFC

To my parents, Sylvia Sondak and Ben Miller,
and to my daughter, Ariana Jessica Miller.
    JLM

Credits

Contents

Welcome to NorthStar

Second Edition

NorthStar leads the way in integrated skills series. The Second Edition remains an innovative, five-level series written for students with academic as well as personal language goals. Each unit of the thematically linked Reading and Writing strand and Listening and Speaking strand explores intellectually challenging, contemporary themes to stimulate critical thinking skills while building language competence.

Four easy to follow sections—Focus on the Topic, Focus on Reading/Focus on Listening, Focus on Vocabulary, and Focus on Writing/Focus on Speaking— invite students to focus on the process of learning through **NorthStar**.

Thematically Based Units

NorthStar engages students by organizing language study thematically. Themes provide stimulating topics for reading, writing, listening, and speaking.

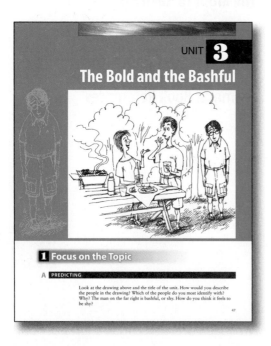

NORTHSTAR

READING AND WRITING

Advanced

SECOND EDITION

Robert F. Cohen
Judy L. Miller

Series Editors
Frances Boyd
Carol Numrich

NorthStar: Reading and Writing, Advanced, Second Edition

Pearson Education, 10 Bank Street, White Plains, NY 10606

Development director: Penny Laporte
Project manager: Debbie Sistino
Senior development editor: Paula H. Van Ells
Vice president, director of design and production: Rhea Banker
Executive managing editor: Linda Moser
Production coordinator: Melissa Leyva
Senior production editor: Kathleen Silloway
Production editor: Alice Vigliani
Director of manufacturing: Patrice Fraccio
Senior manufacturing buyer: Dave Dickey
Photo research: Aerin Csigay
Cover design: Rhea Banker
Cover art: Detail of Der Rhein bei Duisburg, 1937, 145(R 5) Rhine near
    Duisburg 19 × 27.5 cm; water-based on cardboard; The Metropolitan
    Museum of Art, N.Y. The Berggruen Klee Collection, 1984.
    (1984.315.56) Photograph © 1985 The Metropolitan Museum of Art.
    © 2003 Artists Rights Society (ARS), New York / VG Bild-Kunst, Bonn
Text design: Quorum Creative Services
Text composition: ElectraGraphics, Inc.
Text font: 11/13 Sabon
Text art: Duśan Petricic
Text credits: see page iv
Photo credits: see page iv

Der Rhein bei Duisburg
Paul Klee

Library of Congress Cataloging-in-Publication Data

Cohen, Robert F.
   NorthStar. Reading and writing, advanced/Robert F. Cohen,
Judy L. Miller.—2nd ed.
       p. cm.
     Includes index.
     1. English language—Textbooks for foreign speakers. 2. English
language—Rhetoric—Problems, exercises, etc. 3. Reading
comprehension—Problems, exercises, etc. 4. Report writing—Problems,
exercises, etc. I. Title: Reading and writing, advanced. II. Miller, Judy L.
III. Title.

PE1128.C684 2004
428.6'4–dc21

2003044732

ISBN: 0-201-75575-0 (Student Book)
          0-13-184673-6 (Student Book with Audio CDs)

Printed in the United States of America
10—CRK—09 08
5 6 7 8 9 10—CRK—09 08 07

Extensive Support to Build Skills for Academic Success

Creative activities help students develop language-learning strategies, such as predicting and identifying main ideas and details.

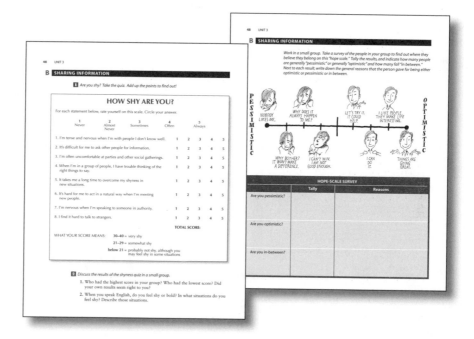

High-Interest Listening and Reading Selections

The two listening or reading selections in each unit present contrasting viewpoints to enrich students' understanding of the content while building language skills.

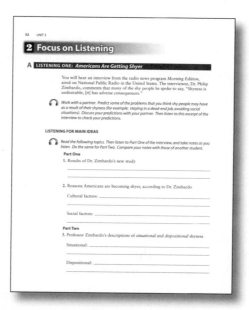

Critical Thinking Skill Development

Critical thinking skills, such as synthesizing information or reacting to the different viewpoints in the two reading or listening selections, are practiced throughout each unit, making language learning meaningful.

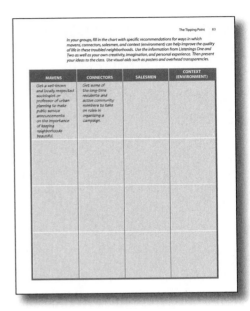

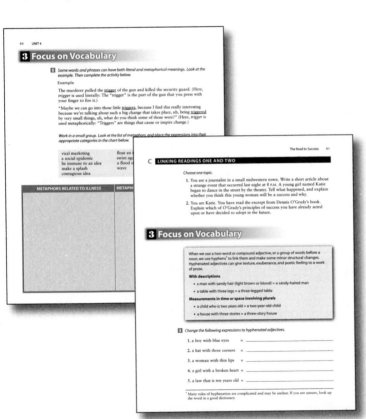

Extensive Vocabulary Practice

Students are introduced to key, contextualized vocabulary to help them comprehend the listening and reading selections. They also learn idioms, collocations, and word forms to help them explore, review, play with, and expand their spoken and written expression.

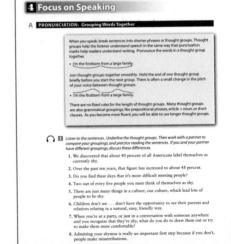

Powerful Pronunciation Practice

A carefully designed pronunciation syllabus in the Listening and Speaking strand focuses on topics such as stress, rhythm, and intonation. Theme-based pronunciation practice reinforces the vocabulary and content of the unit.

Content-Rich Grammar Practice

Each thematic unit integrates the study of grammar with related vocabulary and cultural information. The grammatical structures are drawn from the listening or reading selections and offer an opportunity for students to develop accuracy in speaking or writing about the topic.

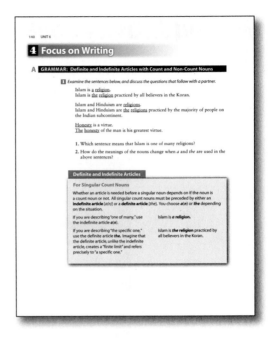

Extensive Opportunity for Discussion and Writing

Challenging and imaginative speaking activities, writing topics, and research assignments allow students to apply the language, grammar, style, and content they've learned.

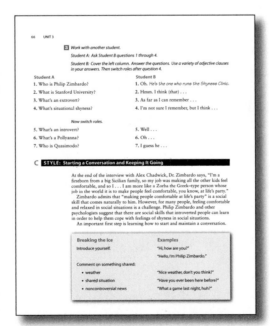

Writing Activity Book

The companion *Writing Activity Book* leads students through the writing process with engaging writing assignments. Skills and vocabulary from **NorthStar: Reading and Writing,** are reviewed and expanded as students learn the process of prewriting, organizing, revising, and editing.

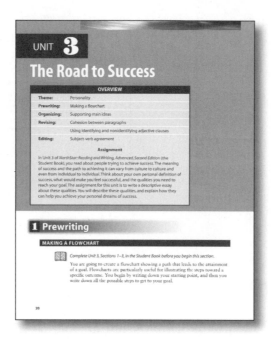
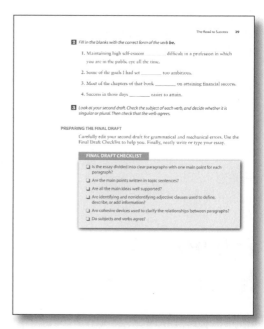

Audio Program

All the pronunciation, listening, and reading selections have been professionally recorded. The audio program includes audio CDs as well as audio cassettes.

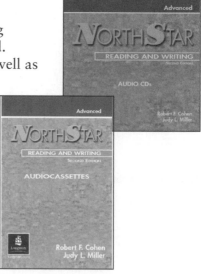

Teacher's Manual with Achievement Tests

Each book in the series has an accompanying *Teacher's Manual* with step-by-step teaching suggestions, time guidelines, and expansion activities. Also included in each *Teacher's Manual* are reproducible unit-by-unit tests. The Listening and Speaking strand tests are recorded on CD and included in the *Teacher's Manual*. Packaged with each *Teacher's Manual* for the Reading and Writing strand is a TestGen CD-ROM that allows teachers to create and customize their own **NorthStar** tests. Answer Keys to both the Student Book and the Tests are included, along with a unit-by-unit word list of key vocabulary.

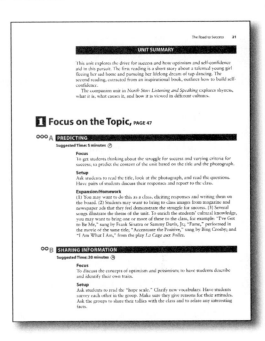

NorthStar Video Series

The *Northstar* video presents authentic, engaging segments from ABC broadcasts including *20/20, World News Tonight,* and *Primetime* as well as documentaries, cartoons, narratives, and interviews correlated to the themes in *Northstar, Second Edition,* containing two to five minute segments for each unit. Packaged with each video is a Video Guide with complete scripts, vocabulary for comprehension and background notes to enhance the accessability and enjoyment of the material. Worksheets for the video can be found on the *Northstar* Companion Website.

Companion Website

http://www.longman.com/northstar includes resources for students and teachers such as additional vocabulary activities, Web-based links and research, video worksheets, and correlations to state standards.

Scope and Sequence

Unit	Critical Thinking Skills	Reading Tasks
1 **Mickey's Team** Theme: Addiction Reading One: *Time in a Bottle* An autobiographical magazine article Reading Two: *Mick's Toughest Inning* A newspaper op-ed column	Support answers with evidence from the readings Infer information not explicit in the reading Hypothesize another's point of view Identify the logic of an argument Identify an author's biases Classify information	Preview vocabulary Make predictions Read for main ideas Read for details Order information according to a timeline Interpret a graph Research issues in organ transplants
2 **A Season in Utopia** Theme: Utopian Movements Reading One: *Early Life at Brook Farm and Concord* An historical account Reading Two: *Making Ends Meet* A book review	Recognize personal attitudes and values Infer word meaning from context Use a graphic organizer to categorize information Support answers with information from the text Interpret an author's tone and attitude Hypothesize another's point of view Propose solutions to contemporary problems	Preview vocabulary Make predictions Identify the historical setting of the reading Restate main facts in the reading Summarize main ideas Locate information in the text Relate an historical text to present-day issues Compare and contrast a common theme in divergent genres Research an American utopian society using multiple sources
3 **The Road to Success** Theme: Personality Reading One: *Gotta Dance* A short story Reading Two: *Keeping Your Confidence Up* An excerpt from a self-help book	Interpret a photograph Identify personality traits Identify assumptions through surveys Support answers with information from the text Analyze character and motivation in fiction Hypothesize information not explicit in the text Apply principles to real-life situations	Preview vocabulary Make predictions Summarize main ideas Read for details Locate information in the text Interpret a poem Identify connecting themes between texts
4 **Silent Spring** Theme: Trends Reading One: *A Fable for Tomorrow* A moral tale Reading Two: *The Story of Silent Spring* An essay	Identify and interpret trends Infer word meaning from context Examine imagery and symbolism in a fictional text Analyze author's purpose Hypothesize another's point of view Relate text to broader historical context	Make predictions Identify the historic context of a book Restate main ideas Recognize the organization of a text Identify cause and effect Research a trend

Writing Tasks	Vocabulary	Grammar
Develop the elements of character, technique, and theme in autobiographical writing Write a summary paragraph Write a personal letter Take notes on research Write a report summarizing data	Synonyms Context clues Word forms with suffixes	Past unreal conditionals
Develop thesis statements and introductory paragraphs Write a paragraph critique using new vocabulary Write statements of opinion using noun clauses Summarize research in a report	Synonyms Idioms Word forms	Noun clauses
Develop a paragraph with a topic sentence, illustration, and a conclusion Write short statements of advice Combine sentences using relative pronouns Write a short article Develop a "career ladder" Summarize an interview	Hyphenated adjectives Context clues Idioms	Identifying and nonidentifying adjective clauses
Write cause-and-effect paragraph and essay Develop a logical organizational pattern Write a paragraph analysis using new vocabulary Combine sentences using discourse connectors and adverb clauses Present research graphically in a poster	Word forms with prefixes and suffixes Context clues	Adverb clauses and discourse connectors to express cause and effect

Unit	Critical Thinking Skills	Reading Tasks
5 **What Is Lost in Translation?** Theme: Cross-cultural Insights Reading One: *Lost in Translation;* *The Struggle to Be an All-American Girl* Two autobiographical accounts Reading Two: *In One School, Many Sagas* A newspaper report	Recognize personal assumptions and biases Compare and contrast cultural customs Identify an author's point of view Infer characters' attitudes and feelings Hypothesize another's point of view	Preview vocabulary Predict content of the reading Read for main ideas Read for details Compare and contrast two readings Relate the text to personal experiences Synthesize information from three different texts Recognize the organization of a text
6 **The Landscape of Faith** Theme: Religion Reading One: *Peace Prevails* An interview Reading Two: *Religion* A definition essay	Compare religious backgrounds Infer word meaning from context Relate supporting details to main ideas Support answers with information from the text Hypothesize another's point of view Identify the purpose of a text Classify information	Make predictions Summarize main ideas Read for details Relate text to personal values Interpret a poem Research a world religion using multiple sources
7 **Going into Business** Theme: Business Reading One: From *Who Wants to Be an* *Entrepreneur?* A college magazine article Reading Two: *Coca Cola Thinks International* An excerpt from a business school textbook	Interpret a cartoon Assess personal traits Infer word meaning from context Infer information not explicit in the text Hypothesize another's point of view Analyze a case study Evaluate advantages and disadvantages	Preview vocabulary Read a limerick Make predictions Summarize main ideas Scan for supporting details Synthesize information from two texts
8 **When the Soldier Is a Woman ...** Theme: The Military Reading One: *Women at War* Personal letters Reading Two: *Asmara Journal: In Peace, Women* *Warriors Rank Low* A news report	Recognize personal values and assumptions Make generalizations Support opinions with information from the text Hypothesize another's point of view Compare and contrast soldiers' experiences Evaluate characters' motivation Relate broad themes to specific situations	Make predictions Identify main ideas Locate specific information in the text Summarize information Research military enrollment practices

Writing Tasks	Vocabulary	Grammar
Write a compare-and-contrast essay Write statements of comparison and contrast Develop a logical organizational pattern for comparison and contrast Write a personal letter Take notes in outline form Develop an outline Construct a dialogue using new vocabulary	Vocabulary classification Synonyms Word forms with suffixes	Adverb clauses of comparison and contrast
Write a definition essay Develop definitions Paraphrase quotations Write summary statements Write essay responses Write a report on research findings	Synonyms Context clues Analogies Word categorization	Definite and indefinite articles
Write an essay showing advantages and disadvantages Write persuasive statements Develop thesis statements Compose transitional sentences Write a questionnaire Summarize questionnaire data	Synonyms Context clues Word forms Idioms	Infinitives and gerunds
Write paragraph summaries Write a summary of divergent texts Write a personal letter Construct a dialogue Write an essay response Summarize research	Vocabulary categorization Word forms with suffixes Idioms	Direct and indirect speech

Unit	Critical Thinking Skills	Reading Tasks
9 **The Cellist of Sarajevo** Theme: The Arts Reading One: *The Cellist of Sarajevo* A magazine article Reading Two: *The Soloist* Fiction	Interpret a photograph Compare tastes and preferences in the arts Infer information not explicit in the text Compare and contrast two artists' careers Theorize characters' motivation Analyze descriptive language	Interpret quotations Make predictions Identify the main ideas Locate details in the text Identify similarities and differences in a text Recognize the organization of a text
10 **The Right to Read** Theme: First Amendment Issues Reading One: *Book Banning Must Be Stopped* An essay Reading Two: *Some Books That Have Been Banned from School Libraries* An annotated list	Identify personal assumptions Identify opinions through a survey Infer information not explicit in the reading Hypothesize another's point of view Develop a logical argument for and against an issue Analyze use of argumentative language	Make predictions Paraphrase main ideas Locate information in the text Restate arguments in the text Relate text to personal values Read a time line Research free-speech issues using multiple sources

Writing Tasks	Vocabulary	Grammar
Analyze descriptive language Write a descriptive paragraph Summarize the reading using new vocabulary Evaluate passive voice usage Write interview questions Summarize an interview	Synonyms Context clues Vocabulary categorization Participles as adjectives Antonyms Figurative language	Use of the passive voice
Write an argumentative essay Write short argumentative responses Write an argumentative letter Write an opinion statement Write a letter of response using new vocabulary Summarize research	Synonyms Context clues Word forms	Verb tense review

Acknowledgments

Our greatest debt is to Carol Numrich, whose expertise, optimism, and creative insight have guided us throughout this project. We are also grateful to Frances Boyd, whose expression of confidence in our work has been a constant source of encouragement.

In addition, we would like to thank Debbie Sistino for her coordination of this effort, Paula Van Ells for her meticulous work in the development phase of this edition, and Kathleen Silloway and Alice Vigliani for their contributions as production editors. We also wish to thank Allen Ascher and Penny Laporte for their continued support.

Finally, our heartfelt thanks go to our colleagues at the Department of Language and Cognition at Eugenio Maria de Hostos Community College and the American Language Program at Columbia University, and to our students, who are our inspiration.

Robert F. Cohen and *Judy L. Miller*

Reviewers

For the comments and insights they graciously offered to help shape the direction of the Second Edition of *Northstar*, the publisher would like to thank the following reviewers and institutions.

Lubie G. Alatriste, Lehman College; A. Morgan Andaluz, Leeward Community College; Chris Antonellis, Boston University CELOP; Christine Baez, Universidad de las Américas, Mexico City, Mexico; Betty Baron, Johnson County Community College; Rudy Besikof, University of California San Diego; Mary Black, Institute of North American Studies; Dorothy Buroh, University of California, San Diego; Kay Caldwell, Leeward Community College; Margarita Canales; Universidad Latinoamericana, Mexico City, Mexico; Jose Carvalho, University of Massachusetts Boston; Philip R. Condorelli, University of Massachusetts Boston; Pamela Couch, Boston University CELOP; Barbara F. Dingee, University of Massachusetts Boston; Jeanne M. Dunnet, Central Connecticut State University; Samuela Eckstut-Didier, Boston University CELOP; Patricia Hedden, Yonsei University; Hostos Community College; GEOS Language Institute; Jennifer M. Gerrity, University of Massachusetts Boston; Lis Jenkinson, Northern Virginia Community College; Glenna Jennings, University of California, San Diego; Diana Jones, Instituto Angloamericano, Mexico City, Mexico; Matt Kaeiser, Old Dominion University; Regina Kandraska, University of Massachusetts Boston; King Fahd University of Petroleum & Minerals; Chris Ko, Kyang Hee University; Charalambos Kollias, The Hellenic-American Union; Barbara Kruchin, Columbia University ALP; Language Training Institute; Jacqueline LoConde, Boston University CELOP; Mary Lynch, University of Massachusetts Boston; Julia Paranionova, Moscow State Pedagogical University; Pasadena City College; Pontifical Xavier University; Natalya Morozova, Moscow State Pedagogical University; Mary Carole Ramiowski, University of Seoul; Jon Robinson, University of Seoul; Michael Sagliano, Leeward Community College; Janet Shanks, Columbia University ALP; Eric Tejeda; PROULEX, Guadalajara, Mexico; Truman College; United Arab Emirates University; University of Minnesota; Karen Whitlow, Johnson County Community College

Mickey's Team

1 Focus on the Topic

A PREDICTING

Look at the photo of Mickey Mantle, a famous baseball player elected to the Baseball Hall of Fame. What do you already know about Mickey Mantle? What do you already know about the kinds of personal problems that famous people often have? Discuss your ideas with a partner.

1

B SHARING INFORMATION

Mickey Mantle credited his skill as a baseball player to the influence of one person. Think of all the people who have influenced your development. What did they contribute to your personality? Was their influence always positive? How old were you when their influence was felt?

Fill in the following chart. Then share your answers with a small group.

WHO INFLUENCED YOU?	HOW DID THIS PERSON INFLUENCE YOU?	HOW OLD WERE YOU?
Family member		
Friend		
Teacher or religious leader		
National celebrity (athlete, politician, movie star, performer)		
Other		

C PREPARING TO READ

BACKGROUND

Read this information, and do the exercise that follows.

Mickey Mantle was one of the greatest baseball players of all time. He played for the New York Yankees in their years of glory. From the time Mantle began to play in 1951 to his last year in 1968, baseball was the most popular game in the United States. For many people, Mantle symbolized the hope, prosperity, and confidence of America at that time.

Mantle was a fast and powerful player, a "switch-hitter" who could bat both right-handed and left-handed. He won game after game, one World Series championship after another, for his team. He was a wonderful athlete, but this alone cannot explain America's fascination with him.

Perhaps it was because he was a handsome, red-haired country boy, the son of a poor miner from Oklahoma. His career, from the lead mines of the West to the heights of success and fame, was a fairy-tale version of the American dream. Or perhaps it was because America always loves a "natural": a person who wins without seeming to try, whose talent appears to come from an inner grace. That was Mickey Mantle.

But like many celebrities, Mickey Mantle had a private life that was full of problems. He played without complaint despite constant pain from injuries. He lived to fulfill his father's dreams and drank to forget his father's early death. Alcohol was part of his friendships, his family life, his retirement distractions.

It was a terrible addiction that finally destroyed his body. It gave him cirrhosis of the liver and accelerated the advance of liver cancer. Even when Mickey Mantle had turned away from his old life and warned young people not to follow his example, the destructive process could not be stopped. Despite a liver transplant operation that had all those who loved and admired him hoping for a recovery, Mickey Mantle died of cancer at the age of 63.

We all have a public life and a private life, but people who are much in the public eye, like Mickey Mantle, are forced to pay a price for fame. Many sports players, fashion models, and others become celebrities but do not necessarily have happy lives. Complete the following sentences, and compare your answers with a partner's.

1. Many people want to become famous because _____

   _____

2. Some celebrities become famous because _____

   _____

3. People want to know everything about celebrities because _____

   _____

4. We admire sports heroes because _____

   _____

VOCABULARY FOR COMPREHENSION

Work in a small group, and help each other to guess the meaning of the boldfaced words. In each set of words, underline the two words that have similar meanings to the boldfaced word. Use your dictionaries if necessary.

1. **hereditary**	<u>genetic</u>	<u>inherited</u>	environmental
2. **instruct**	train	learn	prepare
3. **tough**	delicate	demanding	strong
4. **devastated**	cynical	crushed	desolate

5. blame	accuse	hold dear	hold responsible
6. depression	dejection	gloom	thrill
7. avoid	dodge	evade	confront
8. controversial	debatable	agreeable	disputable
9. choked up	filled with tears	unable to speak	unable to breathe
10. sober	dry	intoxicated	abstinent
11. slogan	memorandum	motto	saying
12. donor	supplier	receiver	giver

2 Focus on Reading

A   READING ONE: *Time in a Bottle*

Before you read, discuss this question with a partner.

What effect can a parent's addiction have on a child?

TIME IN A BOTTLE

By Mickey Mantle (from *Sports Illustrated*)

1   If alcoholism is hereditary, if it's in the genes, then I think mine came from my mother's side of the family. Her brothers were all alcoholics. My mother, Lovell, and my father, Mutt, weren't big drinkers. Dad would buy a pint of whiskey on Saturday night and put it in the icebox. Then every night when he came home from working eight hours in the lead mines of Oklahoma, he'd head for the icebox and take a swig[1] of whiskey.

2   My dad loved baseball, played semi-professional ball on the weekends, and was a tremendous St. Louis Cardinals fan. In fact, he named me after Mickey Cochrane, the Hall of Fame catcher for Philadelphia and Detroit who was a great hitter. Dad had

[1] *swig:* a gulp of a liquid, usually alcohol

high hopes for me. He thought I could be the greatest ballplayer who ever lived, and he did everything to help me realize his dream.

3   Even though he was dog tired after long days at the mine, Dad would still pitch batting practice to me in the backyard when he got home from work, beginning from the time I was four years old. My mother would call us to dinner, but the meal would wait until Dad was finished instructing me from the right and left sides of the plate. Dad was a tough man. If I'd done something wrong, he could just look at me—he didn't have to say anything—and I'd say, "I won't do it no more, Dad." I loved my father, although I couldn't tell him that, just like he couldn't tell me.

4   I joined the Yankees at 19. The following spring, when Dad died of Hodgkin's disease[2] at age 39, I was devastated, and that's when I started drinking. I guess alcohol helped me escape the pain of losing him.

5   God gave me a great body to play with, and I didn't take care of it. And I blame a lot of it on alcohol. Everyone likes to make the excuse that injuries shortened my career. Truth is, after I'd had a knee operation, the doctors would give me rehab[3] work to do, but I wouldn't do it. I'd be out drinking. . . . Everything had always come naturally to me. I didn't work hard at it.

6   After I retired at 37, my drinking got really bad. I went through a deep depression. Billy Martin, Whitey Ford, Hank Bauer, Moose Skowron [my Yankee teammates], I left all those guys and I think it left a hole in

Mickey Mantle with his parents and family.

me. . . . We were as close as brothers. I haven't met anyone else I've felt as close to.

7   I never thought about anything serious in my life for a continuous period of days and weeks until I checked into the Betty Ford Center.[4] I've always tried to avoid anything emotional, anything controversial, anything serious, and I did it through the use of alcohol. Alcohol always protected me from reality.

8   You are supposed to say why you ended up at the Center. I said I had a bad liver and I was depressed. Whenever I tried to talk about my family, I got all choked up. One of the things I really messed up, besides baseball, was being

---

[2] *Hodgkin's disease:* a cancer of the blood characterized by enlargement of the spleen, lymph nodes, and liver. It is hereditary. For a long time, Mickey Mantle thought he would develop the disease. One of his sons had it and died around the same age as Mantle's father.

[3] *rehab, rehabilitation:* training to restore a person to good physical condition

[4] *Betty Ford Center:* a live-in treatment center for drug and alcohol addiction located in Rancho Mirage, California. It is named in honor of the wife of former U.S. president Gerald Ford, and many celebrities have been helped there.

a father. I wasn't a good family man. I was always out, running around with my friends. My son Mickey Jr. could have been a wonderful athlete. If he had had my dad, he could have been a major league baseball player. My kids never blamed me for not being there. They don't have to. I blame myself.

9   During my time at the Betty Ford Center, I had to write my father a letter and tell him how I felt about him. It only took me ten minutes to write the letter, and I cried the whole time, but after it was over, I felt better. I said that I missed him, and I wish he could have lived to see that I did a lot better than my first season with the Yankees. I told him I had four boys—he died before my first son, Mickey Jr., was born—and I told him I loved him. I would have been better off if I could have told him that a long time ago.

10   Dad would have been proud of me today, knowing that I've completed treatment at Betty Ford and have been sober for three months. But he would have been mad that I had to go there in the first place.

11   For all those years I lived the life of someone I didn't know: a cartoon character. From now on, Mickey Mantle is going to be a real person.

Epilogue

12   As one of Mickey Mantle's last wishes, he wanted to establish a donor awareness program, called "Mickey's Team," at Baylor Hospital in Texas, where he received a liver transplant. He planned to tape a series of public service announcements for the program and even invented a slogan before he died: "Be a hero, be a donor." Mickey's painful problems have inspired a twofold increase in the number of people requesting donor cards. "That program," says Mickey Jr., "will probably be the biggest thing he's going to be known for." (Richard Jerome et al., "Courage at the End of the Road," *People*)

READING FOR MAIN IDEAS

Answer the following questions based on your understanding of the reading. Write your answers on a separate piece of paper.

1. What effect did Mickey Mantle's addiction have on:
   • his ability to play baseball?
   • his relationship with family members?
   • his friendships?

2. How did Mickey Mantle feel about his father?

READING FOR DETAILS

Fill in the time line on page 7 by creating sentences using the following phrases.

was cured at the Betty Ford Center	joined the Yankees
left baseball	started a campaign for donor awareness
father died	father began teaching him baseball

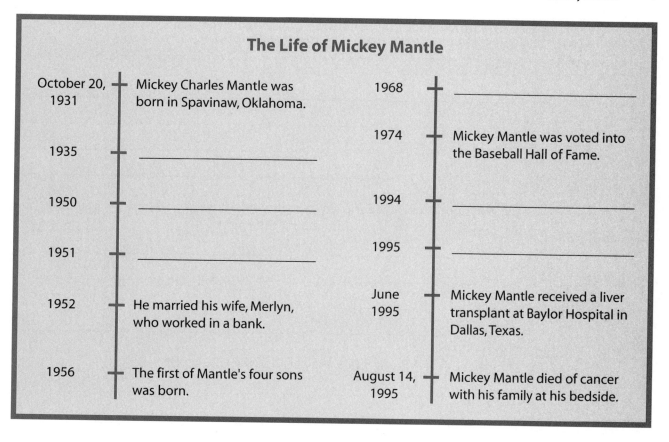

The Life of Mickey Mantle

October 20, 1931	Mickey Charles Mantle was born in Spavinaw, Oklahoma.
1935	_____
1950	_____
1951	_____
1952	He married his wife, Merlyn, who worked in a bank.
1956	The first of Mantle's four sons was born.
1968	_____
1974	Mickey Mantle was voted into the Baseball Hall of Fame.
1994	_____
1995	_____
June 1995	Mickey Mantle received a liver transplant at Baylor Hospital in Dallas, Texas.
August 14, 1995	Mickey Mantle died of cancer with his family at his bedside.

REACTING TO THE READING

1 *Working with a partner, circle the choice(s) that best complete these sentences. There can be more than one correct answer. Refer to Reading One to support your choices.*

1. Mickey Mantle's father _____.
   a. had a drinking problem
   b. had nothing to do with Mickey's drinking problem
   c. had confidence in his son's abilities
   d. had an easygoing personality

2. Mickey Mantle liked to go out with his friends because _____.
   a. they had many things in common
   b. they were like family
   c. he was disappointed with his family
   d. he had trouble dealing with his father's death

3. If Mickey Mantle's father had known about his son's problem, _____.
   a. he would have been very disappointed
   b. he would have been angry with him
   c. he would have forgiven him
   d. he would have made him get treatment much sooner

2 *Discuss the following questions with a partner, and write your answers in the space provided.*

1. Why did Mickey Mantle become addicted?

_____

_____

_____

_____

2. Why did Mickey Mantle say that it would have been better for him if he had told his father he loved him a long time ago?

_____

_____

_____

_____

3. Did Mickey Mantle think that his life was a success?

_____

_____

_____

_____

3 *Discuss these questions in a small group.*

1. Do you think Mickey Mantle was a hero? In your opinion, what makes a person a hero?

2. In your opinion, who, if anyone, should get priority for organ transplants? Important people, young people, people with money? The sickest people, or the people who can best survive a transplant?

B   READING TWO: *Mick's Toughest Inning*

Mickey Mantle's illness and transplant renewed the debate about who gets priority for donated organs. In this article from the New York Post, *Cathy Burke discusses Mantle's situation and gives her opinions.*

First answer the question, and then read Burke's article.

Do you think Mickey Mantle's celebrity status influenced the type of medical treatment he obtained?

Mick's Toughest Inning[1]

By Cathy Burke (from the *New York Post*)

1   Mickey Mantle played his way into the pantheon[2] of baseball gods, and drank his way to the brink of death.[3] So in today's cynical debate over health-care priorities, Mick's record drinking[4] would drop him to the bottom of the list for a life-saving transplant. Chilling but true. He's over 60 and was an alcoholic for most of his life, a choice that helped make him as sick as he is today. Then there's his age and medical condition, which would put his chances at about 60 percent for surviving a liver transplant for five years or more.

2   The cynics would say Mick is a poor risk indeed. They are wrong.

3   Such a heartless and politicized point of view has gained strength ever since 1984, when former Colorado governor Richard Lamm made the famous declaration that the terminally ill have a "duty to die and get out of the way. Let the others in society, our children, build a reasonable life," he said. What kind of a reasonable life is it when politicians decide whether it is a good risk to save a human life?

4   But Lamm had more to say on modern technology, exactly the kind that could save Mickey Mantle. "How many hearts should we give to a smoker . . . how many liver transplants can we afford to give to an alcoholic," he asked, implying that one was too many.

5   In Oregon, Lamm's legacy lives on in something called the Oregon Health Plan, a "medical rationing" welfare program started in February 1994. The plan prioritizes 565 diseases and their treatments based on how effective the treatments are and how much they cost. Transplants for liver cancer patients are not funded.

6   Can we trust the politicians to do the right thing for the sickest and poorest among us? In Oregon, the health professionals decide what diseases and treatments go on the list and then a computer determines treatment priorities based on death rates and costs.

7   But the politicians decide how much money is spent.

8   No matter what the proponents[5] say, the Oregon system rations people out of care simply by denying them medical services because some politician doesn't like the survival odds or costs.

9   Fortunately, Mick won't have to worry about getting a chance at a liver transplant. Get well, Mick, before the most cynical of the health-care reformers do us all in.[6]

---

[1] *inning:* two baseball teams' turns at bat
[2] *pantheon:* a temple of all the gods; a group of famous people or national heroes
[3] *the brink of death:* the state of being near death
[4] *record drinking:* drinking great amounts of alcohol
[5] *proponents:* supporters
[6] *do us all in:* kill us all

With a partner, examine the following statements of opinion. Based on your understanding of Reading Two, decide whether Cathy Burke, a journalist, and Governor Lamm, a politician, would agree or disagree with the statements. Check (✓) off your answers.

OPINION	CATHY BURKE		GOVERNOR LAMM	
	Agree	Disagree	Agree	Disagree
1. Deciding health-care priorities according to money or cost is lacking in compassion.				
2. People must take responsibility for their lives. It is not the business of government to assume responsibility for them.				
3. Everyone should be able to get health care in matters of life and death.				
4. It goes against medical ethics to let politicians decide who gets medical treatment just because they control the money.				
5. It is wiser to use money to find a cure for childhood diseases than to find a cure for diseases of old age.				
6. A nonsmoker is more worthy of a lung transplant than someone who smoked for many years.				
7. Taxpayers' money is being spent to make insurance companies rich.				

C   LINKING READINGS ONE AND TWO

You have read the opinions, thoughts, and observations of the sports hero Mickey Mantle and the journalist Cathy Burke. Choose one topic below, and write a paragraph in reply.

1. What do you think Cathy Burke would write about Mickey Mantle's autobiography? How does she feel about Mickey Mantle? Does she think he is a hero? Does she think he deserves special treatment as a hero? Does she think he should get an organ transplant?

2. What is your reaction to the issues that Cathy Burke raises in her article? Do you think that all people have a right to medical treatment, even if they can't pay? Should health care be rationed? What should the government's role be?

3 Focus on Vocabulary

1 *Working in small groups, fill in the chart with the correct forms of the words. Use your dictionary if necessary. (An **X** indicates that no word belongs in that space either because no such word exists or because it is not commonly used.)*

Noun	Verb	Adjective	Adverb
1.	manage		
2. devastation			
3. priority		X	X
4.	avoid		
5.		tough	
6.			strongly
7. survival			X
8.	deny		
9.		determined	X
10.	celebrate		X

Common Suffixes

A suffix comes at the end of the word. When you recognize certain suffixes, you will be able to understand what part of speech a word belongs to and where the word can be used in the structure of a sentence.

Complete the following sentences with information from the chart above. Then check your answers with a partner's.

1. Common suffixes for _____ are *-al, -ity, -ment, -ness,* and *-tion (-sion).*

2. The endings *-able, -ed,* and *-ing* are common suffixes for

    _____.

3. To create an adverb from an adjective, all you have to do is to add the suffix

    _____. When you do so, sometimes the last letter (*-e*) of the adjective is dropped.

4. Common suffixes for _____ are *-ate, -en,* and *-ize.*

2 *Imagine that the letter Mickey Mantle wrote at the Betty Ford Center to his long-dead father read something like the letter that follows. Fill in each blank with the correct form of a word from the box.*

| avoidance | denial | ~~devastation~~ | priority | survival |
| celebration | determination | management | strength | toughness |

Dear Dad,

Your death really (**1**) ___devastated___ me. I don't think I have ever recovered from the pain and the fact that I never (**2**) _____ to tell you how much I loved you. The hardest thing I ever had to do was to say good-bye to you.

How do I account for my success? Your faith in me, your love, and your help. If you had lived, you would have seen my four beautiful sons. You would have shared my fame and (**3**) _____ my success. You would have seen me realize those dreams we had so long ago.

More than anything else in the world, I wanted you to be proud of me. When I lost you, I lost my guide, my anchor in life. You were such a (**4**) _____ family man, but I seem to have given my family a low (**5**) _____. I lost my way for a long time and now my very (**6**) _____ is in doubt. Whatever happens, I am (**7**) _____ to use the rest of my life to make things up to my family.

Even though I was elected to the Baseball Hall of Fame, I was not the great father to my sons during their childhood that you were to me during mine. I can't (**8**) _____ that in their own ways, my kids bear the scars of my neglect. What chokes me up about all this is that they don't blame me for my failures as a parent. I only wish that I had been there for my kids in the same way that you were always there for me. You were (**9**) _____ on me, but you always wanted the best. Perhaps I could have (**10**) _____ some of this suffering if, years ago, I had had the courage to tell you how much I loved you.

Your loving son,

Mickey

3 *See below the beginning of a paragraph about why Mickey Mantle felt better about himself at the end of his life. Use at least seven more words from the list below to complete the paragraph. Be sure to use the correct form of each word. Then read your writing to a partner.*

avoid	celebrate	depression	devastated	manage	sober
blame	choked up	determined	donor	priority	strength

How Mickey Mantle Changed

At the end of his life, Mickey Mantle was more in touch with his feelings than he had ever been before. He had overcome his addiction to alcohol and was able to stay sober. _____

_____

_____

_____

_____

_____

_____

4 Focus on Writing

A GRAMMAR: Past Unreal Conditionals

1 *Examine this sentence, and discuss the questions that follow with a partner.*

If I had done the physical rehab work after my injuries, I would have been able to play baseball after age 37.

1. Did Mickey Mantle do the physical rehab work after his injury?

2. Was he able to play baseball after age 37?

3. How are these two ideas connected in the sentence above?

Past Unreal Conditionals

A **past unreal conditional** is used to express past untrue or past imagined situations and their result. A past unreal conditional statement can be used to explain why things happened the way they did or to express a regret about the past. A past unreal conditional statement is formed by combining an **if-clause** and a **result clause.** Both clauses have to be stated in terms that are opposite to what really happened.

Reality	Mickey Mantle didn't do the rehab work after his injuries; therefore, he wasn't able to play baseball after the age of 37.
Past unreal conditional	If Mickey Mantle had done the rehab work after his injuries, he would have been able to play baseball after the age of 37.

Formation

To form a past unreal conditional statement, use **had** (not) + past participle in the *if*-clause and **would, might, could** (not) + **have** + past participle in the result clause.

If-clause	**If** Mickey Mantle **had done** the rehab work,
Result clause	he **would have been** able to play baseball after the age of 37.
If-clause	**If** Mantle **hadn't been** out drinking with his friends all the time,
Result clause	he **would have had** time to do the rehab work.

GRAMMAR TIP: Using *could have* or *might have* in the result clause shows more doubt about the conclusion.

2 *Combine the ideas in the following sentences by using the past unreal conditional. Remember that these conditional sentences must express the opposite of what really happened.*

1. Mickey Mantle needed a transplant.

   There has been a twofold increase in the number of people requesting donor cards from Baylor Hospital.

   If Mickey Mantle hadn't needed a transplant, there might not have been a twofold increase in the number of people requesting donor cards from Baylor Hospital.

2. Mickey Mantle's father trained his son to play baseball from the age of four. Mickey became a champion.

_____

_____

_____

3. Mickey Mantle centered his social life on alcohol. He neglected his wife and sons.

_____

_____

_____

4. Mickey Mantle's father died in 1951. He never saw Mickey Mantle become a champion.

_____

_____

_____

5. Mantle went to the Betty Ford Center the year before he died. He reconciled with his family at the end of his life.

_____

_____

_____

3 _Using the information from the readings, write your own past unreal conditionals about the following themes in Mickey Mantle's life. When you write your sentences, try to use the vocabulary words you have studied in this unit._

1. Mickey's transplant

If Mickey Mantle had been sober all his life, he wouldn't have needed a liver transplant.

2. Mickey's relationship with his father

_____

_____

3. Mickey's relationship with his sons

_____

_____

4. Mickey's addiction to alcohol

_____

_____

B | STYLE: Elements of Autobiographical Writing

1 *Reread the example paragraph below from "My Time in a Bottle," and discuss with a partner the questions that follow.*

"Even though he was dog tired after long days at the mine, Dad would still pitch batting practice to me in the backyard when he got home from work, beginning from the time I was four years old. My mother would call us to dinner, but the meal would wait until Dad was finished instructing me from the right and left sides of the plate. Dad was a tough man. If I'd done something wrong, he could just look at me—he didn't have to say anything—and I'd say, 'I won't do it no more, Dad.' I loved my father, although I couldn't tell him that, just like he couldn't tell me."

1. Who is being described here?

2. Who is the narrator (the person who is telling the story)?

3. During which period in the narrator's life does the action take place?

4. What verb tenses are used?

5. What statement makes us aware of an issue that caused the author a lot of pain?

Character, Technique, and Theme

The person being described here is Mickey Mantle's father. Because the passage is written in the first-person narrative (as shown by the use of the pronoun **I** and the possessive adjective *my*), it is clear to the reader that the narrator is Mickey Mantle himself. The verbs are all in a past tense form (the simple past: "he was dog tired"; the habitual past: "My mother would call"), and the actions that are being described here all refer to the period in the author's childhood starting at age four. The statement at the very end, "I loved my father, although I couldn't tell him that, just like he couldn't tell me," makes us aware of an issue that bothered Mantle a lot.

What we can appreciate in this paragraph are the three major "elements" of autobiography: **character, technique,** and **theme.**

Character

The author of an autobiography provides details about himself and others in his life and about his reactions to the events in his life. From the comfortable distance created by the passage of time, the narrator creates self-portraits and portraits of the principal players in his life. Through the portraits, we discover the writer's character or system of values. We learn how the writer views various character traits (such as generosity, sensitivity, meanness, happiness, and sadness) by examining how such traits were reflected in his own behavior and that of others in his life. In addition, we learn why the writer believes the individuals being described became the way they were and how his present values may now be different from his past values.

In the example paragraph, the author provides details about himself and his father. He writes, "Dad was a tough man," and explains further that his father "could just look at [him]" to get him to do what he wanted. The great influence the author's father had on his character development is thus revealed in these few words.

2 *Write short answers to the following questions, and discuss your answers with a partner.*

1. What did you learn about the character of Mickey Mantle's father in the example paragraph on page 16?

2. By reading Mantle's portrait of his father, we learn about the values Mickey Mantle respected. What are these values?

3. Look at the rest of "My Time in a Bottle." Does Mickey Mantle claim he kept to these values? Underline the sentences where you find the answer.

Technique

Autobiographers must use the past tense and the first-person narrative (for example, language like "I loved my father") if they want their portraits to be effective. At the same time, writers must use interesting language and imagery (for example, language like "dog tired after long days at the mine," which gives us a mental picture of a sense experience) and various other stylistic devices (such as direct quotations or questions) to attract readers to their writing.

3 *Discuss the following questions with a partner.*

1. Suppose that in the example paragraph Mickey Mantle had written, "Every day after work my father practiced pitching balls to me before sitting down to dinner." Would this have been an interesting sentence or a dull one? Why?

2. Underline the descriptive words Mantle uses to tell about his father's days. Why are these words effective? What do they communicate?

3. Underline the sentence where Mantle offers a direct quotation of his own words. Why does he do this? What is wrong with the grammar of the sentence?

> **Theme**
>
> Autobiographers must create an intimate bond with readers by making them aware of the issues or problems that have shaped their lives and that continue to be a major concern to them. For example, one of the themes that surfaces in "My Time in a Bottle" is Mantle's escape from loss through alcoholism.

4 *Write short answers to these questions, and compare them with a partner's.*

1. What is the main theme of the paragraph we examined? Underline the sentence that you think is the most significant.

2. Is there anything in this paragraph that shows the weakness or vulnerability of the narrator?

3. Does this make us feel closer to the narrator? Why or why not?

5 *Imagine that you are a character from Mickey Mantle's childhood: a brother, a sister, a parent, a friend. Write a paragraph from that person's point of view. For example, you may want to describe how a younger brother could have been jealous of the daily sessions Mantle had with his father. You could begin the paragraph this way: "Every day was the same. I sat alone while my father spent all his free time with my brother."*

*Consider **character, technique,** and **theme** as you plan your writing strategy. Remember to write in the first person and to use the past tense.*

C WRITING TOPICS

Write about one of the following topics. Use the vocabulary and grammar from this unit.

1. Using the three major elements of autobiography—character, technique, and theme—write a portrait of yourself at a certain time in your life. Use the first-person narrative and the past tense. Express yourself in interesting and descriptive language. You can:

   a. describe your personality as it was during a particular period or at the time of a special event in your life

   b. consider how that period or special event affected you and how it may have caused your system of values to change or remain the same

   c. describe any individuals who had a great influence on you at the time

   d. share with the reader the issue that was most on your mind at that time

   e. discuss whether there was anything you should have done differently

2. Write a letter to someone who has been very important to you in your life. Mickey Mantle wrote one to his father, but the person you choose can still be alive today. If you hadn't had that person in your life, what would have happened to you? Would your life have been different? How?

3. Choose a famous sports hero, celebrity, or national leader. Make sure you know a lot about the life of this person. Put yourself in his or her shoes, and write an imaginary autobiography from his or her point of view. Discuss the influence of his or her early life, the contributions he or she made, the contradictions between the person's public and private life. What are her strengths and weaknesses? What would her life have been like if her career hadn't been successful? if she hadn't made some mistakes? if certain people hadn't been there to help?

4. Some people think that alcoholics should not be eligible for organ transplants. They say that if alcoholics hadn't abused their bodies, they wouldn't have gotten so sick. Other people feel that it is unfair to deny life-saving help to another human being. Still other people are worried about society's limited number of donor organs and limited economic resources. What do you think? Explain your answer in a well-organized essay.

D   RESEARCH TOPICS

PREPARATION

Mickey Mantle received his liver transplant in Dallas, Texas. Organ distribution in the United States is broken down into different geographical regions (see the graph on page 20), which share organs nationally when there is a surplus in a given region. All are connected on the United Network for Organ Sharing.

Use the graph on page 20 and the information below to discuss the following questions with a partner.

1. What might have happened to Mickey Mantle if he had been a patient in another geographical region of the United States?

2. According to the new rules for liver transplants since Mickey Mantle's death, which patients now get priority for liver transplants?

> ### New Rules for Liver Transplants
>
> In November 1996, the United Network for Organ Sharing changed its rules and introduced rationing. In the past, the sickest patients had top priority. But patients whose livers have been deteriorating for decades, like those with alcoholic cirrhosis or viral hepatitis, are only half as likely to survive a liver transplant as people whose livers have just suddenly failed from a viral infection or toxin (poison). The new rules state that if the two types of people are competing for one liver, it should go to the person who just became ill.

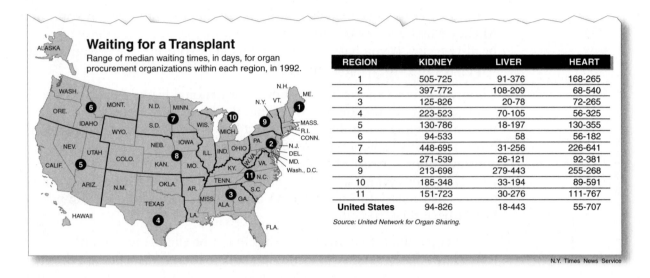

Waiting for a Transplant

Range of median waiting times, in days, for organ procurement organizations within each region, in 1992.

REGION	KIDNEY	LIVER	HEART
1	505-725	91-376	168-265
2	397-772	108-209	68-540
3	125-826	20-78	72-265
4	223-523	70-105	56-325
5	130-786	18-197	130-355
6	94-533	58	56-182
7	448-695	31-256	226-641
8	271-539	26-121	92-381
9	213-698	279-443	255-268
10	185-348	33-194	89-591
11	151-723	30-276	111-767
United States	94-826	18-443	55-707

Source: United Network for Organ Sharing.

N.Y. Times News Service

RESEARCH ACTIVITY

1. Do an Internet search or go to the library, and research organ transplants in your area or country. What are the current issues in organ transplant medicine in your area or country, or in a country of your choice? Can a transplant be bought for money? Where do transplant organs come from? Who decides who will get an organ and according to what criteria?

2. Take notes, and organize the information.

SHARING YOUR FINDINGS

Write a report summarizing your findings, and present a five-minute oral report.

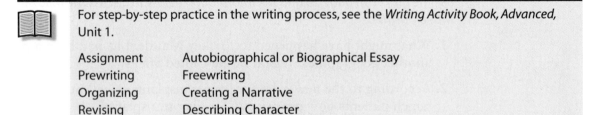

For step-by-step practice in the writing process, see the *Writing Activity Book, Advanced,* Unit 1.

Assignment	Autobiographical or Biographical Essay
Prewriting	Freewriting
Organizing	Creating a Narrative
Revising	Describing Character
	Using Past Unreal Conditionals
Editing	Choosing Word Forms

For Unit 1 Internet activities, visit the NorthStar Companion Website at http://longman.com/northstar.

A Season in Utopia

1 Focus on the Topic

A PREDICTING

Look at the photograph. Why would some people say this is a picture of utopia?* Do you agree? Take ten minutes to write down your thoughts about these questions.

---

* The word *utopia* is based on Greek words that can mean both "a good place" and "nowhere."

B   SHARING INFORMATION

Have you ever dreamed of living the perfect life? What kinds of things would make it "perfect"? Place a check (✓) next to four of the following elements that you consider the most important for your perfect life. You can add other choices. Then discuss the reasons for your choices in a small group.

_____ lots of leisure time   _____ a loving family

_____ a great deal of money   _____ a job you believe in

_____ life with many friends   _____ a chance to be creative

_____ power in the world   _____ beautiful natural surroundings

_____ a spiritual community   _____ _____

_____ success in your career   _____ _____

_____ service to help others   _____ _____

C   PREPARING TO READ

BACKGROUND

Read the information, and complete the sentences that follow based on what you have read.

In the first half of the nineteenth century, many people in Europe and the United States were attracted to the idea of utopian communities. The early industrial society had produced many economic injustices and social problems. Industrial cities were ugly and overcrowded; economic recessions created unemployment and suffering. Most of all, people felt that the dignity of labor was being destroyed by machines and by growing social inequalities. In response to all these problems, utopians set up model communities based on equality.

These utopians, such as Robert Owen in Britain and Charles Fourier in France, hoped that their efforts would influence public opinion and help to change society for the better. Many utopians, including Robert Owen, came to America because they thought that as the "New World" it would be the perfect place to create a more just society. More than 100 religious and socialist communities were created in nineteenth-century America, involving an estimated 100,000 men, women, and children. Some communities, such as the Northampton Association in Massachusetts, were formed by radical Abolitionists,* who worked to end slavery. Others, like the Shaker settlements, were religious efforts. Most of these experiments, including Robert Owen's community in New Harmony,

---

* *Abolitionists:* members of a movement of white and black people working to awaken Americans to the horrors of slavery.

Indiana, and Fanny Wright's in Nashoba, Tennessee, were ultimately failures. Only three or four of these communities lasted longer than a hundred years, but all of them contributed something of value to American life: an expression of idealism; a desire to live in voluntary communities without private property; the importance of working for democracy, equality, and nonviolence.

Brook Farm, Massachusetts, was a utopian community of artists, intellectuals, and farmers established in the 1840s. Its aim was to break down class barriers and end the economic and social separation between mental and physical labor so that all people could develop to their full potential as human beings. Brook Farm was associated with two Boston movements: the Abolitionist movement against slavery and the Transcendentalist movement[*] in art and literature. The famous American author Nathaniel Hawthorne[**] was one of the founders of Brook Farm. Although the Brook Farmers might be considered naïve in many ways, they had a vision of a world where all people would be respected for the work they did. In their community, contrary to the reality of our society today, those who worked long hours at backbreaking tasks would not suffer from low status and poverty in a land of great riches.

1. Utopian communities were _____

_____

2. Utopians criticized their society because _____

_____

3. The people on Brook Farm wanted to _____

_____

VOCABULARY FOR COMPREHENSION

1 *Write your own synonym for the underlined words. Use the context of the sentence to help determine the meaning of the words.*

1. Nathaniel Hawthorne worked as a government worker in a customs house because he had to earn money while he was writing his novels, but his artistic talents were not <u>suited to</u> his boring job.

_____

[*]   *the Transcendentalist movement:* a literary, artistic, and religious movement, related to the Romantic movement in Europe, which emphasized the importance of simplicity and closeness to nature. Transcendentalists were humanists. They believed in spiritual values beyond the world of material concepts, yet they accepted reason and the role of science.

[**]   Hawthorne, whose best-known work is *The Scarlet Letter,* left Brook Farm after about a year and wrote a fictionalized, critical account of his experiences in his novel *Blithedale Romance.*

2. The Transcendentalists considered country life more <u>wholesome</u> than life in the crowded and polluted industrial cities.

_____

3. The Brook Farmers were not concerned with how many material possessions a person could <u>acquire</u>. They were more interested in moral values.

_____

4. At Brook Farm, all members received equal <u>compensation</u> for their labor; they were paid equal amounts for farm labor or intellectual work.

_____

5. A <u>devotion</u> to the ideals of brotherhood and equality is clear in everything that Brook Farm tried to do.

_____

6. Brook Farmers had many goals, but eliminating the poverty of the early working class was of <u>paramount</u> importance to them.

_____

7. The Boston Transcendentalists were educated men and women who enjoyed <u>witty</u> and interesting discussions about society and literature.

_____

8. The Transcendentalists held beliefs similar to those of the Romantic movement in Europe. They feared that the values of the industrial world would <u>overwhelm</u> and destroy humanistic values.

_____

9. Brook Farmers didn't want to <u>impose</u> anything on society; they wanted to convince people by example and persuasion.

_____

10. At Brook Farm, the desire for equality <u>presided over</u> all the relationships in the community.

_____

11. Brook Farmers believed that education would end the <u>vulgarity</u> of the lower classes and lead to more refined and gentle behavior in daily life.

_____

12. To many people, it is <u>inconceivable</u> that society will ever really change. Reforms and revolutions are a great shock to them.

_____

2 *Match the words on the left with their definitions on the right. Compare your answers with a partner's.*

_____ **1.** suited to

_____ **2.** wholesome

_____ **3.** acquire

_____ **4.** compensation

_____ **5.** devotion

_____ **6.** paramount

_____ **7.** witty

_____ **8.** overwhelm

_____ **9.** impose

_____ **10.** presided over

_____ **11.** vulgarity

_____ **12.** inconceivable

a. pay

b. unbelievable

c. more important than anything else

d. appropriate for

e. led, had power over

f. force, oblige

g. dedication

h. healthy

i. coarseness, rudeness

j. gain, obtain

k. clever

l. defeat

2 Focus on Reading

A   READING ONE: *Early Life at Brook Farm and Concord*

Before you read, discuss this question with a partner.

How can ordinary people contribute to changing society for the better?

The following reading is based on an account of Brook Farm written in the nineteenth century by one of its former members.

EARLY LIFE AT
BROOK FARM
AND CONCORD

BASED ON AN ACCOUNT BY GEORGE WILLIS COOKE

1   According to its founder, George Ripley, "the aim of Brook Farm was to insure a more natural union between intellectual and manual labor than now exists, to combine the worker and the thinker as much as possible in one individual, to assure the highest mental freedom by providing everyone with work suited to their tastes and talents, guaranteeing to them the fruits of their toil;[1] to open the benefits of education and the profits of labor to all; and to prepare the way for a society with a more wholesome life than the one we lead amid[2] the pressures of our competitive institutions. To accomplish these purposes, we will take a small tract of land, which under skillful farming will be adequate to support the families. Our farm will be a place for improving the race of men that live on it. Thought will preside over the operations of labor, and labor will contribute to the expansion of thought. We will have work without drudgery[3] and true equality without vulgarity."

2   The Brook Farm Association had two sources of income: the farm of about 200 acres and a school with a six-year college preparation course, of which three years were given to acquiring a knowledge of farming. The Association sold a share for $500, which gave the member one vote, 5 percent interest per year, and one free tuition at the school, which was highly recommended by Harvard. People who did

not live at Brook Farm were required to pay full tuition and board for the children they sent to the Brook Farm School. A person without money could also become a member of Brook Farm in exchange for a year's work (300 days). This entitled the worker to the same share in the Association and 5 percent interest as members who had paid a fee. All work was worth the same amount of money an hour, whatever kind of work it was, because money was not the only compensation of labor. There were compensations of a different kind: all housing, medical attention, nursing, education, and amusements

---

[1] *toil:* labor, work
[2] *amid:* among
[3] *drudgery:* difficult or strenuous physical labor with little creativity

which the community provided free of charge, as well as free board to all those over seventy and under ten and to all those who were sick, unless their 5 percent could support them. Any married couple with their children could live together, eat together, and have a paramount right to each other, or they could go to the common rooms for eating or amusement with no questions asked whatever their decision. Ralph Waldo Emerson wrote, "In Brook Farm there was this peculiarity, there was no head. In every family is the father, in every factory a foreman, in every shop a master, but in this farm, no authority; each was master or mistress of his or her actions."

3   The Association began with 13 friends around the table in the central kitchen. Eventually, it was composed of every kind of person: the finest scholars, men and women of the most aesthetic culture and accomplishment, along with young farmers, clothing workers, mechanics, and preachers.[4] But they were associated in such a spirit and under such conditions that the best of everyone appeared. There was plenty of steady, essential hard work, for the founding of an earthly paradise on a rocky New England farm is no easy pastime.[5]

4   Even with the best intentions, and a great deal of work and devotion, there was an inevitable lack of method. The Farmers were generous to a fault, and poverty was the result of their lack of capital. There were more people applying than the Farmers could house. Financial failure was almost a foregone conclusion. And yet, there have never been such witty potato patches and such sparkling cornfields before or since.

5   Beneath all the lights and shadows of its surface, Brook Farm was a simple, honest effort to create a better life than that in which we find ourselves. Man is miserably half-developed and has not reached his full potential, the proof being the development of modern society in which the few profit and enjoy, and the many work and suffer. If every man did his share of the muscular work of the world, no other man would be overwhelmed by it. The man who does not work imposes the necessity of harder work on those who do. Thereby the one steals from the other the opportunity of mental culture[6]—and at last we reach a world of pariahs[7] and patricians,[8] with all the inconceivable sorrow and suffering that surround us. Our way back to the golden age lies through justice, which substitutes cooperation for competition. The Brook Farm effort wanted to right the wrongs of society, to give all individuals an opportunity in life, and to bring the help of all to the aid of each one.

---

[4] *preachers:* Christian clergymen, evangelical Protestant ministers

[5] *pastime:* something to "pass the time," a leisure activity

[6] Today this sentence would more commonly be written: "The one steals the opportunity of mental culture (education, the leisure to think) from the other."

[7] *pariahs:* outcasts of society, the lower classes

[8] *patricians:* the elite, the upper classes

READING FOR MAIN IDEAS

Fill in the blanks on the left based on the reading about Brook Farm. Then fill in the blanks on the right based on your ideas about the world today. Some information has already been filled in. Compare the two columns, and then compare your answers with a partner's.

CATEGORY	BROOK FARM	OUTSIDE WORLD TODAY
WORK	_____ _____ _____ _____	Each person is paid a different wage according to the market. There is a great separation between mental and physical labor.
HOUSING	All housing was provided freely by the community. People could live separately or in the main house.	_____ _____ _____ _____
EDUCATION	_____ _____ _____ _____	Education is more easily available and of better quality if the family is middle class.
CLASS DISTINCTIONS	_____ _____ _____ _____	_____ _____ _____ _____
WORK ETHIC	_____ _____ _____ _____	Competition among people dominates the workplace.

READING FOR DETAILS

*Read these statements. In the blanks on the left, write **T** (True), **F** (False), or **NS** (Not Stated) if the information isn't in the reading passage. Then write the number of the paragraph in which you found the information.*

Explain your answers to a partner.

___F___ 1. The community failed because no one wanted to join the original founders.

Paragraph ___4___

___NS___ 2. Brook Farm bankrupted its founder, George Ripley.

Paragraph _____

_____ 3. If you had no money to invest, you could not have obtained a share in Brook Farm.

Paragraph _____

_____ 4. Many neighbors of the Brook Farm experiment disagreed with the goals of the Brook Farmers.

Paragraph _____

_____ 5. Everyone who lived at Brook Farm was obliged to work.

Paragraph _____

_____ 6. The Brook Farmers believed in the worth of the individual and allowed individuals to make their own decisions.

Paragraph _____

_____ 7. Brook Farm made money from its school.

Paragraph _____

_____ 8. Farming at Brook Farm was easy work.

Paragraph _____

_____ 9. Couples always ate together.

Paragraph _____

_____ 10. More people left Brook Farm than stayed at it.

Paragraph _____

REACTING TO THE READING

1 *Answer the questions. Discuss your answers with a partner.*

1. The Brook Farmers wanted to "prepare the way for a society with a more wholesome life" (paragraph 1). In what way was Brook Farm wholesome?

   _____

   _____

   _____

   _____

2. "Financial failure was almost a foregone conclusion" (paragraph 4). What does this sentence mean?

   _____

   _____

   _____

   _____

3. "And yet, there have never been such witty potato patches and such sparkling cornfields before or since" (paragraph 4). Is this sentence a compliment or a criticism of Brook Farm? Explain your answer.

   _____

   _____

   _____

   _____

4. What do you think the author's purpose was in writing this article about Brook Farm?

   _____

   _____

   _____

   _____

2 *Would Brook Farmers agree or disagree with these aspects of modern life? Circle* **Agree** *or* **Disagree.** *Write your explanations, and discuss your answers with a partner.*

---

1. The civil rights movement and equality for minorities in society   (AGREE)   DISAGREE

Your Explanation:

*Brook Farmers believed that everyone should be treated
as equals and given equal opportunity.*

---

2. Company directors who make 500 times the salary of one of their workers   AGREE   DISAGREE

Your Explanation:

---

3. The environmental protection movement   AGREE   DISAGREE

Your Explanation:

---

4. Child labor laws that prevent children younger than age 16 from working in factories   AGREE   DISAGREE

Your Explanation:

---

5. Community colleges and the growth of continuing education for adults   AGREE   DISAGREE

Your Explanation:

---

6. Sweatshop factories where immigrants work for less than minimum wage in harsh conditions   AGREE   DISAGREE

Your Explanation:

3 Read these statements, and place a check (✓) in a **Yes, No,** or **Undecided** box. Then discuss your answers in a small group.

	Yes	No	Undecided
1. I would welcome the chance to join an experimental community like Brook Farm.	❏	❏	❏
2. Competition is better than cooperation.	❏	❏	❏
3. It's fair to pay everyone the same salary.	❏	❏	❏
4. I would like to work in a place where I could rotate tasks.	❏	❏	❏
5. Brook Farm could never succeed today.	❏	❏	❏

B   READING TWO: *Making Ends Meet*

1 Discuss the following questions with a partner.

What do you think life is like for people in the United States who try to live on wages of $6 or $7 an hour?

The following reading is taken from a review of a book by Barbara Ehrenreich entitled *Nickel and Dimed: On (Not) Getting by in America.* "To nickel and dime" is an idiom. Nickels and dimes are very small coins that are worth very little. "To nickel and dime" people is to pay them very little or have contempt for them. Another related meaning is to be petty or small-minded, particularly about money.

Barbara Ehrenreich, a writer and social activist, went undercover for three months and lived in three different American cities to find out what it's like to be earning a minimum wage.

Making Ends Meet

From a *New York Times* book review written by Dorothy Gallagher

1   In Key West, Florida, Ehrenreich found a job as a waitress at an inexpensive family restaurant. Her shift ran from 2 P.M. to 10 P.M. Salary: $2.43 an hour plus tips. To find an affordable rent, she had to move 30 miles out of town, a 45-minute commute on a crowded two-lane highway. How did her co-workers manage housing? One waitress shared a room in a $250 a week flophouse,[1] a cook shared a two-room apartment with three others; another worker lived in a van parked behind a shopping center.

---

[1] *flophouse:* a very run-down, shabby place that rents you a bed or a small room

2   "There are no secret economies that nourish the poor," Ehrenreich writes. "If you can't put up the two months' rent you need to get an apartment, you end up paying through the nose for a room by the week. If you have only one room, with a hotplate at best, you can't save by cooking up huge stews that can be frozen for the week ahead. You eat hot dogs and the Styrofoam cups of soup that can be microwaved at a convenience store." Without health insurance from work, you risk a small cut becoming infected because you can afford neither a visit to the doctor nor antibiotics.

3   In the summer tourist slump, Ehrenreich found her salary with tips dropped from about $7 an hour to $5.15. At this rate, the only way to pay her rent was to get a second job. So, for a while she worked 8 A.M. to 2 P.M. and then rushed to her regular shift at the first restaurant—a 14-hour day of brutal physical labor, as anyone who has waitressed for a living knows. With such a schedule, she could not, of course, keep her decent housing so far from town. Ehrenreich's new home was an eight-foot-wide trailer parked among others "in a nest of crime," where "desolation rules night and day. . . . There are not exactly people here but what amounts to canned labor,[2] being preserved between shifts from the heat."

4   Moving to Maine, Ehrenreich took two jobs to make ends meet—a weekend job in a nursing home and a full-time job in a house-cleaning service. At Merry Maids, the cleaning service, the economics were as follows: the customer pays the service $25 an hour per cleaning person; the service pays $6.65 an hour to each cleaner. "How poor are my co-workers?" Ehrenreich asks.

Half-bags of corn chips for lunch; dizziness from malnutrition; a toothache requiring frantic calls to find a free dental clinic; worries about makeshift[3] childcare arrangements because a licensed day-care center at $90 a week is beyond any cleaner's budget; no one sleeping in a car, but everyone crowded into housing with far too many others, strangers or family; "signs of real difficulty if not actual misery."

5   Soon, Ehrenreich starts having money troubles even with two jobs. Housing is the killer. She foresees a weekend without food unless she can find charitable help. More than an hour on the phone with various private charitable agencies (cost of phone calls: $2.50) nets her a severely restricted food voucher[4]—no fresh fruits, vegetables, chicken, or cheese—worth $7.02.

6   Minneapolis is Ehrenreich's last stop. In this city, as in the other two, affordable housing was the major problem. Across the nation, the supply of housing for low-income families was decreasing: 36 units available for every 100 families in need. The old rule that one should pay no more than 30 percent of income for rent has become impossible. For most poor renters, the figure is more than 50 percent. In the Minneapolis–St. Paul region, where the minimum living wage for a parent and one child was calculated to be $11.77 an hour, Ehrenreich has a job at Wal-Mart paying $7 an hour. Many of her fellow workers, even those with working spouses, work two jobs.

7   What does Ehrenreich conclude from her experiences? No surprises here. Even for a worker holding two jobs, wages are too low, housing costs too high, for minimally decent survival in the life of America's working poor.

---

[2] *canned labor:* a reference to the fact that the trailers are made of metal-like cans; the workers are treated like canned food, packed in their inferior housing

[3] *makeshift:* for temporary use, when nothing better is available

[4] *food voucher:* a coupon given to you that you can exchange for food at no cost to you; given to poor people who are destitute or who have very little money

2 *Fill in the chart below based on the information in Reading Two. Use your own words. Then compare your answers with a partner's.*

CATEGORY	WHY IS IT A PROBLEM?	HOW DO WORKERS DEAL WITH IT?
Health care	• no health care from employer • no money for antibiotics • no dental insurance	• don't go to doctors unless it's an emergency • •
Child care	•	• makeshift child care
Housing	• not enough affordable housing for working people • •	• • •

3 *Read the questions and select the best answers. In some cases there is more than one correct answer. Discuss your answers in a small group.*

1. Which of the following jobs did Barbara Ehrenreich have?
   a. waitress, cook, tourist guide, store employee
   b. cook, waitress, housecleaner, store employee
   c. waitress, housecleaner, nursing home attendant, store employee
   d. nursing home attendant, cook, tourist guide, housecleaner

2. Based on Ehrenreich's description of the trailer park in Key West, what are living conditions like for the working poor?
   a. dangerous
   b. congested
   c. depressing
   d. hot

3. What conclusions can we draw about Ehrenreich's job as a housecleaner?
   a. Homeowners pay the cleaning company $50 an hour for two cleaners.
   b. Only about 25 percent of the money goes to the cleaners; 75 percent goes to the cleaning company owners.
   c. Cleaning houses provides Ehrenreich with enough money to live on.
   d. The cleaning workers eat nourishing lunches.

4. What can we conclude about Ehrenreich's attempt to get help from private charities?
   a. She was successful in getting some food.
   b. It was easy to get help from charities.
   c. The charities provided the food she wanted to eat.
   d. The food voucher was really worth only $4.52 to her.

5. "There are not exactly people here [in the trailer park] but what amounts to canned labor, being preserved between shifts from the heat." What does this mean?
   a. The workers are treated well.
   b. Life in the trailer park is not fit for humans.
   c. Employers use robots.
   d. Workers are housed only so that they can continue working.

C   LINKING READINGS ONE AND TWO

Discuss this topic in a group.

Imagine that you are able to design a utopian community for Barbara Ehrenreich and her fellow workers. What would be a good utopian community for them? Would any of the ideas of Brook Farm be useful in setting up this new community? If so, which of Brook Farm's ideas would you implement immediately? Which of Brook Farm's ideas would you not use at all?

As you plan a community to solve the problems of the working poor, consider these categories: work and salaries, housing, health care, education, child care, class distinctions. Try to come up with specific recommendations. Then, in an oral presentation, share your group's plan for a utopian community with the rest of the class.

3 Focus on Vocabulary

1 *Working in pairs, choose the sentences that best express the meaning of the underlined phrases. There can be more than one correct answer.*

1. Are you able to <u>put up</u> the rent, or do you need help?
   a. Can you supply the money?
   b. Are you able to afford the rent?
   c. Can you tolerate this high rent?

2. If you don't have health insurance, you have to <u>pay through the nose</u> to see a doctor or a dentist.
   a. You have to pay cash.
   b. You have to pay a lot.
   c. You have to pay more than others pay.

3. We can't afford a regular babysitter, so we have <u>makeshift</u> childcare arrangements with neighbors and family.
   a. We use temporary solutions.
   b. We are able to use better childcare arrangements.
   c. We are forced to make do with whatever we can get.

4. The tourist <u>slump</u> is badly affecting the hotel and entertainment industry in our city.
   a. Tourists are not coming.
   b. Fewer tourists are coming.
   c. Tourists are too fearful to come.

5. It is very difficult to <u>make ends meet</u> when you earn only $7 an hour.
   a. It is hard to meet others.
   b. It is hard to work in such conditions.
   c. It is hard to earn enough to cover your expenses.

2 *A **noun** is a word that names a person, animal, place, thing, quality, idea, or action. A **verb** is a word that expresses an action, an occurrence, or a mode of being. An **adjective** is a word that describes a noun. An **adverb** is a word that describes a verb, adjective, or another adverb.*

*Circle the correct form of the word to complete the sentence. Then identify your choice as a noun (**n**), verb (**v**), adjective (**adj**), or adverb (**adv**). Check your answers with those of a partner.*

1. Most low-income families cannot make ends meet because there is not enough housing that is (affordable / (affordably)) priced.

   n   v   adj   (adv)

2. Some families live in trailer parks in (desolate/desolation) rural areas and small cities.

   n   v   adj   adv

3. It is not easy for working people to admit that they need (charity/charitable) help because they want to earn their money.

   n   v   adj   adv

4. When people get sick and have no health insurance, they make (frantic/frantically) calls to find an inexpensive clinic.

   n   v   adj   adv

5. People who do hard physical labor must get the proper (nourish/nourishment) from the food they eat.

   n   v   adj   adv

3 *Sir Thomas More wrote his vision of utopia in sixteenth-century Britain. He meant it as a criticism of the society he lived in, and he expressed many of his own views about a just and moral society.*

Read the following selection. Write a synonym from the box below that matches the definition under each blank. (Note that some words will not be used.) Check your answers with a partner's.

acquire	devote	inconceivable	preside over	vulgar
afford	frantic	paramount	severe	witty
desolation	impose	poverty	suitable	

A Book Called "Utopia" by Sir Thomas More

In Utopia, people do not _____ any private property. Everyone
   1. (buy, gain)

dresses alike, and almost all Utopians live in identical cities with nearly

identical houses, which they exchange by lot every ten years. There is no

_____ or homelessness. The Utopians work six hours a day and
   2. (lack of wealth)

_____ the rest of their time to cultivating virtue. No one may be
   3. (dedicate)

idle or engage in any meaningless games or pastimes.

The Utopians believe in a _____ suppression of private life.
   4. (strict)

Meals are served in public halls, and people who choose to eat at home are

regarded with suspicion. No one can travel without permission. Private political

discussion is punishable by death. Citizens considered _____ for
   5. (fit)

learning must attend lectures, which are held before the workday begins. The

lectures are open to the public, and many people attend.

The Utopians are a peaceful people, waging war only when war is obliged

upon them. When their own population expands, they may _____
   6. (force)

war on their neighbors to take over the vacant or unused land of a neighbor

who won't give it to them! They prefer to employ paid foreign soldiers rather

than their own citizens, but when they fight for themselves, Utopia's soldiers do

so with furious bravery.

Judges _____ a system where criminals are enslaved for their
   7. (have control)

first offense. This may seem barbarous to us, but in England at that time, such criminals would be put to death. The Utopians allow only slaves to kill animals because they do not want their free citizens to experience the _____

8. (sadness)

or cruelty associated with the miserable experience of killing beasts.

According to the Utopian philosophy of pleasure, wise people choose

the _____ pleasures of the spirit instead of the more

9. (very important)

_____ pleasures of the flesh.

10. (crude, rude)

4 Choose either the sixteenth-century imaginary utopia of Sir Thomas More or the nineteenth-century community of Brook Farm. Write a paragraph criticizing some of the ideas and practices of the utopia you chose. Explain why certain ideas would not be acceptable today or might lead to failure.

In your writing, use eight of the vocabulary words below in any form you wish.

acquire	frantic	paramount	severely
afford	impose	poverty	suit
desolation	inconceivable	preside	vulgarity
devotion	make ends meet		

4 Focus on Writing

A GRAMMAR: Noun Clauses

1 Examine the underlined clauses in the sentences, and discuss the questions that follow.

- <u>What the founders of Brook Farm wanted to create</u> was a better life.

- <u>That some men in contemporary society were responsible for all the hard, physical labor and others were not</u> was totally unacceptable to <u>whoever joined the Brook Farm experiment</u>.

- The residents of Brook Farm hoped to realize <u>what members of other utopian communities had always dreamed of achieving</u>: to bring justice back into the daily lives of every human being.

    1. Does each of these clauses have a subject and a verb? If so, what are they?

    2. What words do these clauses start with?

    3. What is the subject-verb word order in each of these clauses?

Noun Clauses

Noun clauses are like nouns in a sentence. Noun clauses can be subjects, objects of verbs or prepositions, or complements. The following words often introduce noun clauses: ***what, that, who, whom, whether, why, where, how, whatever, whoever, whomever, wherever, however.***

Noun clause as SUBJECT	**What the founders of Brook Farm wanted to create** was a better life for all of us.
Noun clause as OBJECT	It is important to understand **what the founders of Brook Farm wanted to create.**
Noun clause as COMPLEMENT	This is **what the founders of Brook Farm wanted to create.**

GRAMMAR TIP: Like all clauses, noun clauses must have a subject and a verb. Although some noun clauses start with question words, the word order is not the inverted subject-verb word order that is used in questions. In all noun clauses, the subject comes before the verb- Note that sometimes the question word itself is the "subject" of the noun clause, as in "whoever joined the Brook Farm experiment."

---

2 *Fill in the blanks with **what, that, who, why, where, how,** and **whoever** and the subject and correct form of the indicated verb. You will use some of the words more than once.*

If a utopia is supposed to be a dream come true, a dystopia is a nightmare world. One of the most famous stories of a dystopia is *Fahrenheit 451,*[*] written by the American Ray Bradbury.[**] <u>   What this book describes   </u> is a

1. (this book/describe)
society where violent teenagers, constant meaningless television, censorship, and police state conformity have made people into mindless sheep. The hero of the book is Guy Montag. _____ is a way to be able to

2. (he/look for)
think for himself and enjoy a sense of personal freedom.

After meeting a 17-year-old girl who gives him a glimpse into the past when books were not banned and people were not afraid to be themselves, Montag begins to wonder _____ ten years of his life

3. (he/spend)
burning books and the houses in which they are hidden. The author describes

---

[*] Fahrenheit 451 means 451° Fahrenheit (233° Celsius), the temperature at which books burn.
[**] Bradbury's book was made into a movie by the French film director François Truffaut.

_____ a book from one of the midnight "runs"
    4. (Montag/smuggle)

and soon becomes so obsessed with books that he is no longer able to report to

work. _____ to flames is the natural outcome of
    5. (his house and books/eventually be set)

this drama. Subject to arrest, he escapes with the help of an old English professor

he once met on a park bench. _____ to go is to the
    6. (he/have)

edge of the city. There, he finally realizes _____
    7. (he/be)

meant to be as he joins a network of men and women who have been memorizing

all the great masterpieces of world literature for future generations.

_____ this story of social criticism will be moved
    8. (read)

by its message.

3 _Express your opinions on the following topics. Using the noun clauses given, write one
or two sentences for each topic. Vary the position of the noun clauses by using them as
subjects, objects, and complements._

1. that some people desire a life without pain

   Example

   That some people desire a life without pain is understandable. It is a

   wonderful dream to have, but it is not very realistic.

   Your sentence:

   _____

   _____

2. whoever reads books

   _____

   _____

3. how video surveillance can create a sense of security

   _____

   _____

4. why giving dignity to all work is important

   _____

   _____

5. what makes communal living difficult

_____

_____

6. that Ehrenreich is a good journalist

_____

_____

B STYLE: Introductory Paragraphs and Thesis Statements

1 *Working with a partner, read the introductory paragraph below. Then discuss the questions that follow.*

Should a garbage man be paid the same salary as a college professor? Most people would consider this to be a foolish question. They would immediately answer "No!" because one does physical labor and the other engages in mental labor. Society teaches us to respect and reward one type of work more than another. This kind of thinking was exactly what the founders of Brook Farm were reacting against when they started their utopian experiment in the 1840s. Because the dignity of all human beings was of paramount importance to them, they believed that no matter what kind of work a person did, everyone's contribution to society was of equal value. As a result, all Brook Farm residents received the same wages. Nevertheless, despite these good intentions, Brook Farm failed because of its residents' lack of capital in a world unfavorable to generosity.

1. How does the writer attract the reader's attention in the first sentence?

2. How do you think the ideas develop throughout the paragraph: from the general to the specific? from the specific to the general?

3. Which sentence tells the reader what the writer will focus on in the body of the essay?

Introductory Paragraphs

An essay is composed of an introduction, a body, and a conclusion. In the introductory paragraph the author writes a statement to attract the reader's attention. This statement is the first of the paragraph's general statements, which introduce the general topic of the essay. There are many ways the writer can spark the reader's interest: with a question, a humorous remark, a shocking statement.

The flow of ideas in the paragraph goes from the general (large, broad ideas) to the specific (details, examples, particular cases). The most specific statement is the thesis statement, which is usually the last sentence of the paragraph.

(continued)

Thesis Statements

The **thesis statement** communicates the main idea of the essay. It reflects the writer's narrow focus and point of view, attitude, or opinion, and it also forecasts which aspects of the subject the writer will discuss to support the thesis in the body of the essay. A good thesis statement should have all of the criteria mentioned above.

The thesis statement is not a statement of fact, nor is it a statement that simply announces the general topic of the essay.

Utopias are visions of perfect political or social systems.	THIS IS NOT A THESIS STATEMENT. It states a fact; no point of view is given.
I am going to write about utopias.	THIS IS NOT A THESIS STATEMENT. It only announces the general topic.
Reading about utopias can be valuable.	THIS IS NOT A THESIS STATEMENT. Although it gives us the writer's point of view, there is no focus here. What exactly makes reading about utopias "valuable"?
Reading about utopias can be valuable because what we learn from books can help us to deal with the social, economic, and moral problems of contemporary life.	THIS IS A THESIS STATEMENT. It explains why the writer believes reading about utopias can be valuable. The writer will most likely explain this in three body paragraphs dealing with: 1. social problems 2. economic problems 3. moral problems

2 *Read the following sentences of an introduction to an essay. Working with a partner, put the sentences in order. Using* **1** *for the first sentence and* **5** *for the last sentence (the thesis statement), write the numbers in the blanks.*

_____ However, we all like a good success story.

_____ Known for their furniture and their many inventions, such as the first circular saw in America, the Shakers came here in 1774 and ran successful communities in the United States for 150 years.

_____ We often learn more from our failures than from our successes.

_____ Their simple, celibate life without excessive material wealth was the key to their success.

_____ For example, because of the Shakers' success in running a religious utopian community for many years, people today enjoy reading about their lifestyle.

3 *Working in pairs, evaluate the following statements, and put checks (✓) next to the ones that are good thesis statements. In your evaluation, do not automatically think that the longer the statement, the better a thesis statement it is. For those you identify as good thesis statements, discuss how you think the writer could develop each of these statements in the body of the essay.*

_____ **1.** If we provide everyone in our society with a living wage, good housing conditions, and adequate social services, we will be on the road to creating a utopia.

_____ **2.** The idea of utopia existed in China, India, and various Buddhist and Islamic cultures before More's publication of *Utopia* in 1516.

_____ **3.** The origin of the word *utopia* is Greek; it means "no place."

_____ **4.** People who do a combination of physical and mental work lead wholesome lives.

_____ **5.** Authors often write dystopias to warn us about the dangers of modern-day society: conformity, selfishness, and violence.

_____ **6.** In this essay, the writer will discuss science fiction and utopianism.

_____ **7.** Justice cannot possibly prevail in a society where the majority of the people do the physical labor under the supervision of the privileged few.

_____ **8.** Although this book is not read much today, Samuel Butler's *Erehwon* is a major work in utopian literature that deserves careful consideration.

4 *Read the following introductory paragraphs, and put a check (✓) next to the best thesis statement from the choices given. Discuss your answers with a partner.*

   1. Considering the fact that the nineteenth century is the period in which the United States greatly expanded its territory and its economy, it is not surprising to learn that more than 200 experimental utopian communities were started in the 1800s. In a hundred years, the United States experienced great growth and went from a country of 16 states and 5 million people to one of 42 states and 76 million people. As the country developed, many settlers seeking a better life founded utopian communities and struggled—often with little success—to transform their ideals into reality. Noteworthy in this period are three Tennessee communities, Nashoba, Rugby, and Ruskin, all of which found their inspiration in the economic and social ideas of Robert Owen.

Thesis Statement

_____ **a.** In this essay, the writer will discuss Nashoba, Rugby, and Ruskin.

_____ **b.** Like many other utopian communities, Nashoba, Rugby, and Ruskin failed because of a lack of strong leadership in the absence of their founders, internal mismanagement, and an inability to state priorities and stick to them.

_____ **c.** Robert Owen's community, New Harmony, Indiana, was one of the first and most influential utopian communities in the United States.

2. Could you ever imagine living in a society where books were banned? This is the main theme of *Fahrenheit 451,* Ray Bradbury's tale of a dystopia in which firefighters spend their days burning the books found in readers' houses. Although the story may seem extreme, totalitarian governments throughout the course of history have forbidden people to think for themselves and express their own views. Books have been banned in countries governed by totalitarian regimes because free access to all books and other publications could give people information that their governments might not want them to have. Unfortunately, today we have found that this effort to control citizens' access to information and their right to free expression is not limited to totalitarian societies alone. Even in democratic societies, where freedom is supposed to exist, there is sometimes pressure to censor and eliminate certain kinds of publications. "This publication will offend someone," the guardians of public morality declare. I don't agree with such a line of reasoning.

Thesis Statement

_____ **a.** Censorship in any shape or form is not compatible with freedom.

_____ **b.** People will be offended by what they hear, but this is unavoidable.

_____ **c.** Freedom has its limits.

5 *Using what you have now learned about writing introductory paragraphs, write an introduction to an essay on your own concept of utopia. What kind of utopian world would you create if you were given the opportunity to invent one?*

C   WRITING TOPICS

Write an essay on one of the following topics. Try to include vocabulary and grammar you have studied in the unit. In writing the essay, pay particular attention to:

- making your introduction interesting and relevant to the topic.

- expressing the main idea of the essay in a well-formulated thesis statement.

1. If you were given the opportunity to invent a utopian world, what kind of world would you create? You may use the introductory paragraph you wrote in the previous section and complete the essay here.

2. Imagine a society in which people are not allowed to live beyond the age of 35. Upon reaching their thirty-fifth birthday, people in this society are routinely terminated because it is thought that they are no longer useful to society. Discuss the strengths and weaknesses of such a society. Could this be a perfect society? Why or why not?

3. What would it take to transform a contemporary society that you know about into a more perfect society? Consider any country of your choice, and respond to this question by identifying current problems in that country and explaining what you would do to solve them.

4. Read the title of Samuel Butler's *Erehwon* backwards. What word do you see? To most people, utopia seems to be an elusive dream. After all, we human beings are not perfect. So how can we presume to consider creating a perfect place? What do you think? Is utopia possible?

5. If you could go back and live for a while in the past, what era and place would you choose? In what ways do you think life in the past would be an improvement over the life you are leading today?

6. As an investigative journalist, Barbara Ehrenreich wrote *Nickel and Dimed* by living the lives of the people she was writing about—in this case, America's working poor. What kind of investigative journalism would you like to do, and how would you do it?

D RESEARCH TOPICS

PREPARATION

The following is a list of three famous utopian communities:

Nashoba	a community in Tennessee that intended to educate and free American slaves
New Harmony	one of the first and most influential utopian communities in the United States
The Shakers	a religious community that enjoyed considerable success

Decide which community you would like to research.

RESEARCH ACTIVITY

Go to the library or online to do your research. Take notes, and summarize the information you obtain. Use at least two different sources.

Find out the following:

- who founded the society
- when it was founded
- why it was founded
- where it was established
- how it was organized
- how many people became members

- what its mission statement was

- what special challenges it faced

- what its accomplishments were; what its failures were

- how it ended up

SHARING YOUR FINDINGS

Write a report.

1. In the introduction, give the main idea that ties your research findings together.

2. In the body, summarize your findings in detail.

3. In the conclusion, give your opinion about the community you have studied.

4. After your teacher has commented on your paper, share what you have learned by presenting a five-minute summary to your classmates.

For step-by-step practice in the writing process, see the *Writing Activity Book, Advanced,* Unit 2.

Assignment	Opinion Essay
Prewriting	Critical Listing
Organizing	Reviewing the Basic Features of an Essay
Revising	Analyzing Introductions and Thesis Sentences
	Using Noun Clauses
Editing	Correcting Run-on Sentences

For Unit 2 Internet activities, visit the NorthStar Companion Website at
http://longman.com/northstar.

The Road to Success

1 Focus on the Topic

A PREDICTING

Do you think this photo is a good representation of the struggle for success? Why or why not? Share your thoughts with another student.

B   SHARING INFORMATION

Work in a small group. Take a survey of the people in your group to find out where they believe they belong on this "hope scale." Tally the results, and indicate how many people are generally "pessimistic" or generally "optimistic" and how many fall "in between." Next to each result, write down the general reasons that the person gave for being either optimistic or pessimistic or in between.

HOPE-SCALE SURVEY		
	Tally	**Reasons**
Are you pessimistic?		
Are you optimistic?		
Are you in-between?		

C PREPARING TO READ

BACKGROUND

Read this information, and take the Self-Discovery Quiz that follows. Discuss your responses and your goal with a partner.

People's outlook on life has a lot to do with their potential for success. Some researchers have found a direct link between hope and success. They have found that optimists—people who always see the bright side of things—are more likely to succeed in life than pessimists, their direct opposites. Hope does not just involve having a belief in good results. It involves having both the will and the means to reach one's goal. People with hope have some traits in common: They turn to friends for advice; they regard setbacks as challenges and not as failures; they know how to break a big goal into smaller chunks and work on one aspect at a time.

Hope is the driving force of Katie, the main character in "Gotta Dance," the short story that you will read in this unit. It is the first published short story of Jackson Jodie Daviss, a freelance writer who lives in New Hampshire. In speaking of this story, the author stated that it allowed her to "say some things about the need to find acceptance on our own terms, and to define our own ideas of home and family."

SELF-DISCOVERY QUIZ

Achieving success has a lot to do with how you look at yourself.

1. Write down three things that you like about yourself.

   _____

   _____

   _____

2. Write down a goal that you would like to achieve.

   _____

3. What is your target date for achieving it?

   _____

4. What obstacles or opposition to your goal might you encounter?

   _____

5. What are some first steps you could take toward your goal?

   _____

keep on = keep going

VOCABULARY FOR COMPREHENSION

Work in pairs to match the underlined expressions with the meanings below.

_B_ 1. My uncle's remark that I would never succeed in life, no matter how much I tried, <u>lit a fire under</u> me.

_i_ 2. My old room was <u>dim</u> because the curtains were drawn across the windows and the sunshine could not enter.

_L_ 3. The <u>pace</u> of life is slower and quieter in the countryside, but I couldn't wait to travel to the cities.

_A_ 4. The passengers enjoyed the smoothness of the new train, which <u>eased in and out</u> of stations <u>with no jolts to their systems</u>.

_D_ 5. Waiting on tables and serving food for eight hours a day with no break can really <u>take it out of you</u>, no matter how strong you are.

_F_ 6. Because I was not hungry and eating was the last thing on my mind, I only <u>picked at</u> the food they brought me.

_H_ 7. Even though I insisted that I was no longer hungry, the young man was <u>reluctant</u> to take the dinner I offered to give him.

_J_ 8. I didn't want to draw attention to the fact that I was alone and carrying a lot of money. I kept quiet about everything because it is better to use <u>discretion</u> with strangers.

_K_ 9. The young people begging for <u>spare change</u> outside the theater looked hopeless and lost.

_g_ 10. Once I started dancing, I danced so well that I didn't <u>miss a beat</u>.

_C_ 11. When I finally realized what I had to do in order to succeed, everything <u>came together</u> and I knew success was around the corner.

_e_ 12. Because I had no doubts that the decision I had made was the right one, I <u>had no weights, no worries</u>.

a. arrived in and departed from quietly, without creating a shock

b. angered and motivated

c. made sense

d. exhaust you, knock you out

e. felt free, with no burdens

f. ate very little with no appetite

g. hesitate, make a mistake

h. unwilling

i. dark

j. good judgment, prudence

k. extra coins

l. rhythm, tempo

2 Focus on Reading

Discuss these questions with a partner. Then read the story.

Did you ever have a compulsion—something you felt you had to do, no matter what the obstacles or consequences? Did you act on your feelings? Were you glad you did?

GOTTA DANCE¹

BY JACKSON JODIE DAVISS

1   Maybe I shouldn't have mentioned it to anyone. Before I knew it, it was all through the family, and they'd all made it their business to challenge me. I wouldn't tell them my plans, other than to say I was leaving, but that was enough to set them off. Uncle Mike called from Oregon to say, "Katie, don't do it," and I wouldn't have hung up on him except that he added, "Haven't you caused enough disappointment?" That did it. Nine people had already told me no, and Uncle Mike lit the fire under me when he made it ten. Nine-eight-seven-six-five-four-three-two-one. Kaboom.

2   On my way to the bus station, I stopped by the old house. I still had my key, and I knew no one was home. After ducking my head into each room, including my old one, just to be sure I was alone, I went into my brother's room and set my duffel bag and myself on his bed.

3   The blinds were shut so the room was dim, but I looked around at all the things I knew by heart and welcomed the softening effect of the low light. I sat there a very long time in the silence until I began to think I might never rise from that bed or come out of that gray light, so I pushed myself to my feet. I eased off my sneakers and pushed the rug aside so I could have some polished floor, then I pulled the door shut.

¹ *gotta dance:* slang expression for "I have got to dance," "I must dance"

4   Anyone passing in the hall outside might've heard a soft sound, a gentle sweeping sound, maybe a creak of the floor, but not much more as I danced a very soft shoe[2] in my stocking feet. Arms outstretched but loose and swaying, head laid back and to one side, like falling asleep, eyes very nearly closed in that room like twilight, I danced to the beat of my heart.

5   After a while, I straightened the rug, opened the blinds to the bright day, and walked out of what was now just another room without him in it. He was the only one I said good-bye to, and the only one I asked to come with me, if he could.

6   At the bus station, I asked the guy for a ticket to the nearest city of some size. Most of them are far apart in the Midwest, and I liked the idea of those long rides with time to think. I like buses—the long-haul kind, anyway—because they're so public that they're private. I also like the pace, easing you out of one place before easing you into the next, no big jolts to your system.

7   My bus had very few people in it and the long ride was uneventful, except when the little boy threw his hat out the window. The mother got upset, but the kid was happy. He clearly hated that hat; I'd seen him come close to launching it twice before he finally let fly. The thing sailed in a beautiful arc, then settled on a fence post, a ringer, just the way you never can do it when you try. The woman asked the driver if he'd mind going back for the hat. He said he'd mind. So the woman stayed upset and the kid stayed happy. I liked her well enough, but the boy was maybe the most annoying kid I've come across, so I didn't offer him the money to buy a hat he and his mother could agree on. Money would have been no problem. Money has never been my problem.

8   There are some who say money is precisely my problem, in that I give it so little thought. I don't own much. I lose things all the time. I'm told I dress lousy. I'm told, too, that I have no appreciation of money because I've never had to do without it. That may be true. But even if it is, it's not all there is to say about a person.

9   There is one thing I do well, and money didn't buy it, couldn't have bought it for me. I am one fine dancer. I can dance like nobody you've ever seen. Heck, I can dance like everybody you've ever seen. I didn't take lessons, not the usual kind, because I'm a natural, but I've worn out a few sets of tapes and a VCR. I'd watch Gene Kelly and practice until I had his steps. Watch Fred Astaire, practice, get his steps. I practice all the time. Bill Robinson. Eleanor Powell. Donald O'Connor. Ginger Rogers. You know, movie dancers. I'm a movie dancer. I don't dance in the movies though. Never have. Who does, anymore? I dance where and when I can.

10   My many and vocal relatives don't think much, have never thought much, of my dancing—largely, I believe, because they are not dancers

---

[2] *a soft shoe:* tap dance steps but without taps (metal caps) on the shoes; a silent dance

themselves. To be honest, they don't think much of anything I do, not since I left the path they'd set for me, and that's been most of my 23 years. These people, critical of achievement they don't understand, without praise for talents and dreams or the elegant risk, are terrified of being left behind but haven't the grace to come along in spirit.

11   Mutts and I talked a lot about that. He was a family exception, as I am, and he thought whatever I did was more than fine. He was my brother, and I backed everything he did, too. He played blues harmonica. He told bad jokes. We did have plans. His name was Ronald, but everyone's called him Mutts since he was a baby. No one remembers why. He never got his chance to fly, and I figure if I don't do this now, I maybe never will. I need to do it for both of us.

12   The bus depot was crowded and crummy, like most city depots seem to be. I stored my bag in a locker, bought a paper, and headed for where the bright lights would be. I carried my tap shoes and tape player.

13   When I reached the area I wanted it was still early, so I looked for a place to wait. I found a clean diner, with a big front window where I could read the paper and watch for the lines to form. I told the waitress I wanted a large cup of coffee before ordering. After half an hour or so, she brought another refill and asked if I was ready. She was kind and patient, and I wondered what she was doing in the job. It seems like nothing takes it out of you like waitress work. She was young; maybe that was it. I asked her what was good, and she recommended the baked chicken special and said it was what she had on her break. That's what I had, and she was right, but I only picked at it. I wanted something for energy, but I didn't want to court a side-ache, so the only thing I really ate was the salad. She brought an extra dinner roll and stayed as pleasant the whole time I was there, which was the better part of two hours, so I put down a good tip when I left.

14   While I was in the diner, a truly gaunt[3] young man came in. He ordered only soup, but he ate it like he'd been hungry a long time. He asked politely for extra crackers, and the waitress gave them to him. When he left he was full of baked chicken special with an extra dinner roll. He wouldn't take a loan. Pride, maybe, or maybe he didn't believe I could spare it, and I didn't want to be sitting in a public place pushing the idea that I had plenty of money. Maybe I don't know the value of money, but I do know what discretion is worth. The guy was reluctant even to take the chicken dinner, but I convinced him that if he didn't eat it, nobody would. He reminded me of Mutts, except that Mutts had never been hungry like that.

15   When the lines were forming, I started on over. While I waited, I watched the people. There were some kids on the street, dressed a lot like me in my worn jeans, faded turtleneck, and jersey warm-up jacket. They were working the crowd like their hopes amounted to spare

---

[3] *gaunt:* very thin

change. The theater patrons waiting in line were dressed to the nines,[4] as they say. There is something that makes the well-dressed not look at the shabby. Maybe it's guilt. Maybe it's embarrassment because, relatively, they're overdressed. I don't know. I do know it makes it easy to study them in detail. Probably makes them easy marks[5] for pickpockets, too. The smell of them was rich: warm wool, sweet spice and alcohol, peppermint and shoe polish. I thought I saw Mutts at the other edge of the crowd, just for a moment, but I remembered he couldn't be.

16   I was wearing my sneakers, carrying my taps. They're slickery[6] black shoes that answer me back. They're among the few things I've bought for myself, and I keep them shiny. I sat on the curb and changed my shoes. I tied the sneakers together and draped them over my shoulder.

17   I turned on my tape player, and the first of my favorite show tunes began as I got to my feet. I waited a few beats, but no one paid attention until I started to dance. My first taps rang off the concrete clear and clean, measured, a telegraphed message: Takka-takka-takka-tak! Takka-takka-takka-tak! Takka-takka-takka-tak-tak-tak! I paused; everyone turned.

18   I tapped an oh-so-easy, wait-a-minute time-step while I lifted the sneakers from around my neck. I gripped the laces in my right hand and gave the shoes a couple of overhead, bola-style swings, tossing them to land beside the tape player, neat as you please. I didn't miss a beat. The audience liked it. I knew they would. Then I let the rhythm take me, and I started to fly. Everything came together. I had no weight, no worries, just the sweet, solid beat. Feets, do your stuff.[7]

19   Didn't I dance. And wasn't I smooth. Quick taps and slow-rolling, jazz it, swing it, on the beat, off the beat, out of one tune right into the next and the next and I never took one break. It was a chill of a night, but didn't I sweat, didn't that jacket just have to come off. Didn't I feel the solid jar to the backbone from the heavy heel steps, and the pump of my heart on the beat on the beat.

20   Time passed. I danced. A sandy-haired man came out of the theater. He looked confused. He said, "Ladies and Gentlemen, curtain in five minutes." I'm sure that's what he said. Didn't I dance and didn't they all stay. The sandy-haired man, he was tall and slim and he looked like a dancer. Didn't he stay, too.

21   Every move I knew, I made, every step I learned, I took, until the tape had run out, until they set my rhythm with the clap of their hands, until the sweet sound of the overture drifted out, until I knew for certain they had held the curtain for want of an audience. Then I did my knock-down, drag-out, could-you-just-die, great big Broadway-baby finish.

---

[4] *dressed to the nines:* dressed in expensive clothes
[5] *easy marks:* easy victims
[6] *slickery:* patent leather, shiny and smooth
[7] *Feets, do your stuff:* Feet, start dancing.

22   Didn't they applaud, oh honey, didn't they yell, and didn't they throw money. I dug coins from my own pockets and dropped them, too, leaving it all for the street kids. Wasn't the slender man with the sandy hair saying, "See me after the show"? I'm almost sure that's what he said as I gripped my tape recorder, grabbed my sneakers, my jacket, and ran away, ran with a plan and a purpose, farther with each step from my beginnings and into the world, truly heading home.

23   The blood that drummed in my ears set the rhythm as I ran, ran easy, taps ringing off the pavement, on the beat, on the beat, on the beat. Everything was pounding, but I had to make the next bus, that I knew, catch that bus and get on to the next town, and the next, and the next, and the next. Funeral tomorrow, but Mutts will not be there, no, and neither will I. I'm on tour.

READING FOR MAIN IDEAS

"Gotta Dance" can be divided into three parts. Write a sentence that summarizes the main idea of each part of the story. Use your own words.

Part I: Saying Good-bye (paragraphs 1–5)

After saying good-bye to her childhood home and the memory of her brother,

Katie decides to change her life.

Part II: On the Road (paragraphs 6–14)

_____

_____

_____

Part III: Meeting the Challenge (paragraphs 15–23)

_____

_____

_____

READING FOR DETAILS

First circle your answers to the questions below. Then compare your answers with another student's. There is only one correct answer for each item.

1. How would you describe the attitude of the majority of Katie's family?
   a. They were critical of Katie's desire to be a dancer.
   b. They encouraged her risk-taking.
   c. They were very supportive of all her plans.

2. Which statement is not true of Mutts?
   a. He loved playing the blues.
   b. He died before he could realize his dream.
   c. His sister was very upset at his funeral.

3. Which of the following did Katie do before setting out for the bus depot?
   a. She went straight to her brother's room after entering her old house.
   b. She danced a soft shoe in her brother's room to the beat of a jazz album.
   c. She danced with a lot of emotion in her brother's room knowing full well that no one else was in the house.

4. Which one of Katie's ideas must she re-evaluate as a result of her experiences?
   a. The pace of a long bus trip allows her time for reflection.
   b. Waiters and waitresses are generally impatient and unkind.
   c. Bus depots are usually dirty and packed with a lot of people.

5. What did Katie observe when she was in the bus?
   a. On his third attempt, the boy succeeded in throwing his hat out the window.
   b. The boy showed his perfect aim when his hat landed on a fence post.
   c. The bus driver responded to the mother with a lot of compassion.

6. Why did Katie go to the diner?
   a. She needed to be in a quiet place to think more about her brother.
   b. She needed to wait for her audience to arrive and to mentally and physically prepare for her performance.
   c. She needed to sit down for a while to take care of a pain in her side.

7. What thoughts did Katie have when she was watching the lines form in front of the theater?
   a. She considered how differences in dress can cause people to be uncomfortable with each other.
   b. She realized that one should dress up when going to the theater.
   c. She thought the street kids would be chased away by the police.

8. Which of the following is true about Katie's performance?
   a. The theatergoers liked it so much that they missed the first five minutes of the show they had been waiting in line to see.
   b. Katie was offered a job.
   c. Katie was satisfied with her performance.

REACTING TO THE READING

1 *Based on what is implied in the short story, discuss with your partner whether these statements are true or false, and write **T** or **F** on the line to the left. Then write a sentence explaining your decision. Include points in the story that support your inference.*

_____ **1.** Katie was a very private person.

Support: _____

_____ **2.** Family was important to Katie.

Support: _____

_____ **3.** Dancing came easily to Katie.

Support: _____

_____ **4.** Katie was ambitious.

Support: _____

_____ **5.** Katie sympathized with children who rebel against their families.

Support: _____

_____ **6.** Katie was careless with money.

Support: _____

_____ **7.** To Katie, "heading home" meant fulfilling her dreams.

Support: _____

2 *Discuss these questions in a small group.*

1. If one of your relatives said to you, "You are a big disappointment to me," what would you say or do? Would you react the way Katie did?

2. Do you think rebelling against the family is part of growing up? Is it necessary or dangerous, or both?

3. How would you describe Katie's relationship with her brother Mutts? How did her feelings about him affect her decisions?

4. In the story, Katie left the money people gave her for the street kids who had been begging from the theatergoers. What do you do when strangers ask you for money?

B READING TWO: *Keeping Your Confidence Up*

1 *Before you read "Keeping Your Confidence Up," write down three qualities that you consider essential for success, and explain why. Then share your answers with the class, and discuss your reasons.*

KEEPING YOUR CONFIDENCE UP

BY DENNIS O'GRADY
(from *Taking the Fear out of Changing*)

1   **S**uccess seeks to help you become more accepting of your genuine strengths. Self-approval unleashes[1] your best traits to be expressed in your work and family life, and in the world. How can you learn to accept your successes without panicking? Here are some practical ways to learn to celebrate all of your SUCCESSES.

2   SELF-ESTEEM. Being a genuine achiever means you acknowledge your strengths, hunt for your secret talents, and give your best to the world without being a braggart.[2]

Build Self-Confidence: Learn from your failures.

3   UNDERSTANDING. Achievement means you are an intense person who expresses who you really are while staying open to growing and changing each and every day.

Build Self-Confidence: Thrive on[3] responsibility.

4   CHILD DRIVE. You pay attention to inner urges that speak to you about what work you love to do and what insights[4] you have to give the world.

Build Self-Confidence: Make work fun.

---

[1] *to unleash:* to release
[2] *braggart:* someone who boasts a lot
[3] *to thrive on:* to draw success from
[4] *insights:* clear, perceptive thoughts

5   CURIOSITY. You talk, talk, and talk some more to people to find out what makes them tick. You soak up information like a sunbather taking in sunshine.
    Build Self-Confidence: Take good advice.

6   ENERGY. You maximize your energy by eating, sleeping, exercising, and working in recognition of your own special rhythms. You do what makes you feel most alive.
    Build Self-Confidence: Keep your energy high.

7   SET GOALS. You dignify life with long-term goals and mark your progression toward them.
    Build Self-Confidence: Choose commitment.

8   STAY FOCUSED. You intensely focus single-mindedly on the most important tasks to accomplish, and you say "No way!" to nifty distractions.[5]
    Build Self-Confidence: Accept self-discipline.

9   ERRORS. You make errors every day and know that if you aren't failing at least once a day then you aren't succeeding. You try again to hit the mark after you've missed it.
    Build Self-Confidence: Never accept failure as a permanent state.

10 SATISFACTION. You endorse[6] yourself for your wins, follow a consistent set of values, and take humble pride in all of your accomplishments.
    Build Self-Confidence: Feel gratified.

11 Permit yourself to be a genuine achiever instead of an impostor. Real people aren't impostors—we are the genuine article. Take the risk, and be the real McCoy![7]

[5] *nifty distractions:* pleasurable amusements
[6] *to endorse:* to show approval of
[7] *the real McCoy:* the real thing, not something artificial or phony (after Kid McCoy, professional name for American boxer Norman Selby, 1873–1940)

2 *Dennis O'Grady's principles of success can be applied to typical problems that come up in business. Read the situations below, and determine what O'Grady would recommend. Discuss your answers with a partner, and refer to specific parts of the text that support your interpretation. Write your answers on the lines.*

1. You have been working seven days a week on a project that must be completed two weeks from now. Because it requires your full attention, you will need to make use of your every waking minute in the next two weeks to complete the project. Yet you are tempted to take advantage of an airline's cheap four-day "getaway" in the Florida sun. What should you do?

2. After being in business for several years, it is clear that you are on the road to becoming a real success. You are not sure what kind of image you need to project in public. Should you flaunt your success and boast about your great fortune, or should you act like a regular person and behave as if you are just like everyone else?

_____

_____

_____

3. You have a very important decision to make about a policy that will have a great impact on the future of your company. You know that there will be dissatisfaction no matter which direction you take. You usually make all your decisions on your own. Should you consult your staff or go it alone?

_____

_____

_____

4. The promotion you had been hoping for does not come through because of a poor performance evaluation. You have lost confidence in yourself. How should you deal with this situation?

_____

_____

_____

5. You are offered a high-paying job in a field that really doesn't interest you. Nevertheless, the increase in salary would dramatically change your current lifestyle. You are now earning a much lower salary while taking courses in the field of your choice. What should you do?

_____

_____

_____

6. You are a valued employee. Nevertheless, your supervisor has complained to your boss that you nap and take exercise at unauthorized times. He would like you to follow the normal break and lunch schedule. What should you explain to your boss?

_____

_____

_____

C   LINKING READINGS ONE AND TWO

Choose one topic.

1. You are a journalist in a small midwestern town. Write a short article about a strange event that occurred last night at 8 P.M. A young girl named Katie began to dance in the street by the theater. Tell what happened, and explain whether you think this young woman will be a success and why.

2. You are Katie. You have read the excerpt from Dennis O'Grady's book. Explain which of O'Grady's principles of success you have already acted upon or have decided to adopt in the future.

3 | Focus on Vocabulary

When we use a two-word or compound adjective, or a group of words before a noun, we use hyphens* to link them and make some minor structural changes. Hyphenated adjectives can give texture, exuberance, and poetic feeling to a work of prose.

With descriptions

- a man with sandy hair (light brown or blond) = a sandy-haired man

- a table with three legs = a three-legged table

Measurements in time or space involving plurals

- a child who is two years old = a two-year-old child

- a house with three stories = a three-story house

1 *Change the following expressions to hyphenated adjectives.*

1. a boy with blue eyes   = _____

2. a hat with three corners   = _____

3. a woman with thin lips   = _____

4. a girl with a broken heart = _____

5. a law that is ten years old = _____

---

* Many rules of hyphenation are complicated and may be unclear. If you are unsure, look up the word in a good dictionary.

2 *Look back at the story "Gotta Dance," and find two sentences that use a number of hyphenated adjectives in the climax of the story (the last six paragraphs). Then rewrite the expressions below as hyphenated adjectives.*

1. a step that tells the audience to wait a minute = _____

_____

2. an ending similar to what a performer in a Broadway musical would do = ___

_____

3. a finish that makes you want to die from happiness = _____

_____

4. a finish that knocks the audience out because it is so good = _____

_____

3 *As you read the possible thoughts of the sandy-haired man in "Gotta Dance," fill in the blanks with the expressions from the box below. The expressions are synonyms for the words in parentheses.*

backed	picked up the pace	the better part
for want of	reluctantly	the long haul
hold the curtain	shabby	to the nines
miss a beat	take it out of you	

It may seem glamorous, but let me tell you, working in the theater can really

_____ . I've been a dancer, singer, ticket taker, scenery
   1. (wear you out)

painter, and everything else you can think of for _____ of the
                                                          2. (most)

last twenty years. Of course, sometimes show business can really surprise you

and then, all of a sudden, it all comes together.

I remember one time we were on tour in a _____ little
                                                   3. (run-down)

theater in a small city in the Midwest. The locals were all dressed

_____ , waiting for the show to begin. But when we finally
   4. (in their fancy clothes)

opened the doors, no one came in! No one! We couldn't understand it. All we

could hear was music from the street. _____ , I went outside
                                              5. (With unwilling steps)

to announce the curtain and saw a young woman in jeans and tap shoes dancing for the crowd. She didn't _____ as she danced her heart out.

6. (hesitate for a minute)

I couldn't take my eyes off her, and neither could anyone else. As she

_____, we all began clapping with her, marking the rhythm,

7. (went faster and faster)

showing our pleasure. _____ an audience, the company even

8. (Lacking)

agreed to _____.

9. (start the show late)

I would've _____ her to get a job dancing. I knew that

10. (helped)

right away as soon as I saw her, with no time needed to think it over. She was a

natural! Sure, she needed training and polish, but she had the fire and joy in her

eyes that would keep her out there for _____. I guess she

11. (a long time)

didn't hear what I said to her that night. We were all pretty shocked and

surprised. She asked for nothing, didn't even tell us her name. I can still see her

running off into the night and wonder what happened to her.

4 *Answer the following questions about yourself and other people you know. Use the underlined expressions in your answer.*

1. When Katie's relatives criticized her, it <u>lit a fire under</u> her and she had to do something. What kinds of things make you angry?

   Answer: *When my brother talks back to my mother, it lights a fire under me and I end up yelling at him about his awful behavior.*

2. When Katie first started to work on her dance routine, it must have seemed like an impossible task, but after she practiced again and again, things started to <u>come together</u> and she did very well. How did you deal with a difficulty that you eventually conquered?

   Answer: _____

   _____

   _____

3. Leaving home was not easy for Katie. Saying good-bye to her old room really <u>took it out of her</u>, and she felt drained of energy. What kind of physical or mental activity totally exhausts you?

   Answer: _____

   _____

   _____

4. Katie wanted to travel to a big city. She seemed to like the rapid, hectic <u>pace</u> of the city more than the tranquil rhythm of a small town. What do you prefer?

Answer: _____

_____

_____

5. For a long time, Katie was <u>reluctant</u> to start out on her own. But after her brother's death, she decided that she had to follow her dream. Can you think of anything that you were reluctant to do and then found the courage to do?

Answer: _____

_____

_____

4 Focus on Writing

A GRAMMAR: Identifying and Nonidentifying Adjective Clauses

1 *Working in pairs, examine the sentences and discuss the questions that follow.*

- People <u>who are unwilling to risk failure</u> are not capable of achieving big successes.

- The waitress stayed as pleasant the whole time I was there, <u>which was the better part of two hours</u>, so I put down a good tip when I left.

    1. In the first sentence, which people are being discussed?

    2. In the second sentence, how much time did Katie spend in the restaurant?

    3. Which words come at the beginning of the underlined phrases?

    4. Do you notice any difference in punctuation in the two sentences?

Adjective Clauses

Adjective clauses define, describe, or add information about nouns just as adjectives do. These clauses must have a subject and a verb, but they are fragments, not full sentences. The adjective clause can begin with the relative pronouns **who, whom, which, that,** and **whose,** or the relative adverbs **when** and **where. Who** is used for people, **which** is used for things, and **that** can be used for both people and things.

Identifying Adjective Clauses

Identifying adjective clauses give information that is essential to the meaning of the sentence.

- People **who are unwilling to risk failure** are not capable of achieving big successes.

If you take the adjective clause out of this sentence, the sentence itself no longer has any precise meaning. "People are not capable of achieving big successes" is vague and unclear because it implies that no one can ever succeed. The adjective clause is needed because it tells us specifically which people the statement is referring to. Identifying adjective clauses do not have any commas.

Nonidentifying Adjective Clauses

Nonidentifying adjective clauses have a different function in the sentence: They only provide extra or additional information. If nonidentifying adjective clauses are left out, the sentence still retains its basic meaning.

- The waitress stayed as pleasant the whole time I was there, **which was the better part of two hours,** so I put down a good tip when I left.

The significant clauses of this sentence are "The waitress stayed as pleasant the whole time I was there," and "so I put down a good tip when I left." The adjective clause is not essential to the meaning of the sentence. It provides only an additional piece of information about the time.

GRAMMAR TIP: In nonidentifying adjective clauses
—we do not use *that*
—we place commas at the beginning and end of the clause unless the clause comes at the end of a sentence.

2 *Underline the adjective clauses in the sentences that follow. Decide whether they are identifying or nonidentifying, and write **I** or **N** on the line. Then add the appropriate punctuation. Note that there is at least one sentence here that could be both I and N.*

_____ 1. People who lack the courage to fail also lack what it takes to achieve big successes.

_____ 2. Attitudes that help you feel positive about yourself are the key to success.

_____ 3. Dennis O'Grady who is quoted in this unit is a popular writer on motivational thinking.

_____ 4. A company whose executives are highly motivated will succeed.

_____ 5. A college speaker whose exact name I've now forgotten helped us to understand the power of positive thinking.

_____ 6. A modern idea which I do not share at all is that success can only be measured in financial terms.

_____ 7. The research director patiently pursued theories which others had discovered and developed.

_____ 8. The executive who wants to climb the corporate ladder will have to "go the extra mile" and work long hours.

3 *Combine the following phrases into a complete sentence, using relative pronouns and adjective clauses.*

1. Katie was a self-taught dancer. She considered herself a "natural."

   Katie, who considered herself a "natural," was a self-taught dancer.

2. A young man entered the restaurant hungry. He left it with a full belly.

   _____

3. Katie was off to find a new place in the world. Katie's brother had just died.

   _____

4. Katie was thinking about a mother. The mother's son had just thrown his hat out the window of the bus.

   _____

5. Katie waited two hours at a diner. At the diner she had an excellent view of the people lining up for the theater.

   _____

6. Tap dancing is an American dance form. It was popularized by Hollywood movies.

   _____

B   STYLE: Supporting a Topic Sentence with Illustration and Conclusion

1 *Working in pairs, examine the paragraph below and discuss the questions that follow.*

People who are unwilling to risk failure are not capable of achieving big successes. The careers of the inventor Thomas Edison and the comedian Charlie Chaplin serve as good examples. Without Thomas Edison, we might still be reading in the dark today. But did you know that Edison discovered the lightbulb after a thousand different attempts? When asked what he had learned from those one thousand mistakes, Edison responded that he had found one thousand ways in which a lightbulb could not be made. During his early days in London, people threw things at Charlie Chaplin to make him get off the stage. Would we be enjoying the starring film roles of this famous comedian today if he had taken those audiences' reactions to heart and stopped pursuing his dream to become an actor? Learning to cope with failure makes you strong enough to view every defeat as another step toward success.

1. What kind of information does the first sentence provide?

2. What do the next six sentences have to do with the first sentence?

3. Which sentence does the last sentence refer back to?

Illustration

Illustration, an essential ingredient of effective writing, is used to clarify or support the main idea that has been expressed in the **topic sentence** of a paragraph. To illustrate an idea, a writer provides clear and concise examples, persuasive explanations, appropriate statistics, and relevant anecdotes (brief stories) that support the topic sentence.

In the example paragraph above, the writer provides statistics and anecdotes about the lives of Thomas Edison and Charlie Chaplin to show how both these famous people would not have become great successes if they had not risked failure. Thomas Edison's one thousand failed attempts before discovering the lightbulb and Charlie Chaplin's experiences of having things thrown at him when he first started to act are two examples that not only convince the reader of the logic of the topic sentence, but also prepare the reader for the **concluding sentence,** which reinforces the main idea of the paragraph.

2 *Work with a partner on developing an appropriate topic sentence for the fully developed paragraph below.*

Topic Sentence: _____

_____

Both Judy Garland and Marilyn Monroe were wonderful entertainers. Although they died in the 1960s, they are still remembered today for their genius as performers. Judy Garland was a fine actress and singer. There isn't a child who doesn't know her as Dorothy in the classic film *The Wizard of Oz*. Moreover, adults are still buying compact discs of her many record albums. Marilyn Monroe played comic and tragic roles in films and on the live stage. People today still watch videos of *Some Like It Hot*, *The Misfits*, and *Bus Stop*, her most famous films. Yet both these actresses tried to commit suicide many times. It is not clear if their actual deaths were the result of suicide attempts. What is clear, however, is that despite their great successes, they were not happy people.

3 *Work in a small group. Analyze Katie's character. Find the supporting statements in "Gotta Dance" which illustrate the descriptions below. Write them on a separate piece of paper.*

> Katie is a loving and caring person.
> Katie is a generous person.
> Katie is an ambitious person.

4 *Develop the idea of this topic sentence. Write a complete paragraph with the necessary supporting and concluding statements. Then, in a small group, compare your paragraphs.*

Topic Sentence: "People who decide to follow their dreams sometimes have to go against the wishes of those who love them the most."

C WRITING TOPICS

Write an essay on one of the following topics. Be sure to write an introduction with a thesis statement and topic sentences in each of your paragraphs. Support your views with examples and explanations.

1. Discuss the three main qualities that you feel are needed to achieve success.

2. The CEO (chief executive officer) of a major company once said that the most successful person he knew was his gardener—a man loved by his family and respected by his friends, a man who worked hard and had a full life. Would you agree or disagree with this statement? Comment on the definition of success expressed here. Do you think the CEO would agree to change places with the gardener? Would you?

3. What do you think Katie's life will be like after the end of her story? Explain how certain aspects of her life and personality will influence her future. (You may want to refer to the work you did on page 68 as you work on this topic.)

4. Read the following poem. Explain what you believe Mary Oliver is saying in her poem, and compare her "journey" with Katie's in "Gotta Dance."

The Journey

One day you finally knew
what you had to do, and began,
though the voices around you
kept shouting
their bad advice—
though the whole house
began to tremble
and you felt the old tug
at your ankles.
"Mend my life!"
each voice cried.
But you didn't stop.
You knew what you had to do,
though the wind pried
with its stiff fingers
at the very foundations—
though their melancholy
was terrible.

It was already late
enough, and a wild night,
and the road full of fallen
branches and stones.
But little by little,
as you left their voices behind,
the stars began to burn
through the sheets of clouds,
and there was a new voice,
which you slowly
recognized as your own,
that kept you company
as you strode deeper and deeper
into the world,
determined to do
the only thing you could do—
determined to save
the only life you could save.

Mary Oliver

D   RESEARCH TOPICS

PREPARATION

Identifying Career Goals

One measure of success is achieving career goals. Before interviewing a person with a successful career, think about your own career goals by making a career ladder.

1. At the top of the ladder, identify your **long-term goal.**

2. Consider the plan you will follow to get there. Include on each step of the ladder the **short-term goals** that you will need to meet in order to achieve your long-term goal.

3. Set a **timetable** for each step. That is, determine how long you are mentally prepared to work on each phase of your climb on this ladder.

4. Next to each short-term goal, write down the **difficulties** that you believe you will encounter and how you hope to deal with them.

RESEARCH ACTIVITY

Interviewing a Successful Person

Now that you've analyzed your own career goals, interview a successful person. Write down the name of a successful person:

_____

1. Explain why you think this person is successful:

_____

_____

2. Prepare to interview this person. Use the four factors you have already considered—long-term goal, short-term goals, timetable, difficulties encountered—to prepare questions for the interview. Next, brainstorm with a partner to come up with a list of questions for each factor that you believe will be worth considering.

SHARING YOUR FINDINGS

1. Examine your notes taken during the interview.

2. Write a summary of the interview. What have you learned? What can be applied to your own career?

For step-by-step practice in the writing process, see the *Writing Activity Book, Advanced,* Unit 3.

Assignment	Descriptive Essay
Prewriting	Making a Flowchart
Organizing	Supporting Main Ideas
Revising	Cohesion Between Paragraphs
	Using Identifying and Nonidentifying Adjective Clauses
Editing	Subject-Verb Agreement

For Unit 3 Internet activities, visit the NorthStar Companion Website at http://longman.com/northstar.

Silent Spring

1 Focus on the Topic

A PREDICTING

In the place you live now, what are some of the trends in the way people think about things like the environment, technology, fashion, music, politics, or other topics? Think about one trend in particular. Is this trend expressed in other countries? How do trends grow and develop? Why do people go along with them? Take five minutes to write down your thoughts about these questions.

B   SHARING INFORMATION

Study the pictures below. Explain how the product in each picture represents a trend and what you think of each trend.

cell phones

easier to use

faster

_____

_____

_____

_____

DVDs

_____

_____

_____

_____

_____

the Internet

_____

_____

_____

_____

_____

Velcro material

_____

_____

_____

_____

_____

C   PREPARING TO READ

BACKGROUND

Read this information, and answer the questions that follow.

Have you ever wondered why people believe what they believe, wear what they wear, and do what they do? In his book *The Tipping Point: How Little Things Can Make a Big Difference*, Malcolm Gladwell examines ideas and trends, and he discusses how they spread and eventually change people's lives. For Gladwell, "the tipping point" is the exact moment when ideas become accepted by the general public. It is "the boiling point," the moment when a previously stable situation undergoes rapid change. In this unit, you will read the first chapter of Rachel Carson's book *Silent Spring*. When the book was published in 1962, Rachel Carson brought America to the tipping point: The modern environmental protection movement was born.

Rachel Carson was a highly respected writer on scientific topics. She was born in 1907 on a farm in Pennsylvania, where she developed her great love of nature. Encouraged by her mother to read books and write, she became a prize-winning author as a child. Carson entered college as a writing major but switched to zoology. She completed a master's degree in zoology at Johns Hopkins University and taught zoology at the University of Maryland for several years. During this period, she became very interested in the sea. In 1936, when she accepted an editorial position with the U.S. Fish and Wildlife Service, Rachel Carson the scientist and Rachel Carson the writer were finally united.

Carson worked for the government for 17 years and received praise in scientific circles for the books and articles she wrote about the environment. In 1951, her book *The Sea Around Us* was a best-seller; as a result, Carson retired from her government position and devoted the rest of her life to writing. By the time *Silent Spring* was published 11 years later, the author was known to both the science community and the general public. That is why her book created such a great deal of discussion and controversy. Although Carson was aware of the immediate impact of her book, especially the movement to ban, or prohibit, the use of DDT,* she did not live long enough to see the extent to which it would transform attitudes toward nature. She died of breast cancer on April 14, 1964, two years after *Silent Spring*'s publication.

1. When does a tipping point occur?

2. How did Rachel Carson's childhood and education prepare her for her work?

3. Why was Rachel Carson able to influence many other people?

4. Can you think of any other books, ideas, or products that have reached the tipping point?

---

* **DDT:** a chemical pesticide that remains in the food chain and that is harmful to humans. Carson protested the large-scale, indiscriminate use of DDT, especially in crops.

VOCABULARY FOR COMPREHENSION

Choose the word that best expresses the same meaning as the underlined word in these sentences. Compare your answers with those of a partner.

1. Rachel Carson wrote about preserving nature and our natural <u>surroundings</u> in her best-seller, *The Sea Around Us*.
   a. zone
   b. climate
   c. environment

2. Many people feel that in order to be <u>prosperous</u> and productive, American agriculture has to rely on chemicals to kill all the insects.
   a. profitable
   b. healthy
   c. happy

3. Chemicals can <u>drift</u> on the wind and fall on areas and people far away.
   a. catch
   b. float
   c. hold

4. The <u>countless</u> delights of nature—the food, the flowers, the animals—are so varied that we often take them for granted.
   a. unaccountable
   b. countable
   c. infinite

5. Insects and bacteria threaten to reduce the <u>abundance</u> of our food supply.
   a. quantity
   b. success
   c. happiness

6. When <u>blight</u> creeps over a crop, all the food decays or dies.
   a. sickness
   b. cold
   c. invasion

7. Some people were <u>puzzled</u> about the effects of a chemical like DDT; they were pleased that it killed insects, but they were not sure if it was safe to use around humans and other animals.
   a. annoyed
   b. confused
   c. disturbed

8. Many diseases develop very quickly and do their damage before people even realize they have been <u>stricken</u>.
   a. impressed
   b. attacked
   c. warned

9. Farmers use pesticides to protect their crops, but some pesticides can kill so many living things that nature itself may <u>wither</u> and die.
   a. grow
   (b.) dry up
   c. condense

10. The American government and many <u>of its counterparts</u> all over the world have banned DDT from agricultural use.
    a. opposing countries
    (b.) governments with similar concerns
    c. friends

11. Chemical companies considered the banning of DDT a <u>misfortune</u> because they lost a considerable amount of money.
    (a.) disaster
    b. boon
    c. mistake

12. Chemical pesticides like DDT are powerful and dangerous. They can create the <u>specter</u> of a dying planet.
    a. financial result
    b. beautiful vision
    (c.) threatening possibility

2 Focus on Reading

A   READING ONE: *A Fable for Tomorrow*

Before you read, discuss these questions with a partner.

What are the sounds of spring in the place where you live? What could cause these sounds to go "silent"?

Before Rachel Carson's book *Silent Spring* was published in 1962, not very many Americans worried about air and water pollution. Moreover, people were unaware of the long-term dangers of DDT. The book alerted millions to the dangers of DDT and inspired them to act to protect nature. This started the modern environmentalist movement, which seeks to protect the earth from the harmful effects of industrialization. "A Fable for Tomorrow" is the first chapter of *Silent Spring*.

A FABLE FOR TOMORROW

BY RACHEL CARSON

1   There was once a town in the heart of America where all life seemed to live in harmony with its surroundings. The town lay in the midst of a checkerboard of prosperous farms, with fields of grain and hillsides of orchards where, in spring, white clouds of bloom drifted above the green fields. In autumn, oak and maple and birch trees set up a blaze of color that flamed and flickered across a backdrop of pines. Then foxes barked in the hills and deer silently crossed the fields, half hidden in the mists of the fall mornings.

2   Along the roads, laurel, viburnum and alder,[1] great ferns and wild-flowers delighted the traveler's eye through much of the year. Even in winter the roadsides were places of beauty, where countless birds came to feed on the berries and on the seed heads of the dried weeds rising above the snow. The countryside was, in fact, famous for the abundance and variety of its bird life, and when the flood of migrants was pouring through in spring and fall, people traveled from great distances to observe them. Others came to fish the streams, which  flowed clear and cold out of the hills and contained shady pools where trout lay. So it had been from the days many years ago when the first settlers raised their houses, sank their wells, and built their barns.

3   Then a strange blight crept over the area and everything began to change. Some evil spell[2] had settled on the community: mysterious maladies swept the flocks of chickens; the cattle and sheep sickened and died. Everywhere was a shadow of death. The farmers spoke of much illness among their families. In the town the doctors had become more and more puzzled by new kinds of sickness appearing among their patients. There had been several sudden and unexplained deaths, not only among adults but even among children, who would be stricken suddenly while at play and die within a few hours.

4   There was a strange stillness. The birds, for example—where had they gone? Many people spoke of them, puzzled and disturbed. The

---

[1] *laurel, viburnum and alder:* types of plants
[2] *evil spell:* in old superstitions, an act of harmful magic. (The witch cast an evil spell on the prince, turning him into a frog.)

feeding stations in the backyards were deserted. The few birds seen anywhere were moribund;³ they trembled violently and could not fly. It was a spring without voices. On the mornings that had once throbbed with the dawn chorus of robins, catbirds, doves, jays, wrens, and scores of other bird voices there was now no sound; only silence lay over the fields and woods and marsh.

5   On the farms the hens brooded, but no chicks hatched.⁴ The farmers complained that they were unable to raise any pigs—the litters were small and the young survived only a few days. The apple trees were coming into bloom, but no bees droned among the blossoms, so there was no pollination and there would be no fruit.

6   The roadsides, once so attractive, were now lined with browned and withered vegetation as though swept by fire. These, too, were silent, deserted by all living things. Even the streams were now lifeless. Anglers⁵ no longer visited them, for all the fish had died.

7   In the gutters⁶ under the eaves and between the shingles of the roofs, a white granular powder still showed a few patches; some weeks before it had fallen like snow upon the roofs and the lawns, the fields and the streams.

8   No witchcraft, no enemy action had silenced the rebirth of new life in this stricken world. The people had done it themselves.

9   This town does not actually exist, but it might easily have a thousand counterparts in America or elsewhere in the world. I know of no community that has experienced all the misfortunes I describe. Yet every one of these disasters has actually happened somewhere, and many real communities have already suffered a substantial number of them. A grim specter has crept upon us almost unnoticed, and this imagined tragedy may easily become a stark reality we all shall know.

³ *moribund:* dying
⁴ *brooded, but no chicks hatched:* the hens sat on their eggs, but no new chicks were born
⁵ *anglers:* fishermen
⁶ *gutters:* drain pipes for rainwater; usually found on the roofs of houses

READING FOR MAIN IDEAS

1 *Summarize the main points of this fable.*

1. The way the town was before:

_____

_____

_____

2. The way it is now:

_____

_____

_____

3. Rachel Carson's predictions for the future:

_____

_____

_____

2 _A fable is a story with a lesson. In one sentence, summarize the lesson you think this fable teaches._

_____

_____

READING FOR DETAILS

"A Fable for Tomorrow" illustrates the idea that DDT could have many disastrous, long-term consequences for the environment. What are the negative effects of DDT that Rachel Carson foresaw?

Cause: _The use of DDT_

Effects:

REACTING TO THE READING

1 *Discuss these questions with a partner, and choose the best answers. There can be more than one correct answer for each question.*

1. Why did Rachel Carson start her book with a fable?
   a. The fable was poetic, and people would remember it.
   b. The fable was an easy way to state the issue.
   c. The fable would prove she was right.

2. Who was the intended audience for this fable?
   a. scientists
   b. farmers
   c. the general public

3. What do you think the response of people in the chemical industry would be to this fable?
   a. The chemical industry creates a strong economy.
   b. Not all chemicals are bad.
   c. Rachel Carson is exaggerating.

4. What would be Rachel Carson's defense of the use of a fable?
   a. The disasters included in the fable could really happen.
   b. It's OK to use a fictional story to persuade people of a real danger.
   c. Rachel Carson didn't have adequate statistics to offer.

5. What best summarizes Rachel Carson's view of the relationship between humankind and nature?
   a. Humankind is the most splendid creation of nature.
   b. Nature must be made to serve humankind.
   c. Humans and nature must live in harmony.

2 *Discuss these questions in a small group. Share your group's conclusions with the rest of the class.*

1. What was your opinion of DDT after reading "A Fable for Tomorrow"? Do you think Rachel Carson was objective in her treatment of the problem of DDT? Did she present both sides of the story? Why or why not?

2. Rachel Carson uses a symbol, a spring that is "silent." What is she trying to communicate with the use of the word *silent*?

3. When Rachel Carson says "The people had done it themselves," what does she mean? Explain.

B   READING TWO: *The Story of* Silent Spring

Before reading the following essay, discuss this question with a partner.

How do you think people responded to *Silent Spring* when it first appeared?

FROM A BOOK TO A MOVEMENT
THE STORY OF SILENT SPRING

1   Developed in 1939, DDT was the most powerful pesticide the world had ever known. It was used throughout the 1940s and 1950s to clear regions of mosquitos carrying malaria. Its inventor was awarded the Nobel Prize. When DDT became available for purely commercial use and was sprayed over crops, only a few people, like Rachel Carson, felt that there was some danger. When she finally published her book, *Silent Spring*, her fears were heard loud and clear. The impact of *Silent Spring* was great; with this book, Rachel Carson laid the foundation for the modern environmental protection movement.

2   Carson did not originally intend to write a book about the harmful effects of DDT. Her interest in the subject was sparked by a letter from old friends telling about the damage that aerial spraying had done to the ecological system[1] on their land. Although Rachel Carson was a best-selling author, no magazine would agree to her idea for an article investigating the negative effects of DDT. She decided to go ahead and deal with the issue in a book, *Silent Spring,* which took her four years to complete. It described how DDT entered the food chain and accumulated in the fatty tissues of animals, including human beings, and caused cancer and genetic damage. The book's most famous chapter, "A Fable for Tomorrow," depicted a nameless American town where all life—from fish to birds to apple blossoms to children—had been "silenced" by the insidious[2] effects of DDT.

3   First serialized in *The New Yorker* magazine in June 1962, the book alarmed readers across the country and, not surprisingly, brought howls of anger from the chemical industry. "If man were to faithfully follow the teachings of Miss Carson," complained an executive of the American Cyanamid Company, "we would return to the Dark Ages,[3] and the insects and diseases would once again inherit the earth." Some of the attacks were more personal, questioning Carson's integrity and even her sanity.

"The Story of *Silent Spring*" is adapted from a Natural Resources Defense Council Publication.

[1] *ecological system:* the system showing how plants, animals, and people depend on each other and their environment
[2] *insidious:* gradually and secretly causing serious harm
[3] *Dark Ages:* a time in western Europe (about A.D. 400–1000) when Roman civilization had been destroyed and with it almost all learning and trade

4   Her careful preparation, however, had paid off. Foreseeing the reaction of the chemical industry, she had written *Silent Spring* like a lawyer's brief, with no fewer than 55 pages of notes and a list of experts who had read and approved the manuscript. Many well-known and respected scientists rose to her defense, and when President John F. Kennedy ordered the President's Science Advisory Committee to examine the issues the book raised, its report supported both *Silent Spring* and its author. As a result, DDT came under much closer government supervision and was eventually banned.

5   Conservation had never attracted much public interest before Rachel Carson's book, but the dangers she analyzed were too frightening to ignore. For the first time, the need to regulate industry[4] in order to protect the environment became widely accepted, and environmentalism was born. Carson was well aware of the implications of her book. Appearing on a CBS documentary about her work shortly before her death from breast cancer in 1964, she remarked:

> The public must decide whether it wishes to continue on the present road, and it can only do so when in full possession of the facts. We still talk in terms of conquest. We haven't become mature enough to think of ourselves as only a tiny part of a vast and incredible universe. Man's attitude toward nature is today critically important simply because we have now acquired a fateful power to alter and destroy nature. But man is part of nature, and his war against nature is inevitably a war against himself.

6   One of the landmark books[5] of the twentieth century, *Silent Spring* still speaks to us today, many years after its publication. Equally inspiring is the example of Rachel Carson herself. Against overwhelming difficulties and hardship, despite her own shyness and reserve, and motivated only by her love of nature, she rose like a gladiator in its defense.

---

[4] *regulate industry:* limit the activities of business in the public interest through laws passed by the government
[5] *landmark book:* a book that changes history

Working with a partner, answer these questions based on Reading Two.

1. According to Rachel Carson, why is DDT so dangerous?

_____

_____

_____

2. At first, no magazine would agree to publish an article on DDT. Why do you think magazine editors were so reluctant?

_____

_____

_____

3. "If man were to faithfully follow the teachings of Miss Carson, we would return to the Dark Ages, and the insects and diseases would once again inherit the earth."

What did the executive of the American Cyanamid Company mean here?

_____

_____

_____

4. What did Carson do to prepare for the criticism that her book would receive?

_____

_____

_____

5. According to Carson, how should people think of themselves in relation to nature?

_____

_____

_____

6. How does the reading describe Carson as a person?

_____

_____

_____

C **LINKING READINGS ONE AND TWO**

In his book The Tipping Point: How Little Things Can Make a Big Difference, *Malcolm Gladwell examines how major changes can suddenly take place in society when they are least expected. The "tipping point" is the exact moment when new ideas set off a major change. Read a summary of his ideas about the "tipping point."*

THE TIPPING POINT

Three Factors in Popularizing an Idea

- The "stickiness factor": An idea has to be presented in a way that will impress people so that the idea will "stick," or stay in their minds.

- The power of context: The world has to be ready to receive an idea.

- The law of the few: Only very few exceptional people are capable of making great changes.

Three Types of People Who Contribute to Change

- Mavens: teachers and people who have knowledge and want to share it

- Connectors: people who can spread the message by word of mouth through their network of contacts

- Salesmen: people who know how to persuade and influence the public

---

Discuss these questions in a small group.

1. Does the first chapter of *Silent Spring* (Reading One) follow *The Tipping Point* rules about popularizing an idea? Which rule or rules does it demonstrate? Why is it such a persuasive piece of writing?

2. You have read Malcolm Gladwell's categories describing "three types of people who contribute to change." Based on "The Story of *Silent Spring*" (Reading Two), in which category or categories would you place Rachel Carson and why? What other people or organizations helped her to get her message to the people?

3 Focus on Vocabulary

1 *Study the following chart of prefixes, suffixes, and example words.*

Prefix	Meaning	Example
1. *mis-*	bad or badly	misfortune (bad luck, or what happens as a result of bad luck)
2. *un-* *im-* *in-* *dis-* *non-*	not	unclear (not clear) impossible (not possible) incredible (not believable) disrespectful (not respectful) nontoxic (not poisonous)
3. *re-*	again	rebirth (born again)
4. *fore-*	ahead	foresee (to see the future)

Suffix	Meaning	Example
1. *-cide*	killing	pesticide (killing bugs)
2. *-craft*	art or skill	witchcraft (the art of being a witch)
3. *-ful*	full of	powerful (full of power)
4. *-less*	without	nameless (without a name)
5. *-ship*	the state of or condition of	friendship (the state of being a friend)

2 *Choose a prefix or suffix (in parentheses) for the word on the line, and complete the sentences with the correct form of the word.*

1. In *Silent Spring*, Rachel Carson (un-/fore-) _____told a grim future where nature's abundance had been destroyed.

2. However, Rachel Carson wanted to prove that it was not (im-/fore-) _____possible to change the way people treated the environment.

3. If people would agree to eliminate DDT, the destruction of nature and the life_____ (-ful/-less) future she foresaw could be avoided.

4. She made a good case for the <u>harm</u>_____ (-ful/-less) nature of certain pesticides.

5. Banning DDT created economic <u>hard</u>_____ (-ship/-craft) for chemical companies.

3 *Read these sentences from "A Fable for Tomorrow." Circle the correct answer to complete each sentence that follows.*

1. "The countryside was . . . famous for the abundance and variety of its bird life, and when the flood of migrants was pouring through in spring and fall, people traveled from great distances to observe them."

   A _____ number of birds lived in the district.
   a. harmful   **b.** countless   **c.** uninteresting

2. "In autumn, oak and maple and birch trees set up a blaze of color that flamed and flickered across a backdrop of pines."

   In autumn, the trees were very _____.
   a. colorful   **b.** incredible   **c.** powerful

3. "Deer silently crossed the fields, half hidden in the mists of the fall mornings."

   The deer were almost _____.
   a. invisible   **b.** colorless   **c.** misplaced

4. "The roadsides, once so attractive, were now lined with browned and withered vegetation as though swept by fire."

   The roadsides are now very _____.
   a. refreshed   **b.** disorganized   **c.** unattractive

   Everything looks washed out and _____.
   d. cheerful   **e.** colorless   **f.** nonstop

5. "Everywhere was a shadow of death."

   We could see death coming. It was a death _____.
   a. foreseen   **b.** unforeseen   **c.** reborn

4 *Read the following selection. Fill in each blank with the word from the box that matches the definition under the blank. Not all the words are used.*

abundance	countless	insidious	stricken
accumulate	~~damage~~	misfortune	surroundings
alter	depicted	prosperous	
ban	harmful	puzzled	

The struggle to save the food supply from _____*damage*_____ did not end
                                          1. (harm)

with *Silent Spring*. The need to maintain a __*prosperous*__ agricultural
                                              2. (successful)

economy has led to many difficulties. For example, in order to increase the

protein in cattle feed, people began to _____*alter*_____ the diet of cows.
                                          3. (change)

Cows do not eat meat in their natural __*surroundings*__, but farm industries
                                        4. (environment)

in many countries began feeding cows the ground-up parts of dead sheep. Many

scientists believe that some cows' nervous systems were __*stricken*__ by
                                                          5. (attacked)

a sheep disease called scrapie. According to them, this __*insidious*__
                                                          6. (gradual and harmful)

process, begun by humans for greater profits, has led to outbreaks of "mad cow

disease" in several countries of Europe and Asia.

Farmers also often feed large amounts of antibiotics and hormones to their

animals to make them stronger. These large doses __*accumulate*__ in animal
                                                    7. (collect)

organs and are eaten by humans. This is __*harmful*__ to us all because
                                          8. (damaging)

human diseases are becoming less responsive to antibiotics and the hormones are

not good for children.

Recently, food manufacturers in the United States have developed a new

method of irradiating food to kill bacteria. Many people want to

_____*ban*_____ irradiated food because they are not sure such food is safe.
9. (eliminate)

The dangers to the food supply __*depicted*__ by the environmental
                                10. (described)

movement have led many people to buy only natural products from organic

farms, which do not use chemical pesticides. But organic foods are expensive

and hard to find. People in many countries are __*puzzled*__ about how
                                                 11. (unsure)

to carry on the legacy of *Silent Spring*.

5 Write a paragraph describing the change inspired by a trend in popular culture. You may use a trend you listed on page 72 or another trend of your choice. Discuss the causes and results of this change. Use at least eight vocabulary words from the box below.

abundance	damage	misfortune
accumulated	depict	prosperous
alter	drift	puzzled
blight	faithful	specter
counterpart	hardship	surroundings
countless	insidious	wither

4 Focus on Writing

A   GRAMMAR: Adverb Clauses and Discourse Connectors Expressing Cause and Effect

1 Working in pairs, examine these sentences and the underlined phrases. Then discuss the questions that follow.

- <u>Because it was a very powerful pesticide,</u> DDT cleared regions of malaria throughout the 1940s and 1950s.

- Rachel Carson's *Silent Spring* made people aware of the dangerous effects of DDT; <u>consequently, DDT came under closer government supervision and was eventually banned</u>.

- Every detail in *Silent Spring* has <u>such</u> good documentation <u>that not one factual error has ever been found in the book</u>.

   1. In the first sentence, what word suggests that a reason is going to be given?

   2. In the second sentence, what word suggests that a result is going to be given?

   3. In the third sentence, what words suggest that a reason and a result are going to be given?

Adverb Clauses and Discourse Connectors Expressing Cause and Effect

Adverb clauses and **discourse connectors** can be used to link ideas and to express cause and effect. In compound sentences these **cause-and-effect structures** reveal the connection between the reason for an event or a situation (the *cause*) and the influence this event or situation has on people, places, or things (the *result*, or the *effect*).

CAUSE: Stating a reason with adverb clauses that begin with *because* and *since*

- *Because/Since* **it was a very powerful pesticide,** DDT cleared regions of malaria throughout the 1940s and 1950s.

- DDT cleared regions of malaria throughout the 1940s and 1950s *because/since* **it was a very powerful pesticide.**

PUNCTUATION TIP: When the adverb clause beginning with *because* or *since* comes at the beginning of a sentence, a comma separates the clause from the result.

EFFECT: Stating a result with the discourse connectors *consequently, thus, therefore,* and *so*

- Rachel Carson's *Silent Spring* made people aware of the dangerous effects of DDT; *consequently/thus/therefore* **DDT came under much closer government supervision and was eventually banned.**

- Rachel Carson's *Silent Spring* made people aware of the dangerous effects of DDT, *so* **DDT came under much closer government supervision and was eventually banned.**

PUNCTUATION TIP: When using discourse connectors, you may write one sentence and join the other as above with a semicolon (*consequently/thus/therefore*) or a comma (*so*). If you decide to separate the two sentences with a period, the discourse connectors are capitalized and followed by a comma.

DEGREE OF EFFECT: *such* and *so . . . that*

Compound sentences using the pattern "***such*** (+ noun) or ***so*** (+ adjective or adverb) *...that...*" dramatically describe the great degree to which the cause has had an effect (*that* + the explanation) on the situation.

- Every detail in *Silent Spring* has **such** good **documentation that** not one factual error has ever been found in the book.

- Every detail in *Silent Spring* is **so well documented that** not one factual error has ever been found in the book.

2 *Combine the following pairs of sentences to show cause and effect. Write two sentences for each item. Use patterns with **because/since** and **consequently/therefore/thus/so.***

1. Rachel Carson spent her childhood on a Pennsylvania farm. She developed a love of nature at a young age.

   Because Rachel Carson spent her childhood on a Pennsylvania farm; she developed a love of nature at a young age.

2. Rachel Carson was a wonderful writer. Her books about nature were a blend of scientific as well as beautiful poetic prose.

   Because Rachel Carson was a wonderful writer, her books about nature were a blend of scientific as well as beautiful poetic prose.

3. Rachel Carson was very respected in scientific circles. She had the opportunity to speak out on various issues that were important to her.

4. The content of *Silent Spring* posed a threat to the manufacturers of chemical pesticides. *Silent Spring* disturbed the business world immediately.

5. The angry protests of the big chemical companies were not heeded. The government listened to the message of *Silent Spring*, and the modern environmental protection movement was born.

[handwritten top margin: Such + noun + That / So + adj/adv + That]

3 *Combine the following sentences with **such/so . . . that** patterns.*

1. Rachel Carson was brought up with a great love of nature. *[handwritten: so great That]*
It was not surprising that she changed her major from writing to zoology in her third year of college.

   [handwritten: Rachel Carson was brought up with a love of nature so great, that it was not surprising that she changed her major form writing to Zoology in her third year of college]

2. She became very interested in the sea when she spent a summer at Woods Hole, Massachusetts, in her early twenties.

   The first three books she wrote were about the sea environment.

   _____

   _____

   _____

3. By 1952 Rachel Carson was enjoying a great deal of success as a writer.

   She was able to retire from the U.S. Fish and Wildlife Service to write full-time.

   _____

   _____

   _____

4. Magazine publishers were very afraid to lose their advertisers.

   They refused to publish Rachel Carson's articles about the dangers of DDT.

   _____

   _____

   _____

5. Rachel Carson was very upset about how DDT was being used without regard for the consequences.

   She decided to write her own book on the topic.

   _____

   _____

   _____

4 *Working with a partner, complete the following paragraphs by filling in the blanks with the cause-and-effect structure (**because, since, consequently, therefore, thus, so, such, so . . . that**) that is missing.*

a. *Silent Spring* made (1) ___such___ an impact in America at the time it was published (2) ___that___ people's general thinking about nature changed dramatically from that point on. (3) ___since / because___ the book made people see that whatever they did to nature they were also doing to themselves, their blind faith in science and industry was shaken. (4) ___Consequently___, our modern era of environmental awareness was launched. In the years immediately following the book's publication, people became (5) ___so___ interested in the concept of their "interconnectedness" with the natural world (6) ___that___ TV shows such as Marlin Perkins's *Wild Kingdom* became very popular in the early 1960s. By 1970, the United States had celebrated its first Earth Day.

b. Within the first year of *Silent Spring*'s publication, over 40 state laws were proposed to regulate pesticide use (7) ___because___ government scientists had backed Rachel Carson fully after their researchers corroborated all her claims. This initial momentum of legislation passed was (8) ___so___ great (9) ___that___ many national laws were created afterwards to protect the environment: The National Environment Protection Act (1969), the Clean Air Act (1970), the Clean Water Act (1972), and the Endangered Species Act (1973) are just a few of them.

B STYLE: Cause-and-Effect Essays

1 *Reread the essay entitled "The Story of* Silent Spring*" on pages 80–81. Working with a partner, complete the following activities.*

1. In the introduction, underline the *thesis statement*, the sentence that communicates the main idea of the essay (see page 42).

2. According to the essay, what caused Rachel Carson to write *Silent Spring*?

   a. _____

   b. _____

   c. _____

3. List the effects of the publication of *Silent Spring*, according to the writer.

   a. _____

   b. _____

   c. _____

   d. _____

   e. _____

4. Does this essay focus more on what caused Rachel Carson to write *Silent Spring* or on the effects of the book after its publication?

Cause-and-Effect Essays

Thesis Statement

A cause-and-effect essay most often focuses on either the causes or the effects of an event or a situation. This focus is reflected in the thesis statement.

In a causal analysis, the thesis statement can briefly state the causes of an event or situation, or it can mention only the most important cause. In an effect analysis, the thesis statement can simply summarize the main consequences of the event or the situation. In the essay entitled "The Story of *Silent Spring*," we can see that the writer introduces both causes and effects; however, the focus of the essay, as reflected in the thesis statement, is on the effects of Rachel Carson's book.

Organization

The essay must follow a logical pattern of organization. Some common ways of organizing cause-and-effect essays are:

- *Immediate versus long-term:* If you are discussing what caused Rachel Carson to write *Silent Spring,* you may want to begin with the immediate cause—the

1deia

1 Sub top
2 Sub top
3 Sub top

letter that she received from friends about ecological damage caused by aerial spraying. Or you may want to discuss the author's general concern about tampering with the natural environment, and her lifelong preoccupation with nature.

- *A coherent order of importance:* You may want to begin with the least important effects of an event and work up to the most important. Or you may find that you need to begin with the historical background of a situation and then go on to the present-day situation. The choice will be determined by the nature of the material, but you must give a logical order to your essay. Much of the model essay (Reading Two), for example, follows chronological order.

- *Order of familiarity or interest:* You may want to work from what your readers know or would be most interested in, to what is new and different from what they expect.

- *Causal chain:* Another type of cause-and-effect essay is the causal chain. As in "A Fable for Tomorrow," one effect can become the cause of another effect, which, in turn, can become the cause of another effect. This kind of pattern is also used to a certain extent in "The Story of *Silent Spring*" (Reading Two), where one effect of the book is seen to be the cause of another effect:

an alarmed public and an angry chemical industry → the government takes notice → the government investigates and confirms Rachel Carson's claims → DDT is put under close government scrutiny → DDT is ultimately banned.

2 *In a causal chain, one effect can be the cause of another. Work with a partner to fill in the blanks in this causal chain based on Reading Two.*

READING TWO: CAUSAL CHAIN			
1	**2**	**3**	**4**
→	Carson wants to write a magazine article about DDT. →	→	She decides to write a book about DDT. →
5	**6**	**7**	**8**
Carson's book is published. →	People are very alarmed about the effects of DDT. →	The government agrees to supervise the use of DDT more closely. →	

3 *The following sentences present some of the reasons for the popularity of jeans. Work with a partner to organize the sentences to form a paragraph using one of the principles of organization discussed on pages 92–93. Number the sentences from **1** to **11**.*

_____ Levi Strauss, the creator of Levi's jeans, met a gold miner who told him that it was difficult to find sturdy pants that wouldn't tear. It was then that Strauss thought of using the canvas material he had brought to California in 1850 to make the famous jeans we now wear.

_____ Ideas for many popular products often come as a result of a chance occurrence, as was the case for jeans.

_____ At that meeting, Strauss measured the miner and tailored the canvas into a pair of stiff and rugged pants.

_____ When Strauss ran out of canvas material, his brothers in New York sent him the denim material that we now associate with jeans, and Levi dyed it blue.

_____ Soon after the pants became "blue" jeans, copper rivets were added in response to the complaint of a miner by the name of Alkali Ike, who said that the pockets of his pants always tore when he stuffed them with ore samples.

_____ Because the miner was very satisfied with the results, other miners started to look for "Levi's canvas pants," and Levi Strauss went into business.

_____ However, their popularity spread during the 1930s, when Levi's blue jeans were introduced to the East after vacationers returned home and showed off the wonderful pants with the rivets.

_____ Although the invention of jeans was a chance occurrence, jeans have become a major part of modern life today.

_____ Up to 1930, the sturdy pants with the copper rivets were worn mostly by working people in the West: miners, cowboys, lumberjacks, and railroad workers.

_____ World War II also contributed to the popularity of the pants because during this period blue jeans were considered an essential commodity and were sold only to defense workers.

_____ Since the war, more and more companies around the world have competed with the Levi Strauss company to produce the jeans that so many young people want.

4 *Write a cause-and-effect paragraph. Choose one of these questions, and write a paragraph in response. Remember that your paragraph must have an appropriate topic sentence and a logical pattern of organization.*

1. What made Rachel Carson write *Silent Spring*? (causes)

2. What were the results of its publication? (effects)

C   WRITING TOPICS

Choose one topic, and write a well-organized essay. Use the vocabulary, grammar structures, and style structures from this unit whenever possible.

1. What is your first reaction when you look at nature? When you see a waterfall, do you see the beauty of the light sparkling on the waters, or do you see the threat of roaring waters pounding on the rocks below? In general, do you see the beauty or the danger of nature? What causes this reaction in you? What effect does it have on your choice of a place to live?

2. "The obligation to endure gives us the right to know." It is with these words that Rachel Carson ends the second chapter of *Silent Spring*. Explain what you think this quote means and whether or not you agree with it. How do these words relate to Rachel Carson's motivation to write *Silent Spring*?

3. What do you think of some of the issues that environmental activists raise? Do you support any of their campaigns to save endangered animal species, to oppose the wearing of fur, to save the rain forests, or to help us get away from using too much fossil fuel (oil, coal, and gasoline)? Explain.

4. A scientist usually works for the government, a business, or a university. What do you think the responsibility of the scientist is when he or she is asked to work on projects that may be dangerous for humankind, such as biological or chemical warfare or nuclear weapons?

5. The introduction to the current edition of *Silent Spring* was written by Al Gore, the former vice president. In it, he writes that *Silent Spring* "changed the course of human history." Can you think of other landmark books in the history of civilization for which the same comment would apply? Choose a book that you believe fits this description, and show how it changed the course of human history.

D   RESEARCH TOPICS

PREPARATION

Choose a product or original idea that has started a trend in society, something that created a need so great that it changed the way we live or think about things. It can be anything from fast food to blockbuster movies to technology to a famous book. You can choose one of the trends mentioned in this chapter or discover your own. You can write about today's trends or trends in history.

- Identify the product/idea and the trend it created.

- Identify the company, individual, or government that helped create this product or idea, and give its history.

RESEARCH ACTIVITY

1. Find the history of the product or idea. Describe how it grew in popularity and eventually became a trend.

2. Explain the popularity and success of the product or idea. Consider the categories defined by Malcolm Gladwell: the "stickiness factor" and the "context." Does his "law of the few" hold true?

3. Was the person who thought of the product or idea a "maven," a "connector," or a "salesman"?

4. Indicate your opinion about this trend: Do you think it is positive or negative for society?

SHARING YOUR FINDINGS

When you have found the information you need, create a poster explaining the origin and evolution of the trend you chose, and present the poster to the class.

In designing the poster, make sure you have included a title and all the important information. Show cause and effect. Pay attention to the layout. Work with computer graphics or color markers, crayons, and ink. Use visual imagery that will attract the viewers' attention.

For step-by-step practice in the writing process, see the *Writing Activity Book, Advanced,* Unit 4.

Assignment	Cause-and-Effect Essay
Prewriting	Making a Flowchart
Organizing	Focusing on Cause or Effect
Revising	Writing Unified Essays
	Using Discourse Connectors to Express Cause and Effect
Editing	Identifying Sentence Structure

For Unit 4 Internet activities, visit the NorthStar Companion Website at http://longman.com/northstar.

What Is Lost in Translation?

1 Focus on the Topic

A PREDICTING

Look at the title of this unit and the photo. What are the advantages of living in a multicultural society? What could be "lost in translation" for these young people? Take five minutes to write down your thoughts about these questions.

B   SHARING INFORMATION

Work in a small group, and fill in your answers to the questions in the boxes that follow. Discuss your responses. Are there regional, class, gender, or age variations to these situations in your culture? Have you had any experiences in other cultures that you can share with your group?

Kissing in public

Acceptable? _____

In what circumstances?

_____

_____

What reaction do you get if you go against this social rule?

_____

_____

_____

Commenting on people's choice of clothing

Acceptable? ___No_____

In what circumstances?

_____

_____

What reaction do you get if you go against this social rule?

_____

_____

_____

Touching people you are talking to

Acceptable? ___No_____

In what circumstances?

_____

_____

What reaction do you get if you go against this social rule?

_____

_____

_____

Criticizing people directly and strongly

Acceptable? ___No\Yes_____

In what circumstances?

_____

_____

What reaction do you get if you go against this social rule?

_____

_____

_____

Two women walking arm-in-arm	**Eating as you walk down the street**
Acceptable? __NO__	Acceptable? __NO__
In what circumstances?	In what circumstances?
_____	_____
_____	_____
What reaction do you get if you go against this social rule?	What reaction do you get if you go against this social rule?
_____	_____
_____	_____
_____	_____

C PREPARING TO READ

BACKGROUND

Being a teenager is difficult under any conditions. It is easy to understand how much more complicated it can be when a family immigrates to a new country. Such was the case for Eva Hoffman. Born in Poland in 1945 to Jewish parents who were Holocaust survivors, she left her homeland at age thirteen with her parents and sister to start a new life in Canada. In her autobiography, *Lost in Translation,* she tells about the impact this move had on her and her family.

Ms. Hoffman takes us on the journey from Old World Cracow to New World Vancouver; this journey prepared her for her studies at Harvard University, for her literary career at *The New York Times,* and for her work as a well-known author. Eva Hoffman writes the story of all immigrants. She describes how her Polish identity was transformed into a new Canadian identity as she underwent the physically and emotionally exhausting process of learning to communicate in English. In their attempts to "translate" the essence of their personalities from one language and culture to another, don't all immigrants find themselves both linguistically and culturally "lost in translation"?

Although Elizabeth Wong, who was born in Los Angeles, California, in 1958, was not an immigrant herself, she too may have understood Eva Hoffman's feeling of being "lost in translation" as a young girl. In "The Struggle to Be an All-American Girl," she writes how she was torn between two cultures and how she continually resisted her Chinese mother's attempts to get her to learn Chinese and be aware of her cultural background. Ms. Wong is an award-winning playwright, a teacher of playwriting at several universities, and a writer for television.

*Read the statements in the chart below about the cultural values expressed in the stories that you are going to read. Do you agree or disagree with these statements? Circle **Yes** or **No**. After you study the two readings, you will be asked to return to this chart to compare the authors' points of view with your own.*

STATEMENTS	YOUR OPINION	HOFFMAN	WONG
1. Children have more difficulty adapting to a new culture than their parents do.	Yes / No		
2. When people move to another culture, their native language becomes more important to them.	Yes / No		
3. Parents lose authority over their children when the family moves to another culture.	Yes / No		
4. Families become closer when they must adapt to a new culture.	Yes / No		
5. People who move to a new culture worry about betraying or forgetting their old cultural traditions.	Yes / No		

VOCABULARY FOR COMPREHENSION

Work in a small group, and help each other to guess the meaning of the words listed below. In each set of words, underline the two words that have similar meanings to the boldfaced word on the left. Use your dictionaries if necessary.

1. scold	criticize angrily	reprimand	praise
2. tighten the reins	be more lenient	be stricter	exercise more control
3. fabric	foundation	structure	factory
4. betray	desert	maintain	forsake
5. beleaguered	attacked	joined	pressured
6. demonstrative	affectionate	emotional	reserved
7. restraint	restriction	moderation	freedom
8. give vent to	express	suppress	release
9. stoical	unemotional	uncomplaining	unnerving
10. dissuade	pursue	hinder	advise against
11. nagging	annoying	insistent	pleasing
12. chaotic	toxic	tumultuous	confusing

Handwritten annotations:
- next to 1: Brigar / criticon
- next to 2: mantter controle
- next to 4: Trait
- near 8: ventilador
- next to 10: convencer a ví fazer
- below 12: Querioso
- near 4 (above maintain): manutençã

2 Focus on Reading

A   **READING ONE: *Lost in Translation* and**
        The Struggle to Be an All-American Girl

Before you read, discuss the following information and question with a partner.

The first reading in this section portrays the difficulties of a Polish-Canadian family. This memoir is told from the point of view of Eva, a 13-year-old girl from Poland. Along with her mother, father, and sister Alinka, she becomes an immigrant to Canada after World War II. The second reading is about a Chinese-American family. This story is told from the point of view of 10-year-old Elizabeth. She and her brother were born in the United States. Do you think these families will have many things in common, or do you think they will be very different?

LOST IN TRANSLATION

BY EVA HOFFMAN

1   "In Poland, I would have known how to bring you up, I would have known what to do," my mother says wistfully, but here, she has lost her sureness, her authority. She doesn't know how hard to scold Alinka when she comes home at late hours; she can only worry over her daughter's vague evening activities. She has always been gentle with us, and she doesn't want, doesn't know how, to tighten the reins. But familial bonds seem so dangerously loose here!

2   Truth to tell, I don't want the fabric of loyalty and affection, and even obligation, to unravel either. I don't want my parents to lose us, I don't want to betray our common life. I want to defend our dignity because it is so fragile, so beleaguered. There is only the tiny cluster, the four of us, to know, to preserve whatever fund of human experience we may represent. And so I feel a kind of ferociousness about protecting it. I don't want us to turn into perpetually cheerful suburbanites, with hygienic smiles and equally hygienic feelings. I want to keep even our sadness, the great sadness from which our parents have come.

3   I abjure my sister[1] to treat my parents well; I don't want her to challenge our mother's authority, because it is so easily challenged. It is they who seem more defenseless to me than Alinka, and I want her to protect them. Alinka fights me like a forest animal in danger of being trapped; she too wants to roam throughout the thickets and meadows. She too wants to be free.

4   My mother says I'm becoming "English." This hurts me, because I know she means I'm becoming cold. I'm no colder than I've ever been, but I'm learning to be less demonstrative. I learn this from a teacher who, after contemplating the gesticulations with which I help myself describe the digestive system of a frog, tells me to "sit on my hands and then try talking." I learn my new reserve from people who take a step back when we talk, because I am standing too close, crowding them. Cultural distances are different, I later learn in a sociology class, but I know it already. I learn restraint from Penny, who looks offended when I shake her by the arm in excitement, as if my gesture had been one of aggression instead of friendliness. I learn it from a girl who pulls away when I hook my arm through hers as we walk down the street—this movement of friendly intimacy is an embarrassment to her.

5   I learn also that certain kinds of truth are impolite. One shouldn't criticize the person one is with, at least not directly. You shouldn't say, "You are wrong about that"—although you may say, "On the other hand, there is that to consider." You shouldn't say, "This doesn't look good on you"—though you may say, "I like you better in that other outfit." I learn to tone down my sharpness, to do a more careful conversational minuet.

6   Perhaps my mother is right after all; perhaps I'm becoming colder. After a while, emotion follows action, response grows warmer or cooler according to gesture. I'm more careful about what I say, how loud I laugh, whether I give vent to grief. The storminess of emotion prevailing in our family is in excess of the normal here, and the unwritten rules for the normal have their osmotic effect.[2]

---

[1] *I abjure my sister:* I have made my sister promise
[2] *osmotic effect:* an effect of being gradually absorbed

THE STRUGGLE TO BE AN ALL-AMERICAN GIRL

BY ELIZABETH WONG

1   It's still there, the Chinese school on Yale Street where my brother and I used to go. Despite the new coat of paint and the high wire fence, the school I knew ten years ago remains remarkably, stoically, the same.

2   Every day at 5 P.M., instead of playing with our fourth- and fifth-grade friends or sneaking out to the empty lot to hunt ghosts and animal bones, my brother and I had to go to Chinese school. No amount of kicking, screaming, or pleading could dissuade my mother, who was solidly determined to have us learn the language of our heritage. Forcibly, she walked us the seven long, hilly blocks from our home to school, depositing our defiant tearful faces before the stern principal. My only memory of him is that he swayed on his heels like a palm tree and he always clasped his impatient, twitching hands behind his back. I recognized him as a repressed maniacal child killer, and that if we ever saw his hands, we'd be in big trouble.

3   We all sat in little chairs in an empty auditorium. The room smelled like Chinese medicine, an imported faraway mustiness,[1] like ancient mothballs[2] or dirty closets. I hated that smell. I favored crisp new scents like the soft French perfume that my American teacher wore in public school. There was a stage far to the right, flanked by an American flag and the flag of the Nationalist Republic of China, which was also red, white, and blue but not as pretty.

4   Although the emphasis at school was mainly language—speaking, reading, and writing—the lessons always began with exercises in politeness. With the entrance of the teacher, the best student would tap a bell and everyone would get up, kowtow,[3] and chant "Sing san ho," the phonetic for "How are you, teacher?"

5   Being ten years old, I had better things to learn than ideographs[4] copied painstakingly in lines that ran right to left from the tip of a *moc but,* a real ink pen that had to be held in an awkward way if blotches were to be avoided. After all, I could do the multiplication tables, name the satellites of Mars, and write reports on *Little Women* and *Black Beauty.* Nancy Drew, my favorite heroine, never spoke Chinese.

---

[1] *mustiness:* moldy dampness, a smell of decay
[2] *mothballs:* made of a strong-smelling substance; used to keep moths away from clothes
[3] *kowtow:* to bow with respect
[4] *ideograph:* a written sign, for example in Chinese, that represents an idea or thing rather than the sound of a word

6   The language was a source of embarrassment. More times than not, I had tried to dissociate myself from the nagging loud voice that followed me wherever I wandered in the nearby American supermarket outside Chinatown. The voice belonged to my grandmother, a fragile woman in her seventies who could outshout the best of the street vendors. Her humor was raunchy,[5] her Chinese rhythmless, patternless. It was quick, it was loud, it was unbeautiful. It was not like the quiet, lilting romance of French or the gentle refinement of the American South. Chinese sounded pedestrian. Public.

7   In Chinatown, the comings and goings of hundreds of Chinese on their daily tasks sounded chaotic and frenzied. I did not want to be thought of as mad, as talking gibberish. When I spoke English, people nodded at me, smiled sweetly, said encouraging words. Even the people in my culture would cluck[6] and say that I would do well in life. "My, doesn't she move her lips fast," they would say, meaning that I'd be able to keep up with the world outside Chinatown.

8   My brother was even more fanatical than I about speaking English. He was especially hard on my mother, criticizing her, often cruelly, for her pidgin speech[7]—smatterings of Chinese scattered like chop suey in her conversation. "It's not 'What it is,' Mom," he'd say in exasperation. "It's 'What is it, what is it, what is it.'" Sometimes Mom might leave out an occasional "the" or "a," or perhaps a verb of being. He would stop her in mid-sentence: "Say it again, Mom. Say it right." When he tripped over his own tongue, he'd blame it on her: "See, Mom, it's all your fault. You set a bad example."

9   What infuriated my mother most was when my brother cornered her on her consonants, especially "r." My father had played a cruel joke on Mom by assigning her an American name that her tongue wouldn't allow her to say. No matter how hard she tried, "Ruth" always ended up "Luth" or "Roof."

10   After two years of writing with a *moc but* and reciting words with multiples of meanings, I was finally granted a cultural divorce. I was permitted to stop Chinese school.

11   I thought of myself as multicultural. I preferred tacos to egg rolls; I enjoyed Cinco de Mayo more than Chinese New Year.

12   At last, I was one of you; I wasn't one of them.

13   Sadly, I still am.

---

[5] *raunchy:* obscene
[6] *cluck:* a clicking sound with the tongue showing concern or interest
[7] *pidgin speech:* simplified, uneducated speech

READING FOR MAIN IDEAS

*Work in pairs. Go back to the chart on page 100. In the Hoffman and Wong columns of the chart, put a check (✓) next to the statements supported by the readings and an **X** next to the statements not supported by them. Discuss your own answers with your partner. Are your answers different from the answers expressed by the authors of these readings?*

READING FOR DETAILS

1 *Compare and contrast the cultural customs of Poland and Canada as Eva describes them in "Lost in Translation." Try to find at least five examples.*

POLISH WAYS	CANADIAN WAYS
1. In Poland, Eva was comfortable showing her feelings openly.	1. Eva felt Canadians were more reserved about their feelings.
2.	2.
3.	3.
4.	4.
5.	5.

2 *Compare and contrast Elizabeth's attitude toward Chinese things and her attitude toward American things when she was young, as told in "The Struggle to Be an All-American Girl." Try to find at least five examples.*

ELIZABETH'S ATTITUDE TOWARD CHINESE THINGS	ELIZABETH'S ATTITUDE TOWARD AMERICAN THINGS
1. *Chinese smells were musty like old mothballs or dirty closets.*	**1.** *American smells seem new and crisp like her teacher's perfume.*
2.	**2.**
3.	**3.**
4.	**4.**
5.	**5.**

REACTING TO THE READING

1 *Based on what is implied in the readings, discuss with your partner who might have made the following statements. In the blank space, write **Ev** (Eva), **El** (Elizabeth), **B** (Both girls), or **N** (Neither of them).*

_____ 1. "My mother has no idea what I'm going through."

_____ 2. "I am hurt by my mother's criticism of me."

_____ 3. "I miss the old country."

_____ 4. "I just want to fit in and stop thinking about the past."

_____ 5. "I feel comfortable in two cultures."

_____ 6. "Sometimes I want to express myself in one language and sometimes in another."

_____ 7. "Now that I am older, I regret losing so much of the past."

_____ 8. "When people just look at me, they don't really know who I am."

2 *Answer the following questions based on your understanding of the readings. Then compare your answers with those of your partner.*

a. " 'In Poland, I would have known how to bring you up, I would have known what to do,' my mother says wistfully, but here, she has lost her sureness, her authority."

Why do you think Eva's mother has lost her authority?

_____

_____

_____

_____

b. "I don't want us to turn into perpetually cheerful suburbanites, with hygienic smiles and equally hygienic feelings."

Explain the meaning of this statement.

_____

_____

_____

_____

c. At the end of the story "The Struggle to Be an All-American Girl," Elizabeth Wong writes, "At last, I was one of you; I wasn't one of them. Sadly, I still am."

What do you think she means?

_____

_____

_____

_____

3 *Discuss these questions in a small group.*

1. Are there any ideas, experiences, or feelings that are "lost in translation" when you try to explain them in English? What are they, and why do you think this happens?

2. Elizabeth Wong says that she was granted "a cultural divorce." What does she mean by this? Do you think that a cultural divorce is possible? Is it necessary?

B READING TWO: *In One School, Many Sagas*

1 *Before you read "In One School, Many Sagas," write a short answer to the following question.*

A **saga** is a story. Judging from this title, what do you expect Reading Two to be about?

In One School, Many Sagas

By Alan Riding (from the *New York Times*)

1   Sabine Contrepois well remembers the day two years ago when she explained to her high school class how the Vietnam War eventually spilled into Cambodia. Suddenly, Meak, an Asian girl in the front row, burst into tears. "I asked her what was wrong," Mrs. Contrepois recalled. "She said her father was shot the day the Khmer Rouge took power in Cambodia in 1975. She and her mother spent years in concentration camps before they escaped through Thailand. There was absolute silence in the classroom."

2   The incident set the teacher thinking. A traditional role of French schools is to prepare children of immigrants to become French citizens. Yet Meak's reaction made Mrs. Contrepois realize that she knew nothing of the background of the young people of different races whom she faced every day. Clearly, some students' parents came to France simply to find work. Others came fleeing wars and dictatorships. Yet Mrs. Contrepois, who comes from an immigrant family herself, also wondered whether the teenagers themselves knew why they were in France. Did they know their own family history?

3   A year ago, seeking answers, she gave the 120 students in her six classes a research project titled: "In what way has your family been touched by history?" If they did not know, she told them, they should ask their parents and grandparents. The result is "History, My History," a document in which 41 students, mostly in their late teens, describe the tumultuous paths—wars in Armenia, Spain, Algeria, Vietnam, and the former Yugoslavia; repression in Poland, Portugal, and Cameroon—that brought their families here.

4   Mrs. Contrepois sees the problem through the prism of her students[1] at Frederic Mistral High School in this town south of Paris. Her job is to teach youths who are considered by the school system to be slow learners. Many are immigrant children who have trouble finding jobs after school.

5   To Mrs. Contrepois, the youths' main liability[2] is not a lack of ability, but confusion about their identity. "It's easier for them to accept being French if they can also come to terms with their roots," she said. "This project tried to do that. It made them communicate with their parents. In many cases, they discovered things that made them proud. And I think it taught them tolerance toward each other."

6   Yassine, a 19-year-old born in France of Algerian parents, said he discovered that

---

[1] *through the prism of her students:* through the eyes of her students
[2] *liability:* a disadvantage

his grandfather had been tortured and killed by French troops during Algeria's war of independence. "I didn't know anything about this," he said. "We never spoke about Algeria at home. I had never dared ask before."

7   Stephanie, also 19, said she learned that her grandfather was shot by invading German troops in Poland in 1939. "My father came here illegally in 1946, but this topic was taboo[3] at home," she said. "He died two years ago, and my mother told me the story. When she saw the final project, she cried. She was very proud."

8   To insure the authenticity[4] of the stories, Mrs. Contrepois asked her "student authors," as she now calls them, to provide documentation. Sevana, 16, found newspaper photos of the Turkish atrocities[5] against Armenians in 1915, when her great-grandparents were killed. Slawomir, whose father, a Pole, sought asylum[6] in France in 1981, offered a photograph of her grandmother with Lech Walesa.[7]

9   This month, the work was awarded the "Memories of Immigration" prize by the Foundation for Republican Integration, headed by Kofi Yamgnane, a former Minister for Integration who was born in Togo.

10   Mrs. Contrepois was well equipped to oversee the project. The 36-year-old teacher was born in a run-down Paris hotel shortly after her Spanish-born father and Algerian-born mother arrived here fleeing the Algerian War. "They were penniless immigrants, and they knew all about discrimination," she said. While her family eventually found a place in French society, she knows that it is more difficult for immigrants today. But at least with this group of young people, she has made an impact. "She has changed our lives," Yassine said, speaking for the "student authors" at a recent ceremony here attended by Mr. Yamgnane and the town mayor, Gabriel Bourdin.

11   "History, My History" will soon be published as a book here, and the students have made another plan—they want to visit New York. Their prize brought them $5,000, but they must raise $39,000 more. "We want to compare our experiences with those of young Americans like us, how they study, what their culture is," Yassine said. "The only New York I've seen is on television."

---

[3] *taboo:* forbidden
[4] *authenticity:* truthfulness
[5] *atrocity:* an act of great evil, especially cruelty
[6] *asylum:* refuge, shelter
[7] *Lech Walesa:* leader of a workers' movement in Poland who became the head of state after Poland gained its independence from the former Soviet Union

---

2 *Read the following quotes from "In One School, Many Sagas," and write short answers to the questions. Compare your answers in a small group.*

1. Sabine Contrepois: "It's easier for them to accept being French if they can also come to terms with their roots."

What does this statement mean? Do you agree with Mrs. Contrepois?

_____

_____

2. Yassine: "I didn't know anything about this. We never spoke about Algeria at home. I had never dared ask before."

Why do you think Yassine never asked his family any questions?

_____

_____

3. Stephanie: "When [my mother] saw the final project, she cried."

Why do you think Stephanie's project made her mother cry?

_____

_____

C LINKING READINGS ONE AND TWO

Write a paragraph about one of the topics below. Use your understanding of the three stories in this unit.

1. You are Elizabeth from the story "The Struggle to Be an All-American Girl." Imagine that your grandmother said to you one day, "Only your outside is Chinese; inside you are all American-made." Write a letter to your grandmother explaining how you feel about what she said.

2. You are the father of Yassine or the mother of Stephanie, students in Mrs. Contrepois's classroom from "In One School, Many Sagas." Write a letter to your child explaining why you kept the family history a secret.

3. You are Eva Hoffman (from "Lost in Translation") as a young girl. What do you think about the history project the French students are doing? Would you like to do such a project for your class to read in Canada? Do you think it would help your classmates to understand you, or would it just make you seem too different from the others?

4. You are Elizabeth from "The Struggle to Be an All-American Girl," but you are now an adult. Write a letter to the grown-up Eva explaining how your attitude toward your cultural background changed as you got older.

3 Focus on Vocabulary

> The suffixes **-ness, -ty, -ity,** and **-ment** mean "the state, quality, or condition of being." When you add *-ness, -ty,* and *-ity* to certain adjectives and *-ment* to certain verbs, you create nouns that relate to the state, quality, or condition of being a particular way. For adjectives of two syllables or more that end with a *y*, the *y* changes to *i* after *-ness* is added.
>
> **Examples**
>
> quiet (adjective)
> quietness (noun = "the state, quality, or condition of being quiet")
>
> happy (adjective)
> happiness (noun = "the state, quality, or condition of being happy")
>
> authentic (adjective)
> authenticity (noun = "the state, quality, or condition of being authentic")
>
> move (verb)
> movement (noun = "the state, quality, or condition of moving/being moved")

1 *Work with a partner. Read the following sentences, and identify the noun that can be created from the underlined words. Then write a sentence using the noun form. The sentence you create should not change the meaning of the original sentence, even though some words will have to be changed.*

1. Elizabeth likes the <u>refined</u> manner in which Southerners speak English.

   Noun form: *refinement*

   Sentence: *Elizabeth likes the refinement of Southerners' speech.*

2. Penny does not understand that Eva is being <u>friendly</u> when she shakes her arm in excitement.

   Noun form: _____

   Sentence: _____

3. Eva learns that hooking her arm through Penny's as they walk down the street together <u>embarrasses</u> Penny.

   Noun form: _____

   Sentence: _____

4. Eva does not want her father, mother, and sister to stop being <u>loyal</u> to one another.

Noun form: _____

Sentence: _____

5. Many French immigrant children are surprised to learn that their ancestors were the unfortunate victims of <u>atrocious</u> crimes.

Noun form: _____

Sentence: _____

6. The Hoffman family's <u>stormy</u> emotional state is far beyond the norm in Canada.

Noun form: _____

Sentence: _____

7. Eva is <u>ferocious</u> about protecting her family's common bond.

Noun form: _____

Sentence: _____

2 *Read these thoughts that may have gone through the mind of Alinka, Eva's younger sister. Complete the thoughts with words and expressions from the box below; they are synonyms for the words indicated.*

asylum	cluster	fragile	perpetually
atrocities	come to terms	giving vent to	storminess
beleaguered	with their roots	hygienic	trapped
blend in	fabric	loose	

These have been difficult years for my parents. The _____ of
                                                    1. (structure)
their emotional lives has been made ever so _____ because of their
                                              2. (delicate)
own suffering and their firsthand knowledge of the terrible _____
                                                              3. (torment)
suffered by so many of their loved ones during World War II. My parents sought

to make a new life for us in Canada.

Although they had hoped that their new home in Canada would provide an

_____ for them from their tragic past, my parents' sense of
4. (haven)

sorrow still dominates them. Their every gesture is still _____ by
5. (troubled)

their memories of the past.

You may think that as the youngest family member of our

_____ of four, I have been untouched by all this. Yet it was not
6. (group)

until we moved to Canada that I realized how very _____ I had
7. (imprisoned)

been by my parents' sadness. I had never realized how simple life could be. None

of my Canadian friends seem to have a history or to be troubled by the need to

_____ . Their _____ happy faces, which my
8. (understand who they are   9. (constantly)
in light of their family history)

sister sarcastically describes as reflecting not only "_____ smiles,"
10. (clean, healthy)

but also "_____ feelings," are a welcome sigh of relief to me.
10. (clean, healthy)

While my sister may laugh at my friends and their parents because of their

superficiality, I disagree. I want more than anything else to _____
11. (feel comfortable)

with this Disneyland mentality, with this fairy tale of a life where "everyone lives

happily ever after."

So, if I am putting a lot of makeup on my face and behaving in ways that

make my mother think of the _____ girls in our Polish town, be
12. (immoral)

happy for me! I am doing two things at once. I am rebelling as only teenagers

know how to rebel, and in so doing, I am "painting" a new life for myself.

Through my actions, not only am I _____ my frustrations and
13. (expressing)

liberating myself from the _____ of my family's inner life, but I
14. (turmoil)

am also creating a new identity for myself. I am becoming free!

3 *Working with a partner, complete the following imaginary dialogue between Elizabeth Wong and her mother. Elizabeth is young and does not want to go to Chinese school. Her mother is upset and tries to persuade her daughter to respect traditional culture. The daughter wants to be more American than Chinese. In your dialogue, use at least eight words or phrases from the box below.*

betray	demonstrative	restraint
blend in	embarrass	scold
chaotic	give vent to	stoical
~~come to terms~~ ~~with your roots~~	~~nagging~~	trapped

ELIZABETH: *Why are you always* **nagging** *me about going to Chinese school?*

I hate it there.

MOTHER: *It's important for you learn to speak Chinese and to* **come to**

terms with your roots.

ELIZABETH: _____

_____

MOTHER: _____

_____

ELIZABETH: _____

_____

MOTHER: _____

_____

ELIZABETH: _____

_____

MOTHER: _____

_____

4 Focus on Writing

A GRAMMAR: Adverb Clauses of Comparison and Contrast

1 *Working in pairs, examine the following sentence from "Lost in Translation," and discuss the questions that follow.*

"You shouldn't say, 'You are wrong about that,' although you may say, 'On the other hand, there is that to consider.'"

1. Is this one sentence or two?
2. Which part of the sentence contains words that are polite to say in Canadian culture?
3. What is the difference between the two parts of the sentence?
4. What is a synonym for *although* in this sentence?

Adverb Clauses

Adverb clauses can be used to combine two ideas into one sentence. They can be used in the first or second part of the sentence. They provide variety for the sentence and smooth transitions from one idea to another in your paragraphs. The following adverbials will be particularly helpful in comparison and contrast essays. Look at the examples carefully to see where commas are needed.

Comparison or Similarity	Examples
just as	*Just as* Eva is struggling to be accepted in Canada, Elizabeth is struggling to be accepted in the United States.
in the same way that	*In the same way that* many immigrants have chosen to come to North America, many are choosing France as their new home.

Contrast or Difference	
whereas	*Whereas* **France has an official ministry to help with assimilation of immigrants,** the United States does not have such an institution.

(continued)

while	Mrs. Contrepois felt that children need to know their roots, ***while their parents felt the past was too painful.***
despite the fact that	***Despite the fact that Americans have tolerated the use of many immigrant languages,*** they remain profoundly attached to the English language.
although	***Although Americans have tolerated the use of many immigrant languages,*** they remain profoundly attached to the English language.
while	***While Americans have tolerated the use of many immigrant languages,*** they remain profoundly attached to the English language.

GRAMMAR TIP: As you can see, *while* can be used in two distinct ways: either as a synonym for *whereas* or as a synonym for *despite the fact that* and *although*. Sentences with *despite the fact that* and *although* often include an unexpected idea or a contradiction. In these sentences, the subject of both clauses is usually the same.

2 *For each of the following topics, write one or two sentences with words of comparison and contrast. Use the cues given, and write sentences with **although, despite the fact that, in the same way that, just as, whereas,** and **while**.*

1. *Telling the truth*

   Poles / Canadians

   While Poles may prefer to be honest and direct when giving criticism,

   Canadians may choose to be more diplomatic and keep their opinions

   to themselves.

2. *Cultural identity*

   Elizabeth / Eva

   _____

   _____

   _____

3. *Respecting one's parents*

Elizabeth's brother / Alinka (Eva's sister)

_____

_____

_____

4. *Showing intimacy*

Eva / Penny (Eva's friend)

_____

_____

_____

5. *Obedience*

American children / Chinese children

_____

_____

_____

6. *American ways / Canadian ways*

Elizabeth / Eva's mother

_____

_____

_____

7. *Independence*

Elizabeth / Eva

_____

_____

_____

8. *Personal stories*

"Lost in Translation" / "History, My History"

_____

_____

_____

B STYLE: Comparison and Contrast Essays

1 *Examine this essay, and discuss the questions that follow. Work with a partner.*

A Comparison of Eva and Elizabeth

INTRODUCTORY
PARAGRAPH

Whoever once said that the children of immigrants have an easy time adapting to life in their new country was surely mistaken. Because they usually learn to speak the new language sooner than adults, immigrant children often become the family spokesperson. As the oldest children in their families, both Eva Hoffman and Elizabeth Wong play an active role in helping their family members communicate with the outside world. As a result, they often suffer from the pain and frustration that people who live in two cultures can experience. By examining the relationships that these two girls have with their mothers and other important people in their lives, we can see that although Eva and Elizabeth may have certain hopes and feelings in common, they are at the same time very different from one another.

BODY
PARAGRAPH 1

Like Eva, Elizabeth wants to be accepted by her peers, and she is embarrassed when she is made to feel different from them. In the same way that Eva becomes self-conscious about expressing her feelings, Elizabeth is ashamed as she wanders through the American supermarket and hears her grandmother calling after her in Chinese. Elizabeth also hates it when her mother speaks English. But on the surface at least, she does not seem to be as bothered by this as her younger brother. This brings us to another common area of concern. Eva and Elizabeth are both unhappy about the ways in which their brother and sister treat their mother. Just as Eva is angered when her sister Alinka challenges her mother's authority, Elizabeth views her brother's constant criticisms of her mother's English as fanatical and cruel. Both Eva and Elizabeth are more outwardly protective of their mothers' feelings than their brother and sister are.

BODY
PARAGRAPH 2

Although Eva and Elizabeth share similar attitudes, they also differ from each other in many respects. Unlike Eva, Elizabeth does not feel that her identity is bound to her family's cultural heritage and history. Whereas Eva embraces her Polish heritage, Elizabeth flees her Chinese background. While Eva wants to hold on to the memory of the family's sad past, Elizabeth is happy when her mother grants her a "cultural divorce" and says she no longer has to attend the Chinese school. In contrast to Elizabeth, Eva is flexible: She is willing to compromise and accept the best of both cultures. Whereas Eva sees herself becoming bicultural, Elizabeth adores the sights and sounds of everything American and wants only to be an "all-American girl." How could she want anything else if Nancy Drew, her favorite heroine, never spoke Chinese? Of course, all this can be explained by the different ages and the different circumstances of the two girls. Eva is thirteen years old, while Elizabeth is only ten years old. In addition, whereas Eva herself is an immigrant, Elizabeth was born and raised in the United States. Such basic differences in their lives leave a wide gap between them.

CONCLUSION   Eva and Elizabeth have made different adjustments to their cross-cultural experiences. When children like Eva immigrate, they understand the sacrifices their parents have made in order to provide them with a better life because they themselves have participated in the immigration process. However, children like Elizabeth often don't understand the sacrifices their parents have made for them until they become adults. And when they finally do, can it sometimes be too late?

1. Which words and phrases does the writer use to point out similarities and differences?

2. In the body of the essay, can you readily identify the paragraph that deals with the similarities and the paragraph that deals with the differences? Explain how the writer makes this easy for the reader.

3. What does the writer do to connect the two paragraphs of the body?

4. Are the similarities between the two characters more important than the differences, or are the differences more important than the similarities? Explain.

Purpose of Comparison and Contrast Essays

When you write a comparison and contrast essay, the purpose is not just to point out similarities and differences or advantages and disadvantages. The purpose is—as with all essays—also to persuade, explain, or inform. The emphasis should be on either the similarities or the differences, and details should be included according to which emphasis is chosen.

The thesis statement of the essay you have just read, the last sentence of the introductory paragraph, tells the reader something about the emphasis that will be developed in the body of the essay. "By examining the relationships that these two girls have with their mothers and other important people in their lives, we can see that although Eva and Elizabeth may have certain hopes and feelings in common, they are at the same time very different from one another." We know by the last sentence of the body of the essay that the differences outweigh the similarities: "Such basic differences in their lives leave a wide gap between them." This point of view is reinforced in the conclusion of the essay.

Patterns of Organization

There are two ways to organize a comparison and contrast essay: through block organization or point-by-point organization.

Block Organization	Point-by-Point Organization
• Similarities: *All subjects are discussed.* • Differences: *All subjects are discussed.*	• Subject One: *Similarities and differences are discussed.* • Subject Two: *Similarities and differences are discussed.* • Subject Three: *Similarities and differences are discussed.*

Block Organization

In a **block organization** essay, the writer discusses each part of the comparison in clearly distinct parts (or blocks) of the essay. For example, the writer could first refer only to Eva and then only to Elizabeth, or, as in the essay "A Comparison of Eva and Elizabeth," he could first discuss the similarities between the two girls and then the differences between them.

The paragraph dealing with similarities contains many words and expressions that point out likenesses: *like, in the same way that, just as, both,* and so on. Similarly, the paragraph revealing the differences contains words and expressions that show differences: *unlike, whereas, while, in contrast to,* and so on.

In order to connect one block of the essay with the other, the writer uses a transitional sentence that prepares us for the change in emphasis of the next block: "Although Eva and Elizabeth share similar attitudes, they also differ from each other in many respects."

Point-by-Point Organization

In **point-by-point organization,** the writer organizes the development of ideas according to "points," or categories, that are common to both subjects. In each paragraph of the body, a different point is discussed. For example, a comparison of Eva and Elizabeth might (after the introductory paragraph) begin with a paragraph exploring the differences in their *age and background*. A second paragraph might discuss the similarities and differences in their *family life,* and so on. It is usually better to limit the categories to three or four. A point-by-point organization is usually chosen when there are many complex aspects to a comparison; a block organization is more suitable for a simpler subject.

Organizing Information through Outlines

Whether you choose block or point-by-point organization for your comparison and contrast essay, preparing an outline can help you to organize your main ideas, topic sentences, and supporting details. After you prepare an outline, you know exactly what you want to write and how you want to write it.

2 *Reread the body of the essay "A Comparison of Eva and Elizabeth." Then work with a partner, and complete the block organization outline that follows by filling in the blanks. Do not copy the sentences that appear in the essay. Instead, write notes that reflect the information that is conveyed in each sentence.*

**Outline: A Comparison of Eva and Elizabeth
(Block Organization)**

I. How Eva and Elizabeth are like each other

    A. Embarrassment

        1. Eva:

        _____

        2. Elizabeth:

        _____

    B. Siblings

        1. Eva:

        _____

        2. Elizabeth:

II. _____

    A. Cultural Heritage and History

        1. Eva:

           *does not want to go to Chinese school*_____

        2. Elizabeth:

        _____

    B. Cultural Identity

        1. Eva:

        _____

        2. Elizabeth:

        _____

    C. _____

        1. Eva:

           *immigrant*_____

        2. Elizabeth:

        _____

3 *With your partner, plan an outline based on point-by-point organization for the same essay, "A Comparison of Eva and Elizabeth." Use the following framework as a guide.*

Outline: A Comparison of Eva and Elizabeth
(Point-by-Point Organization)

I. Age and Background

A. Eva:

_____

B. Elizabeth:

_____

II. Family Life

A. Eva:

_____

B. Elizabeth:

_____

III. Cultural Identity

A. Eva:

_____

B. Elizabeth:

_____

C   WRITING TOPICS

Write an essay about one of the following topics. In order to organize your ideas effectively, write a clear thesis statement and create an outline in response to it. Follow the outline as you write the essay. Use vocabulary, grammar structures, and style structures that you studied in this unit.

1. Have you ever had a friend whose culture, background, talents, or qualities were different from yours? Consider how your similarities and differences contributed to your friendship. Did your friendship grow because you were similar or because you were different?

2. When immigrants arrive in a new country, should they assimilate into the new culture or try to preserve their old culture? In what ways do you think people need to assimilate? What kinds of things do people usually want to preserve from their old culture? What is the risk to the nation if assimilation is too extreme? What is the risk if immigrants do not assimilate?

3. What is the meaning of the following extract? In what ways might Luc Sante have felt "other"? How has your own identity been formed? Have you ever had the experience of being "other"?

> "Ethnically, I am about as homogeneous as it is possible to be: Aside from one great-grandmother who came from Luxembourg, my gene pool derives entirely from an area smaller than the five boroughs of New York City. I was born in the same town [Verviers, Belgium] as every one of my Sante forebears at least as far back as the mid-sixteenth century, which is as far back as the records go. Having been transplanted from my native soil [to live in the United States], and having had to construct an identity in response to a double set of demands, one from my background and one from my environment, I have become permanently 'other.' "

—Luc Sante, "Living in Tongues"
(from the *New York Times Magazine*)

D RESEARCH TOPICS

PREPARATION

In what way has your family been touched by history? Prepare to write an essay in response to this question. Interview family members—in person, by mail, or by e-mail—to gather information for your essay. Before starting your research, brainstorm with a partner for other questions that you believe would be worth investigating. Here are some points you may want to consider when you make up the questions for your interviews.

- Has your family always lived in the same place? What influenced the decision to stay or go?

- Has your country undergone any great changes in the last 50 years? wars? revolutions? divisions? reunifications? changes in the political system? What effect have these events had on your family?

- Have the economic circumstances of your family changed in recent generations? What are the reasons for these changes?

- How has your family adjusted to change?

- Do you think it is important for children to know the history of their family?

- Has your family ever had any secrets that were not immediately told to the younger generation? Why were certain facts not discussed in your family?

- Is there any documentation that you would like to show to illustrate your family's history? This can include photos, newspaper articles, or magazines from the period. It can include personal items if you and your family agree to do so.

RESEARCH

When you interview family members, be sure to take good notes. You may want to request permission to use a tape recorder if you are interviewing in person. Ask them if they have any photos, newspaper articles, official announcements, letters, or personal records that you can include with your essay.

SHARING YOUR FINDINGS

Write an essay in which you summarize your findings and explain how this information has affected you. Include relevant documentation.

For step-by-step practice in the writing process, see the *Writing Activity Book, Advanced,* Unit 5.

Assignment	Comparison and Contrast Essay
Prewriting	Creating a Venn Diagram
Organizing	Analyzing Methods of Organization
Revising	Writing Thesis Statements
	Comparing and Contrasting Ideas with Adverb Clauses
Editing	Varying Sentence Types

For Unit 5 Internet activities, visit the NorthStar Companion Website at http://longman.com/northstar.

The Landscape of Faith

1 Focus on the Topic

A PREDICTING

Look at the title of this unit and the photo above. In spite of different practices, why do you think religion is such an important part of life all over the world? Write down your ideas, and share them with the class.

B   SHARING INFORMATION

Interview a partner using this questionnaire about religion. You will need to summarize in a few sentences your partner's answer to question 5.

After you have finished, show your summary to your partner to check the content. Then discuss your answers in a small group.

RELIGION IN YOUR LIFE

	Yes	No
1. Were you brought up in a particular religion?	☒ CATHOLIC	☐
2. Do you still feel a part of that religion today?	☒	☐
3. Do you participate in a religion today?	☒	☐
4. Do you follow all the customs, rules, and traditions of this religion?	☐	☒ Sometimes

5. How has the religion affected your life or your family's life?

Ricordo: He had to go to the church when He was child, was obligation and he didn't like".

Lisane She dosn have a espetific religion she is espiritualist

Faith (fe)

C PREPARING TO READ

BACKGROUND

Read the information below, and discuss the questions that follow in a small group.

In this chapter, there is an interview with one of the most well-known Buddhists in the world, the Dalai Lama, the religious leader of the Tibetan Buddhist community.

The Buddhist religion is based on the teachings of Siddhartha Gautama, a Hindu prince who lived about 2,500 years ago in India. (This was about the same time Confucius was teaching in China.) Siddhartha became the Buddha, or "Enlightened One," after a personal journey of spiritual awakening, and he spent the rest of his life teaching people. Buddhist teachings have spread all over Asia and are followed today by more than 290 million people. Buddhism is divided into many different schools and sects, but all Buddhists share certain basic beliefs.

For Buddhists, all life is suffering. This suffering is caused by selfish efforts and desires. A life goes through many cycles of rebirth because there is always something more to learn. Nirvana, the end of rebirth and suffering, the release into the highest stage of happiness, is achieved only by learning to give up self-interest. Buddhists are taught to speak kindly, to do no harm, and to avoid killing, stealing, lying, drinking alcohol, and committing sexual offenses. Buddhists believe there is no beginning and no end, no creation and no Higher Being.

Tibetan Buddhism suffered greatly in the last generation. In the 1950s the Chinese Communist government invaded Tibet and almost destroyed the spiritual and cultural basis of the religion. In 1959 the Dalai Lama, the head of the religion there, had to leave his country with 70,000 of his followers; he now lives in exile. → Sair do país

1. Do you know of any other religions whose philosophy is based on respect for the life and teachings of an individual? What religions are they?

2. Do you know of other religions that suffered from government persecution in the last century?

3. Why do you think some Westerners are attracted to Eastern religions? Why do you think some Easterners are attracted to Western religions?

VOCABULARY FOR COMPREHENSION

Work in pairs. Read the sentences, and match each underlined word or expression with a synonym from the list.

__h__ 1. The Buddhist religion believes in <u>the idea that individual people can come back in a new life form after death</u>.

__F__
__K__ 2. Some religious doctrines <u>foretell</u> the end of the world.

3. When someone asks you to imagine what the future will <u>bring</u>, you are being asked to <u>theorize</u> about what may happen.

__W__ 4. Spiritual concerns are usually associated with religion, but <u>worldly, material</u> concerns are usually identified with government authority. In some cultures, however, the spiritual leader is also the <u>head of government</u>.

__C__ 5. In some countries, a political, spiritual, or artistic leader who is unpopular with the government can be forced into <u>leaving his or her country and living in a foreign land</u>.

__D__ 6. Although almost all religions defend the need for peace, religious concerns have sometimes been used to <u>prepare</u> people <u>for war</u>.

__B__ 7. Most religions try to teach moral principles, hoping that people will <u>stop</u> their selfish or aggressive behavior.

__A__ 8. In many religions, the leaders are not elected. The heads of the religion <u>choose</u> their successors.

__E__ 9. Many parents give their children a religious education, hoping that when the children grow up they will be <u>observant</u> members of the religion.

__i__ 10. Some young people feel that religious concerns are no longer <u>related</u> to modern life.

__j__ 11. History shows that brutal dictators do not think much about the long-term interests of their people. They are often reckless and <u>interested only in the moment</u>.

__g__ 12. Some religions are practiced only among their own people, but other religions seek to <u>spread</u> their ideas among as many people as possible.

a. designate   g. propagate

b. cease   h. reincarnation

c. exile   i. relevant

d. mobilize   j. short-sighted

e. practicing   k. speculate

f. predict   l. temporal

I'm a worldly person = sou uma pessoa global
conheço o mundo, viaje muito.

The Landscape of Faith   **129**

2 Focus on Reading

Before you read the interview with the Dalai Lama, answer the following question in a written paragraph. Then discuss your answer with a partner.

Do you think the world will be better or worse 100 years from now?

PEACE PREVAILS

By Claudia Dreifus (from the *New York Times Magazine*)

1   In the Buddhist tradition, the future counts for little. Nonetheless, when Tenzin Gyatso, fourteenth Dalai Lama and the spiritual and temporal leader of Tibet in exile, was asked to speculate on the landscape of faith a century from now, he gave it his best try. He was interviewed in Bloomington, Indiana, on a brilliant summer morning, after having laid the cornerstone[1] for a new Buddhist temple.

2   **Question:** In the next hundred years, thanks to organ transplants and genetic therapies, people may be able to live much longer lives. If you had the chance to do that, would you take it?

3   **Dalai Lama:** The mere living is not so important. The important thing is usefulness. So if I could get another hundred years more and be useful, then . . . good. Otherwise, you just create more problems for others. And then, from the Buddhist viewpoint, isn't it better to have another young body [through reincarnation]? There's a Buddhist story about an old monk who was dying and everyone was very sad.

He said, "Don't be sad. Right now, I have an old, decaying body. But very soon . . . I will get a fresh young body."

4   **Question:** Three years ago, you predicted that the next hundred years would be a century of peace, hope, and justice. Since then, there have been massacres in Rwanda and Burundi, the Northern Irish peace discussions have been blown apart, and the Chinese have kidnapped the young boy you designated to be the Panchen Lama.[2] Are you still optimistic about the future?

5   **Dalai Lama:** Oh, yes. Of course. A handful of shortsighted people have always existed. But overall, their day is over because the public's attitude toward war and violence has become much healthier than at any time in history. People used to be much more jingoistic[3] and nationalistic compared with the way they are now.

6   Recently I was talking with the English Queen Mother. She is 96, and I asked her, "What changes have you seen in your lifetime?"[4] She answered, "When I was young,

---

[1] *cornerstone:* a foundation, a stone laid at a formal ceremony
[2] *Panchen Lama:* chief spiritual adviser to the Dalai Lama
[3] *jingoistic:* believing strongly that your own country is better than others
[4] The Queen Mother was born on August 5, 1900, and died on March 29, 2002.

we had not much concern about the outside world. Now people have a great concern about what is happening all over the world." This is a very positive change.

7   So I believe that due to [the revolution in] information, generally speaking, any leader, if he tried to mobilize the whole nation for war, would find it impossible. In previous times, it was quite possible. Well, small-scale wars, perhaps they can still do. But large-scale wars, I think, are not likely. I do believe that in the next century we have to seriously think about putting a complete stop to the arms trade.

8   **Q:** Buddhism has become quite popular in the West. Could you see a future American president who is a practicing Buddhist?

9   **DL:** No, I think someone in the Judeo-Christian tradition would be better. I prefer that people in Western countries follow their own traditions. I have no desire to propagate [my religious beliefs].

10   **Q:** A hundred years in the future, what will be the role of women in religion?

11   **DL:** I think improved. Because the women want it.

12   **Q:** Can you see a situation where there might be a woman as Pope, a woman as Archbishop of Canterbury, a woman as Dalai Lama?

13   **DL:** In the Buddhist world, there's not much of a problem. Some of the Lamas of high reincarnation are women.

14   **Q:** Is it possible that you, the 14th Dalai Lama, might be the last Dalai Lama?

15   **DL:** It is possible. Not as a result of external force, though. If the majority of the Tibetan people feel that the Dalai Lama institution is no longer relevant, then the institution will automatically cease. Now, if that happens while I'm alive or just after my death, then I am obviously the last Dalai Lama. But if my death comes in the next one or two years, then most probably the Tibetan people will want to have another

incarnation. Of that I'm quite certain. Of course, there is the possibility that Tibetans become insignificant in our land and all decisions are made by the Chinese. It is possible and very sad.

16   **Q:** Are you concerned that you might have a violent death?

17   **DL:** It is possible, I don't know. Airplanes trouble me. Dying in the ocean. And ending up in the stomach of a shark.

18   **Q:** One hundred years from now, what would you like to be remembered for?

19   **DL:** As a Buddhist practitioner, I have no interest in that. So long as I am alive, my time and my life must be utilized properly. Then after my death, I don't care how people remember me.

20   **Q:** Is it true that you like to go shopping when you travel?

21   **DL:** I like it. I'm a human being. I think human beings have a lot of curiosity. I go to Los Angeles; sometimes I shop for myself. Shoes . . . small electronic equipment . . . cat food. I go to shopping malls just like they were museums.

22   **Q:** Many people get a sense of God by observing nature. What will religions be like in a hundred years if there is little nature left on earth?

23   **DL:** The world itself is nature. The sun, the moon, they are nature. Even if there were no more animals, nature would still be here. For those religions that believe in a creator, they would have to find reasons to explain why our beautiful blue planet became a desert.

24   If you ask me whether it's good or bad, of course it's bad. But in the Buddhist tradition, something like that would not change our attitude. We believe the whole world will come and disappear, come and disappear—so eventually the world becomes desert and even the ocean dries up. But then again, another new world is reborn. It's endless.

READING FOR MAIN IDEAS

Under each of the questions about the main themes of this reading, write a few sentences summarizing the Dalai Lama's point of view.

1. What does the Dalai Lama say about his philosophy of death?

_____

_____

_____

_____

2. What does the Dalai Lama say about his attitude toward war?

_____

_____

_____

_____

3. What does he say about the role of the Dalai Lama in the future?

_____

_____

_____

_____

4. What does he say about the future of the earth?

_____

_____

_____

_____

READING FOR DETAILS

Read the sentences below. Cross out the sentences that are not part of the Dalai Lama's predictions. Then decide which major theme of the reading each remaining sentence supports. Write the number of the sentence on the blank next to the appropriate main idea.

Predictions

1. The Chinese government may go further in opposing the Tibetan people's religion.

2. Buddhists will be converting thousands of Americans to their religion.

3. Improvements in information technology will continue to create concern for people in other countries.

4. World wars will be less likely than in the twentieth century.

5. Nature may go through a cycle where much is destroyed.

6. Tibetans will be true to their religion unless external force obliges them to change.

7. Nationalism will decrease as different peoples draw closer together.

8. The Dalai Lama will not worry about how people will remember him 100 years from now.

9. Buddhists will have to accept the idea of a creator.

10. Old bodies should be discarded.

Main Ideas/Themes

_____   **a.** The Role of the Dalai Lama in the Future

_____   **b.** The Dalai Lama's Attitude toward War

_____   **c.** The Dalai Lama's Philosophy of Death

_____   **d.** The Future of the Earth

REACTING TO THE READING

1 *Based on what you read in the interview, imagine what the Dalai Lama would say if he were asked the following questions. Write short answers and explain your conclusions, referring to specific parts of the interview. Then compare your answers with those of another student.*

The Dalai Lama

1. **Question:** Should the Tibetans mobilize against the Chinese?

   Answer: *The Dalai Lama would probably say no because he speaks out against war and violence in paragraph 5 of the interview.*

2. **Question:** Should religious people refuse to go to the movies?

   Answer: I believe that if you have a strong personality you can do everything...

3. **Question:** Should society invest a great deal of money in keeping very old and ill people alive as long as possible?

   Answer: _____

   _____

4. **Question:** Should society be concerned about endangered species?

   Answer: _____

   _____

Now invent two questions of your own for the Dalai Lama, and ask a classmate to answer them.

5. **Question:** _____

   Answer: _____

   _____

6. **Question:** _____

   Answer: _____

   _____

2 *Discuss these questions in a small group.*

1. Why do you think the Dalai Lama gives interviews to Western journalists?

2. The Dalai Lama feels that being nationalistic is a bad thing. Do you agree?

3. The Dalai Lama wants to be useful in his old age. Are older people entitled to special respect or privileges because of their age? Do older people have a responsibility to help the younger generation?

4. Do you think it is possible to change a society by using peaceful, nonviolent methods?

B READING TWO: *Religion*

1 *Below is an excerpt from an essay that offers a general definition of the word* **religion.** *Although there can be diverse views on this subject, the passage tries to make broad generalizations applicable to many religions and different periods of history.*

Before you read the passage, answer the question below. Write a short definition, and discuss it with a partner.

How would you define the word *religion*?

RELIGION

FROM *COMPTON'S INTERACTIVE ENCYCLOPEDIA*

1   It has been said that thoughts of death lead necessarily to the development of religion. It is difficult to imagine what need there would be for religion in a world in which no one ever died or became ill. The literatures of all religions attempt to give answers to basic questions: From where did the world come? What is the meaning of human life? Why do people die and what happens afterward? Why is there evil? How should people behave? In the distant past, these questions were answered in terms of mythology. In literature, they are dealt with in poetry. Modern sciences try to investigate them.

2   As a word religion is difficult to define, but as a human experience it seems to be universal. The twentieth-century German-born American theologian Paul Tillich[1] gave a simple and basic definition of the word. "Religion is ultimate concern." This means that religion encompasses that to which people are most devoted or that from which they expect to get the most fundamental satisfaction in life. Consequently, religion provides adequate answers to the most basic questions posed above.

---

[1] *Paul Tillich:* Protestant theologian (religious thinker), 1886–1965

3   Four centuries earlier the German social reformer Martin Luther[2] spoke in similar terms about God. He stated that to have a god was to "have something in which the heart trusts completely." Putting Tillich's and Luther's definitions together, it is possible to see that religion does not necessarily have to be involved with shrines, temples, churches, or synagogues. It does not need complex doctrines or clergy.[3] It can be anything to which people devote themselves that fills their lives with meaning.

4   In Western civilization, religion has traditionally been defined as belief in and worship of one god. This is true for Judaism, Christianity, and Islam. The statements by Tillich and Luther make it clear, however, that such a definition may be too narrow. In original Buddhism in India and Confucianism in China, there was no recognition of a supreme being. Both of these philosophies were basically concerned with patterns of human behavior.

5   Regardless of definition, all religions (as the word is normally used) have certain elements in common: rituals to perform, prayers to recite, places to frequent or avoid, holy days to keep, means by which to predict the future, a body of literature to read and study, truths to affirm, charismatic[4] leaders to follow, and ordinances[5] to obey. Many have buildings set aside for worship, and there are activities such as prayer, sacrifice, contemplation, and perhaps magic.

6   Closely associated with these elements is personal conduct. Although it is possible to separate ritual observances from moral conduct, worship has normally implied a type of relationship with a god from which certain behavior patterns are expected to follow. A notable exception in history is the official state religion of ancient Rome, which was kept separate from personal commitment and morality.

[2] *Martin Luther:* German leader of the Protestant Reformation, 1482–1546
[3] *clergy:* a group of men and women who are religious leaders and servants of God
[4] *charismatic:* embodying a personal magic of leadership, creating great loyalty and enthusiasm among followers
[5] *ordinances:* orders or regulations to follow

2 *Paraphrase the following quotes from the text. Compare your sentences with a partner's.*

   1. "In the distant past, these questions were answered in terms of mythology. In literature, they are dealt with in poetry. Modern sciences try to investigate them." (paragraph 1)

   _____

   _____

   _____

2. "Putting Tillich's and Luther's definitions together, it is possible to see that religion does not necessarily have to be involved with shrines, temples, churches, or synagogues. It does not need complex doctrines or clergy. It can be anything to which people devote themselves that fills their lives with meaning." (paragraph 3)

_____

_____

_____

3. "Although it is possible to separate ritual observances from moral conduct, worship has normally implied a type of relationship with a god from which certain behavior patterns are expected to follow." (paragraph 6)

_____

_____

_____

C   LINKING READINGS ONE AND TWO

Work in pairs. Choose Exercise 1 or 2, and fill in the appropriate answers.

1 *In Reading Two, the writer lists five basic questions which the literatures of all religions attempt to answer. Based on the interview with the Dalai Lama, how do you think he would respond to these questions? Discuss with a partner what answers you would expect to find in Buddhist literature. Then write your answers in the spaces provided.*

1. Where did the world come from?

_____

_____

_____

2. What is the meaning of human life?

_____

_____

_____

3. Why do people die, and what happens afterward?

_____

_____

_____

4. Why is there evil?

_____

_____

_____

5. How should people behave?

_____

_____

_____

2 *Discuss the following questions with a partner, and then write your opinions in the space provided.*

1. Do you agree that world wars are not likely today or in the future? Why or why not?

_____

_____

_____

2. Do you think we should be worried about endangered animal species and the protection of the earth?

_____

_____

_____

3. Do you care how people will remember you after you die?

_____

_____

_____

3 Focus on Vocabulary

1 The following words are all related to religion. Working in a small group, put them in the correct categories on the chart that follows. Add any other words you can think of to these categories.

bishop	Confucianism	monk	rabbi	temple
Buddhism	contemplation	mosque	rituals	theologian
Christianity	Hinduism	ordinances	sacrifice	worship
church	Islam	prayer	shrine	
clergy	Judaism	priest	synagogue	

NAMES OF RELIGIONS	PLACES OF WORSHIP	RELIGIOUS LEADERS	RELIGIOUS PRACTICES

2 Analogies compare relationships between things that are alike in some ways. The analogy **Buddhism : temple :: Judaism : synagogue** is expressed in English as follows: **"Buddhism is to a temple as Judaism is to a synagogue."** In other words, **"Buddhism is practiced in a temple just as Judaism is practiced in a synagogue."**

Complete the following analogies. Circle the correct answer from the choices given.

1. **church : Christianity = ? : Islam**

   A church is to Christianity as a _____ is to Islam.

   a. church   **b.** mosque   **c.** synagogue

2. **? : temple = priest : church**

   A(n) _____ is to a temple as a priest is to a church.

   a. pope   **b.** imam   **c.** monk

3. **Islam : Turkey = ? : China**

Islam is to Turkey as _____ is to China.

a. Confucianism   **b.** Christianity   **c.** Judaism

4. **politician : political scientists = clergy : ?**

Politicians are to political scientists as clergy are to _____.

a. theologians   **b.** practitioners   **c.** worshipers

5. **Roman Catholicism : France = ? : the United States**

Roman Catholicism is to France as _____ is to the United States.

a. Protestantism   **b.** Catholicism   **c.** Christianity

6. **imam : Islam = ? : Protestantism**

An imam is to Islam as a _____ is to Protestantism.

a. rabbi   **b.** priest   **c.** minister

7. **perform : rituals = recite : ?**

Perform is to rituals as recite is to _____.

a. ordinances   **b.** prayers   **c.** practitioners

8. **laws : customs = ? : rituals**

Laws are to customs as _____ are to rituals.

a. prayers   **b.** ordinances   **c.** theologians

9. **Mecca : ? = Vatican City : Roman Catholicism**

Mecca is to _____ as Vatican City is to Roman Catholicism.

a. Judaism   **b.** Buddhism   **c.** Islam

3 *In order to learn more about one of the religions mentioned in this unit (Buddhism, Christianity, Confucianism, Hinduism, Islam, or Judaism), interview a knowledgeable person. On a separate piece of paper, write down the questions that you would ask this expert, using at least six vocabulary words studied in this unit.*

Example: *Thank you for coming to our school. We are very interested in finding out more about _____ . Where do people of your religion go to* **worship***?*

4 Focus on Writing

1 *Examine the sentences below, and discuss the questions that follow with a partner.*

Islam is <u>a</u> <u>religion</u>.
Islam is <u>the</u> <u>religion</u> practiced by all believers in the Koran.

Islam and Hinduism are <u>religions</u>.
Islam and Hinduism are <u>the</u> <u>religions</u> practiced by the majority of people on the Indian subcontinent.

<u>Honesty</u> is a virtue.
<u>The</u> <u>honesty</u> of the man is his greatest virtue.

1. Which sentence means that Islam is one of many religions?

2. How do the meanings of the nouns change when *a* and *the* are used in the above sentences?

Definite and Indefinite Articles

For Singular Count Nouns

Whether an article is needed before a singular noun depends on if the noun is a count noun or not. All singular count nouns must be preceded by either an **indefinite article** [*a(n)*] or a **definite article** [*the*]. You choose *a(**n**)* or *the* depending on the situation.

If you are describing "one of many," use the indefinite article *a(**n**)*.	Islam is *a religion.*
If you are describing "the specific one," use the definite article *the.* Imagine that the definite article, unlike the indefinite article, creates a "finite limit" and refers precisely to "a specific one."	Islam is *the religion* practiced by all believers in the Koran.

For Plural Count Nouns

The same concepts apply to count nouns in the plural. When it is obvious that the plural count noun does not represent all the nouns in a group, no article comes before it.

In the example sentence, we know that Islam and Hinduism are only two of many religions.	Islam and Hinduism are **religions.**
When information given in the sentence limits the plural count noun to a specific category, the definite article **the** is used.	Islam and Hinduism are **the religions** practiced by the majority of the people on the Indian subcontinent.

For Non-Count Nouns

Non-count nouns are always singular because they cannot be counted. **Honesty, knowledge, wisdom, ignorance, information, evidence, research,** and **advice** are examples of non-count nouns. No article comes before them when a specific reference is not being made. But when it is obvious that a specific reference is being made, the definite article is used.

In the example sentence "the man's honesty," and not just "honesty" in general, is the subject.	**The** honesty of the man is his greatest virtue.

2 *With a partner, decide whether the singular nouns in the items below are count or non-count nouns. Circle your choice. Then write two sentences using each noun. For count nouns, show how both the definite and indefinite articles can be used. For non-count nouns, show how the indefinite article is omitted and the definite article can be used.*

1. purity   Count /(Non-Count)

Purity is a state sought by many religious people.

The purity of his intentions was admired by all his friends.

2. church   (Count)/ Non-Count

The people saw a church in the distance.

The church that they saw was the one that had just been built.

3. belief   Count / Non-Count

_____

_____

4. spirituality   **Count / Non-Count**

_____

_____

5. ceremony   **Count / Non-Count**

_____

_____

3 _Work with a partner. In the following paragraphs about the Religious Society of Friends, a Protestant religion, add a definite article or an indefinite article in the spaces provided if you think that an article is necessary. If you think no article is necessary, put an **X** in the space._

(1) _____ Religious Society of Friends, commonly referred to as

(2) _____ Quakers, was founded in Northwest England in 1652 after

George Fox received (3) _____ vision from God at a place called Pendle

Hill. (4) _____* vision helped Fox to realize that (5) _____ spiritual

presence of God was (6) _____ source of all religious truth. Such

(7) _____ realization became the basis for (8) _____ Quaker doctrine

of the inner light. The Quakers believe that (9) _____ spirit of God enters

(10) _____ consciousness of both men and women equally and that it is

evidenced in human beings' most honorable behavior.

The Quakers believe in (11) _____ equality and in (12) _____

pacifism, which involves an opposition to war and service in an army. Their

insistence on (13) _____ equality of all human beings has been

demonstrated in their refusal to show any signs of respect such as removing

one's hat to (14) _____ person regarded as (15) _____ social superior.

It has also been evident in (16) _____ leadership roles that Quaker women

Susan B. Anthony and Lucretia Mott assumed in (17) _____ struggle for

women's rights in (18) _____ United States.

---

*Wherever a definite article is possible, you may also consider using demonstrative adjectives (_this, that, these, those_) if the noun to which they refer has been mentioned—as this one is—in a preceding sentence.

Because of their beliefs, the Quakers faced many conflicts with the political and religious authorities in England, and they were often persecuted as a result. **(19)** _____ founding in 1681 of **(20)** _____ colony of Pennsylvania by William Penn, **(21)** _____ Quaker, provided **(22)** _____ haven for many Quakers and exiles of other persecuted religious groups. Some Quakers also settled in Rhode Island, Massachusetts, and the South. They were not welcome in the South because of their opposition to **(23)** _____ slavery. Nevertheless, despite their pacifist views, they played **(24)** _____ major role during the American Civil War (1861–1865) by helping **(25)** _____ African-American slaves make their way to **(26)** _____ safety of the North.

B   STYLE: Writing a Definition Essay

1 *Reread Reading Two, and discuss the questions below with a partner.*

1. In the first paragraph, how does the writer "unify" all the religions in the world?

2. In the second and third paragraphs, what does the writer do to come closer to a definition of the word *religion*?

3. What kind of comparison do you find in the fourth paragraph?

4. How is the fifth paragraph similar to the first paragraph?

What Is a Definition Essay?

When writing a **definition essay,** the writer enters the world of classification. Through classification, we analyze a subject by dividing it into categories. First we find what all of the categories have in common—the "common characteristics"—and then we seek to determine how each of the categories can be distinguished from one another.

This is precisely what a definition is: the process of putting nouns in categories or "classes." In a definition, we show how the item or concept to be defined is part of a broader category and how it is different from the other members of this category. The box on page 144 gives examples.

(continued)

Classification

Member/Smaller Class	Larger Class	Specific Details
1. a rabbi	a religious leader	Judaism
2. an imam	a religious leader	Islam
3. rabbis and imams	religious leaders	

1. "A rabbi is a religious leader in the Jewish community."

2. "An imam is a religious leader in the Islamic community."

3. "Rabbis and imams are religious leaders."

Research and Preparation

The writer of the definition essay "Religion" went through a similar process of analysis throughout the research stage. After studying "all religions" and analyzing their "common characteristics" and differences, as in the classification box above, the writer was then ready to write an essay defining "religion."

Essay Structure

As is evident in Reading Two, the definition essay goes from the realm of the "indefinite" (a religion is …/religions are …) to the realm of the "definite" (the Muslim religion, unlike the Buddhist religion, is …). The writer first tells us what "all religions" have in common ("all religions attempt to give answers to basic questions"). Then, after interpreting the quotes by Paul Tillich and Martin Luther, the writer shows that the Western belief in one God is not shared by followers of the Eastern religions. The writer then refers to other "elements in common: rituals to perform, prayers to recite, holy days to keep." It is apparent from the way this brief excerpt unfolds that in the rest of the essay the writer will continue to show a pattern of common characteristics and specific differences.

In a definition essay, as in all other kinds of essays, the writer introduces examples, shows similarities and differences, uses quotations, and so on, in order to make sure the information is communicated as effectively as possible. The writer provides a thesis statement ("As a word religion is difficult to define, but as a human experience it seems to be universal."). The writer also permits his point of view to surface. For example, at the beginning of the essay "Religion," the statement "It is difficult to imagine what need there would be for religion in a world in which no one ever died or became ill" immediately familiarizes the reader with the writer's point of view. Thus, despite the difficult task of objective analysis that the writer must go through when preparing a definition essay, one thing is certain: The writer's point of view remains very important.

2 *Work with a partner. Look at each word in the Member/Smaller Class column. Determine its larger class and give specific details if possible. Then write its definition in the space provided below. Use a dictionary if necessary.*

Member/Smaller Class	Larger Class	Specific Details
1. synagogue	*a house of worship*	*Judaism*
2. prayer		
3. sin		
4. prophet		
5. ritual		

Definitions

6. synagogue: *A synagogue is a house of worship where Judaism is practiced.*

7. prayer:

8. sin:

9. prophet:

10. ritual:

3 *Many religions preach "love your fellow human beings." But what exactly is love?*

Work in a small group to brainstorm a definition for the word **love.** *Analyze at least five types of love. Find the common characteristics (Larger Class) and differences (Specific Details) of each type of love. Then write down the definition of love that the group agrees upon.*

Member/Smaller Class	Larger Class	Specific Details
1. *self-love*	_____	_____
_____	_____	_____
2. *the love of a* *parent for a child*	_____	_____
	_____	_____
3. _____	_____	_____
_____	_____	_____
4. _____	_____	_____
_____	_____	_____
5. _____	_____	_____
_____	_____	_____

Definition of *love:* _____

_____

_____

C   WRITING TOPICS

Read the five topics that follow. Choose one, and write a well-organized essay. Remember to provide a thesis statement and sufficient explanations, examples, and support to develop your definition or essay. Use the vocabulary you have studied in this unit.

1. Write a brief definition of the religion you follow or the dominant religion in your native country. Explain its most important beliefs and practices.

2. George Bernard Shaw* wrote, "There is only one religion, though there are a hundred versions of it." Do you agree or disagree? Explain your answer.

---

* *George Bernard Shaw* (1856–1950), Irish-born British playwright and author

3. How has religion influenced and affected your life? Write an essay defining the positive and/or negative effects of religion on various aspects of your life.

4. Would you marry someone of a different faith? Why or why not? What difficulties would you have to overcome, and what would be the positive or negative results?

5. Can a person be "religious" without following a formal religion? Answer the question with reference to the following poem by Emily Dickinson.*

Some keep the Sabbath going to church;
I keep it staying at home,
With a bobolink[1] for a chorister,[2]
And an orchard for a dome.

Some keep the Sabbath in surplice;[3]
I just wear my wings,
And instead of tolling the bell for church,
Our little sexton[4] sings.

God preaches,—a noted clergyman,—
And the sermon is never long;
So instead of getting to heaven at last,
I'm going all along.

                              Emily Dickinson

---

[1] *bobolink:* an American songbird
[2] *chorister:* a singer in a church choir
[3] *surplice:* a loose, white robe worn by members of the clergy
[4] *sexton:* a church officer or employee who takes care of church property and, in some churches, rings the bell for services

---

* *Emily Dickinson* (1830–1886), American poet

D   RESEARCH TOPICS

PREPARATION

In Reading Two you read a general definition of religion. There are many religions in the modern world. Choose one religion with which you are not familiar, and find out as much as you can about it. Begin with the following questions, and add to them as you do your research.

- Does this religion have a belief in a creator? Is there one god or many?

- What kind of behavior is expected of believers? What is the definition of "a good life" according to this religion?

- Where is this religion practiced in the world?

RESEARCH ACTIVITY

If possible, interview a member of the religious community you are interested in, or conduct your research in the library or on the Internet. Be sure to consult several sources of information so that you can reduce the likelihood of prejudice or distortion in your treatment of the religion.

SHARING YOUR FINDINGS

1. After you have taken notes about the religion you chose, write up your findings as a definition essay. The title can be, for example, "What Is the Hindu Religion?" or "What Is Zen Buddhism as Practiced in Japan?" or "What Is the Baptist (Protestant) Religion?"

2. Form a small group, and share your essay with the other members of the group. Comment on each other's essays, and discuss what you have learned.

For step-by-step practice in the writing process, see the *Writing Activity Book, Advanced,* Unit 6.

Assignment	Definition Essay
Prewriting	Looped Freewriting
Organizing	Writing a Definition Essay
Revising	Writing for a Specific Audience
	Using Definite and Indefinite Articles
Editing	Writing Effective Titles

For Unit 6 Internet activities, visit the NorthStar Companion Website at http://longman.com/northstar.

Going into Business

1 Focus on the Topic

A PREDICTING

Discuss the humor of this cartoon with another student. According to the cartoon, how are some employees treated in a big business? Why do you think this happens? What are some alternatives to working in a large corporation?

B   SHARING INFORMATION

Fill out this questionnaire about business aptitude and experience. Do you think you would make a good businessperson? Share your responses in a small group.

What's Your Aptitude for Business?

1. Are you a risk-taker?   Yes   (No)

2. Are you a creative thinker?   Yes   No

3. Can you spend 80 hours at work every week?   Yes   No

4. What jobs have you had?

   part-time work   _____

   summer jobs   _____

   internships   _____

   full-time employment   _____

5. What do you think would be your strengths as a businessperson?
   For ya

   _____

   _____

6. What do you think would be your weaknesses?

   _____

   _____

C   PREPARING TO READ

BACKGROUND

Read the information and poem below. Write short answers to the questions that follow. Then discuss your answers in a small group.

To be your own boss, you have to put in the hours "24/7/365": 24 hours a day, 7 days a week, 365 days of the year. Are you ready to live and die by the ring of your cell phone? Can you imagine working more than 75 hours a week? Do you think about your work all the time? If your answer is "yes," then you can be an entrepreneur, someone who starts a company and takes risks to make a profit. Entrepreneurial skills are not limited to experienced businesspeople;

they are often found in young men and women. As a University of Texas–Austin undergraduate, Michael Dell launched his Dell Computer Corporation empire in his dorm room. He left college after a year and built one of the most profitable companies in the world. Others launched an Internet super-portal in a crowded room at Stanford University. Many of today's most successful people gave birth to their businesses on college campuses. Where else can you find reasonably priced room and board, a great many professors who know all about business, an exhaustive amount of resources, and free high-speed Internet access?

The people in the first reading of this unit are part of a generation of entrepreneurs who are creating opportunities while they are still in college. A poll conducted by Students in Free Enterprise, an organization that helps students develop leadership skills, revealed that 66 percent of American college students believe they will one day own their own business. However, not everyone begins as an entrepreneur. Many young people decide to start in a large corporation. Many start with internships, either before they finish university or right after business school. The second reading in this chapter explores the internships offered by the Coca-Cola Company and the qualities it looks for in its employees.

A Limerick
There was a young genius named Dell
Who broke from academia's cell
Both the bits and the bytes
he assembled just right.
Now this dropout is doing just swell.

—Liz Carpender
(from *www.bga.com/~kirby/dell.html*)

1. What is the meaning of this poem, and what does it tell us about Dell?

2. Why would some young people prefer to join a large corporation rather than start their own business?

3. Why do you think most of the Internet entrepreneurs are young people?

VOCABULARY FOR COMPREHENSION

Work in pairs. Read the sentences that follow, and circle the correct synonym for the underlined word from the choices given. Use a dictionary if necessary.

1. Michael Dell was always interested in business. He underlined launched his first business venture at age twelve selling stamps to collectors.
   a. required   **b.** terminated   **c.** initiated

2. He targeted customers who used auction houses and sent them a twelve-page catalogue. When orders came in, he went out to find the stamps people wanted.
   a. included   **b.** focused on   **c.** needed

3. He may not have <u>amassed</u> very much money at first, but the direct sales, just-in-time inventory model for Dell Computer was born.

   a. gradually collected   **b.** suddenly found   **c.** quickly lost

4. At age fifteen, Dell became a <u>full-fledged</u> salesman selling subscriptions to *The Houston Post* and earning $18,000 in commissions in the first twelve months.

   a. fully developed   **b.** capable   **c.** fledgling

5. Thus, years before he <u>headed for</u> college, Dell knew he had a talent for business.

   a. came from   **b.** took charge of   **c.** went to

6. Today he has the <u>status</u> of CEO (chief executive officer) of a major corporation, but he started his career by selling computers from his dorm room at the University of Texas at Austin.

   a. worries   **b.** career   **c.** rank

7. When he finished his freshman year in college in 1984, he told his parents he wanted to leave school to start his own computer company. They were upset and <u>reluctant</u> to approve his decision. He did it anyway.

   a. anxious   **b.** unwilling   **c.** eager

8. Dell <u>acquired</u> old computers and upgraded them, selling them directly to the customer without a store dealer as the middleman.

   a. purchased   **b.** sold   **c.** improved

9. There was no <u>ambiguity</u> about the results: He was getting a great many orders because people wanted custom-made computers to fit their needs.

   a. difficulty   **b.** uncertainty   **c.** worry

10. Michael Dell's way of <u>tackling</u> the problem of cost was to build the computers only when the orders came in. This reduced inventory and allowed him to use upgraded and cheaper components as soon as they were available.

   a. dealing with   **b.** understanding   **c.** taking away

11. Unlike his <u>peers</u> in the computer business, Dell was able to integrate new products without having to get rid of old models.

   a. people who want computers   **b.** people in other countries   **c.** people in a similar position

12. Michael Dell has left a <u>legacy</u> that many young entrepreneurs admire: In fifteen years, he has built a vast business empire.

   a. example   **b.** inventory   **c.** testament

2 Focus on Reading

A   READING ONE: *Young Entrepreneurs*

Discuss this question with a partner.

What are the qualities needed to become a successful entrepreneur at a young age?

From Who Wants to Be an Entrepreneur?

by Theresa O'Rourke, from *Link: The College Magazine*

Larry Page

1   Larry Page is the co-founder of the search engine Google. Google came to life several years ago, when Page and his partner were Ph.D. students at Stanford University. By the time they got their first funding at the end of the nineties, their product was already creating 10,000 searches a day. Andy Bechtolsheim, co-founder of Sun Microsystems, was immediately impressed. As Page recounts, "He said, 'This is a no-brainer.[1] What if I write you a check for $100,000?' We agreed. So he wrote it out to Google, but we had no company, no lawyer. We hadn't incorporated the company yet, so we couldn't even cash the check!" The pair celebrated the event over Whopper combos at the Burger King down the block.

2   Speaking of satisfying ideas, imagine this work scenario, as conceived by Larry Page.

You head into work. You're a bit hungry. Thankfully, a large selection of breakfast cereals awaits you. At lunchtime, a chef serves up a dish to suit you. The same thing happens at dinner. As the day ends, you're feeling a bit tired, so you head to the office masseuse for a quick rubdown.[2] Sounds like utopia? It's reality. At Google, in Silicon Valley, work and play are the same thing. "People can work whenever they want in Silicon Valley," Page, age 27, explains. "Our employees spend a lot of time on the job, and having a nice environment is important. We also play street hockey two times a week."

Tina Wells

3   Tina Wells was merely 16 when she launched The Buzz,[3] a consulting firm aimed at bridging the gap between teens and the clothing and cosmetic companies that target

---

[1] *a no-brainer:* something that one doesn't need to think about because it is easy to understand or do
[2] *a rubdown:* a massage, which is given by a masseur (m.) or a masseuse (f.)
[3] *the buzz:* a popular expression meaning gossip about the latest fashion

them. Having amassed more than 50 clients, including teen gems like Bongo jeans and Candie's, Wells is now headed for Chicago to expand her business. The Hood College (Maryland) junior will complete her senior year at Chicago's Columbia College. She's ready to build The Buzz into a full-fledged consulting agency, offering product development, project consulting, and market research reports every quarter on teens and trends. "I'm looking for a group of 10 to 20 college consultants," she explains. "I'd offer them internship possibilities in Chicago with my partner. We're trying to keep it a very youthful company, but at the same time very professional."

Dineh Monajer

4   Dineh Monajer says she doesn't want CEO status. Monajer is a reluctant entrepreneur. The founder of Hard Candy cosmetics admits that if she never had to look at a budget again, she'd die happy. "I really didn't want to be an entrepreneur. I'm not interested in the stock market. I'm much more of a creative person."

5   Monajer is sitting on a cosmetic goldmine,[4] worth more than one million dollars. It all started by accident five years ago, when the former University of Southern California pre-med[5] student couldn't find a toenail polish to match her sandals. "I was just doing a summer project and then everything went haywire,"[6] she recalls. "Everyone heard about the polish and liked it. So I realized at that point that there was a really big opportunity for me. And then when people were interested, I made it bigger and bigger." Rather than study for her medical school admissions test, Monajer set up shop in Beverly Hills and she hasn't looked back since. Though her company was acquired by the Louis Vuitton Moet Hennessey fashion house last year, Monajer still maintains complete creative control over her products and the company image. Monajer is grateful for all the help she's received, especially from her mom. "My parents gave me more than a couple of thousand dollars over time," she admits. "My mom ran my father's medical practice, so she understood how to run a business. She really made it happen for me."

Matt Kelley

6   Born to a Korean mother and a Caucasian father, Matt Kelley created *Mavin* when he was a sophomore at Connecticut's Wesleyan University as a much-needed forum for the multiracial population. The magazine was the end result of a long process of self-discovery. "I went through a racial consciousness between senior year in high school and freshman year in college," he explains. "I didn't realize it, but there was definitely a feeling of ambiguity, of placelessness." Having spent two years shaping *Mavin* (the first and only publication to tackle the mixed-race experience), he's been able to give his peers a voice as well as a home, at least in the pages of his magazine. *Mavin* has become a magazine with a subscriber base of 32,000, sold nationally at newsstands and bookstores. Kelley intends to increase the readership to 50,000 and form a not-for-profit Mavin Foundation to help communication and understanding, "to leave a legacy, which is definitely my long-term goal."

---

[4] *sitting on a goldmine:* owning something very valuable that will generate a lot of money
[5] *pre-med:* pre-medical school studies; studies preparing for medical school
[6] *went haywire:* went out of control; here, far beyond expectations

READING FOR MAIN IDEAS

Summarize in one sentence the businesses started by each of these young people. Then compare your answers with a partner's.

1. Larry Page: _____

   _____

2. Tina Wells: _____

   _____

3. Dineh Monajer: _____

   _____

4. Matt Kelley: _____

   _____

READING FOR DETAILS

For each statement, check the entrepreneur(s) for whom the information is true. Discuss your answers with a partner.

	Page	Wells	Monajer	Kelley
1. Got financial help from parents			✓	
2. Sells a product				
3. Sells a service				
4. Studied for a doctorate				
5. Wants to help the community				
6. Didn't plan to be in business				
7. No longer maintains control over the business created				

REACTING TO THE READING

1 *A college student is interviewing the young entrepreneurs. Read these questions, and decide how the young entrepreneurs listed with the question would answer. Write the answers in your notebook. Share what you wrote with a partner.*

1. Do I need a university degree to succeed in business? (Entrepreneurs: Wells, Monajer)

2. Where should I look for investment money? (Entrepreneurs: Page, Monajer)

3. How do I choose what products or services to sell? (Entrepreneurs: Monajer, Kelley)

4. What kind of information can I sell to companies or consumers? (Entrepreneurs: Wells, Kelley)

5. How would you define "a good job"? (Entrepreneurs: Page, Wells, Monajer, Kelley)

2 *Discuss these questions in a small group.*

1. Which of the businesses discussed in the reading seems the most interesting to you? Why? Would you like to own or work for such a business?

2. Matt Kelley says that leaving a legacy to help others is an important goal of his business. Do you think this is an important goal for many businesses?

3. How can parents help children become interested in business?

4. Would you like to start your own business? What kind of business would it be?

B   READING TWO: *Coca-Cola Thinks International*

1 *Discuss this question with a partner, and then read the following article.*

What qualities do you think multinational corporations like Coca-Cola are looking for when they hire management trainees (people they plan to train as managers)?

COCA-COLA THINKS INTERNATIONAL

BY ALAN RUGMAN AND RICHARD M. HODGETTS

1   Coca-Cola has been operating internationally for most of its 100-year history. Today the company has operations in 160 countries and employs over 400,000 people. The firm's human resource management (HRM) strategy helps to explain a great deal of its success. In one recent year Coca-Cola transferred more than 300 professional and

recent year Coca-Cola transferred more than 300 professional and managerial staff from one country to another under its leadership development program, and the number of international transferees is increasing annually. One senior-level HRM manager explained the company strategy by noting:

> We recently concluded that our talent base has to be multilingual and multicultural. . . . To use a sports analogy, you want to be sure that you have a lot of capable and competent bench strength, ready to assume broader responsibilities as they present themselves.

2   In preparing for the future, Coca-Cola includes a human resources recruitment forecast in its annual and long-term business strategies. The firm also has selection standards on which management can focus when recruiting and hiring. For example, the company likes applicants who are fluent in more than one language because they can be transferred to other geographic areas where their fluency will help them be part of Coca-Cola's operation. This multilingual, multicultural emphasis starts at the top with the president, Roberto Goizueta, a Cuban-born American who has been chairman for over a decade, and with the twenty-one members of the board, of whom only four are American.

3   The firm also has a recruitment program that helps it to identify candidates at the college level. Rather than just seeking students abroad, Coca-Cola looks for foreign students who are studying in the United States at domestic universities. The students are recruited stateside and then provided with a year's training before they go back to their home country. Coca-Cola also has an internship program for foreign students who are interested in working for the company during school break, either in the United States or back home. These interns are put into groups and assigned a project that requires them to make a presentation to the operations personnel on their project. This presentation must include a discussion of what worked and what did not work. Each individual intern is then evaluated, and management decides the person's future potential with the company.

4   Coca-Cola believes that these approaches are extremely useful in helping the firm to find talent on a global basis. Not only is the company able to develop internal sources, but the intern program provides a large number of additional individuals who would otherwise end up with other companies. Coca-Cola earns a greater portion of its income and profit overseas than it does in the United States. The company's human resource management strategy helps to explain how Coke is able to achieve this feat.[1]

---

[1] *feat:* a great accomplishment

*Classic Coke
from Egypt*

2 *You are doing a first screening of candidates for an international internship program at the Coca-Cola Company. Based on your understanding of Reading Two, decide whether the people below might be good candidates for such a program. Indicate your decision with a **Yes** or a **No**, and give your reasons. Then share your findings with a partner.*

1. Mr. X is a brilliant student who excelled in his courses on marketing. He likes to work alone and speaks only when his plans are fully developed. He doesn't react well to criticism or join in discussions.

   Decision/why? NO, I think is importante work with people expor ideas

2. Mr. Y is an ambitious, extroverted candidate who tries hard to please and knows how to get along with others. He has studied engineering in the United States for two years.

   Decision/why? Yes, can help the compony a graw up

3. Ms. A has lived and studied outside her country for several years. She has many friends from different backgrounds and fits in well with the American family she lives with in North Carolina. She is easygoing and flexible and got satisfactory grades in business school.

   Decision/why? Yes

4. Ms. B has studied two foreign languages and has an excellent reading knowledge of each one. She is very nationalistic and only likes the way things are done in her country. She has had a first-rate education and is ambitious and smart.

   Decision/why? NO, not open a new ideas

5. Mr. Z has wonderful ideas about marketing and comes highly recommended from his graduate business school teachers. He is shy and speaks slowly. It is hard for him to make presentations in a large group, but he prepares excellent written reports.

   Decision/why? _____

C   LINKING READINGS ONE AND TWO

Read the case study about the career decision Max Daniels must make, and do the activity that follows.

Case Study: Max Daniels's Options

Max is a 24-year-old student at one of the top business schools in the country. He is wondering what to do after graduation. Even though it is hard to turn your back on a good job in corporate America, his heart is not in working for a large corporation. He feels he won't be satisfied until he has his own business. However, he's a bit confused about where to begin.

One possibility is for him to start his own company right away. He has a lot of great ideas for new software and a friend who is willing to work with him. The two friends might ask their parents for money or get a loan at the bank. They could work together to find a way to sell their ideas. Another possibility is for Max and his friend to start as interns in an established software company and acquire some experience in business. They could learn the software needs of the industry and make useful contacts.

In a small group, consider Max's options. In the space below, make a list of the advantages and disadvantages of each career choice. Then choose the one that you consider the best choice for him now. Try to come to a consensus in your group.

MAX'S CHOICES	ADVANTAGES	DISADVANTAGES
Starting his own business right away		
Becoming an intern in a well-known company		

3 Focus on Vocabulary

1 *Working in pairs, fill in the chart below. Then use the words to fill in the blanks in the sentences that follow. Use the synonyms below the blanks to help you choose the correct word.*

Nouns	Verbs	Adjectives
1. agreement	agree	agreeable
2.	create	
3.		departing
4.		expanding
5.	found	founding
6. impression	impress	
7.		obsessive
8.		relieved
9.	resist	
10. target		

1. As a group, entrepreneurs are _____ about work. They can
   (single-minded)
   hardly think of anything else; even their families often complain.

2. Entrepreneurs also tend to be optimistic: They never see a problem. This
   makes the risk-taking of entrepreneurial work _____ to them.
   (acceptable)

3. Entrepreneurs love being their own bosses. They usually _____
   (oppose)
   working in any large organization which they don't control.

4. Entrepreneurs are very good at finding new and _____ ways
   (inventive)
   of doing things. However, they are often _____ to be able to
   (happy)
   turn over management tasks to other employees.

5. Two examples of modern entrepreneurs are Steve Wozniak and Steve Jobs.
   Wozniak dropped out of Berkeley to join Hewlett-Packard. At Hewlitt-
   Packard he met Jobs, who had come there on a summer job from Reed
   College. Together they _____ the Apple Computer Company
   (started)
   in a garage in California.

6. They funded their first computer prototype by selling their car and begging local suppliers to extend their credit so they could _____ their
(develop)
sales. It was only the beginning of a string of successes.

7. Two other recent entrepreneurs are Jerry Yang and David Filo. When the Internet began to develop, they were _____ by its potential
(amazed)
possibilities and started to collect interesting Web sites.

8. They launched Yahoo! from a campus trailer in 1994, originally
_____ other students who also enjoyed this "cool and
(aiming at)
fun hobby."

9. Their _____ from Stanford, where they were Ph.D. candidates
(exit)
in engineering, marked the beginning of a billion-dollar company.

2 *Match these idioms from the readings with their meanings on the right. Write the correct letter in the blank.*

_____ 1. "a no-brainer"
(Reading One, paragraph 1)

_____ 2. "bridging the gap"
(Reading One, paragraph 3)

_____ 3. "the buzz"
(Reading One, paragraph 3)

_____ 4. "a gem"
(Reading One, paragraph 3)

_____ 5. "sitting on a goldmine"
(Reading One, paragraph 5)

_____ 6. "went haywire"
(Reading One, paragraph 5)

_____ 7. "hasn't looked back since"
(Reading One, paragraph 5)

_____ 8. "made it happen for me"
(Reading One, paragraph 5)

_____ 9. "a forum"
(Reading One, paragraph 6)

_____ 10. "what worked"
(Reading Two, paragraph 3)

a. a first-rate company or client

b. something so obvious that it needs no thought

c. got crazy, had more of a reaction than expected

d. connecting two things or people

e. helped me greatly toward success

f. in control of something that can make a great deal of money

g. a place for discussion and the confrontation of ideas

h. things that got the job done

i. news and gossip of the latest trends

j. has had no regrets

3 *Use at least eight of the vocabulary words in the box below to write four sentences explaining the **advantages** of leaving college early to start a business and four sentences explaining the **disadvantages** of such a course of action. Add these sentences to the paragraphs started below.*

acquire	full-fledged	peers
amass	go haywire	relieve
ambiguity	head for	reluctant
bridge the gap	~~launched~~	~~sitting on a goldmine~~
create	legacy	status
expand	never look back	tackling
found	obsess	target

Many student entrepreneurs who want to **launch** businesses see the advantages of leaving college early. _____

_____

_____

_____

_____

_____

_____

However, other student entrepreneurs think it is disadvantageous to leave college early despite the fact that soon after they drop out they may be **sitting on a goldmine.** _____

_____

_____

_____

_____

_____

_____

4 Focus on Writing

A GRAMMAR: Specific Uses of Infinitives and Gerunds

1 *Examine the underlined words in the sentences below, and discuss the questions that follow with a partner.*

- He had the opportunity <u>to work</u> in another country.
- He was committed to <u>going</u> back to school.

　1. What form is underlined in the first sentence?

　2. What form is underlined in the second sentence?

　3. Why are these forms used?

The Infinitive

The **infinitive** (**to + verb;** *to play, to watch*) is commonly used:

1. When it answers the questions "Why?" or "For what purpose?"

- He dropped out of school **to start** his own business.

2. In certain verb + infinitive + object patterns

- The firm's recruiters **try to identify** candidates at the college level.

3. After many adjectives

- The company is more **willing to take** a risk on someone with multicultural knowledge.

4. After certain expressions

Many expressions are followed by the infinitive when "*to do* what?" is the answer that the infinitive gives the reader or the listener. In the sentence "He had the opportunity to work in another country," the infinitive *to work* tells us "what" he had "the opportunity *to do*." Here is a list of expressions that follow this pattern:

be ready	*have a tendency*
be required	*have the time*
have the ability/have an inability	*have the will*
have the courage	*it is difficult*
have the opportunity	*it is easy*
have the option	*it is economical*
have the right	*it is practical*

The Gerund

The **gerund** (a verb form ending in **-ing** used as a noun; *playing, watching*) is commonly used:

1. After such verbs as ***avoid, consider, enjoy, favor, include, involve, spend***

   - You should *consider* **changing** your career if your talents are not used at your present job.

   - You may simply *spend* a lot of time **doing** boring work.

2. After all prepositions (for example, ***about, from, in, to, with***)

   - The CEO was concerned *about* **making** a profit.

3. After certain expressions

   Many expressions are followed by the gerund because they end with prepositions (for example, "have a commitment *to going*," "be concerned *about going*," "be interested *in going*"). The rule regarding the use of gerunds after all prepositions is simple to apply if you remember that the preposition is "a part of" the expression. Thus, in the sentence at the beginning of this section, "He was committed to *going* back to school," the gerund (*going*) is used because the *to* is part of the expression.

   Because it is difficult to remember which expressions end in prepositions, familiarize yourself with the most common expressions that are followed by the gerund. Here is a list:

be accustomed to	***have (no) difficulty (in)****
be committed to/have a commitment to	***have (no) experience (in)****
be concerned about	***have (no) luck (in)****
be dedicated to	***have (no) trouble (in)****
be devoted to	***insist on***
be interested in	***look forward to***
be involved in	***object to***
be responsible for/have the	***plan on***
responsibility of	***succeed in***
choose between/among	
deal with	

   * The preposition *in* is implied. You need not use it; in fact, it is better usage to leave it out.

2 *Read the following letter that the admissions office of a business school sends to future business school applicants. Underline the gerunds and the infinitives first. Then list the verbs or expressions that take the infinitive and those that take the gerund.*

Dear Future M.B.A. Candidate,

If you want to <u>take bold steps to plan</u> your future, we invite you to <u>consider applying</u> to our school. Our School of Management is dedicated to preparing both generalists and specialists for their individual career goals. As a result, we are committed to offering state-of-the-art, research-based management training in all management functions and disciplines. Our educational approach involves a broad range of teaching methods that reflect a balance between theory and practice and individual and team approaches.

Most of our students have had at least five years of experience working in the business world prior to entering this school. During their two years of course work here, they have the opportunity to create a program tailored to their needs. After they complete a certain number of required courses, students gain the right to customize their curriculum from a whole body of joint degree and interdisciplinary programs.

If you are interested in learning more about our M.B.A. program, please be sure to contact us. We look forward to hearing from you.

Sincerely,

John O'Sullivan

John O'Sullivan
Director of Admissions

Expressions with Infinitives

1. *take bold steps to plan*

2. _____

3. _____

4. _____

5. _____

Expressions with Gerunds

1. *consider applying*

2. _____

3. _____

4. _____

5. _____

6. _____

7. _____

3 *Imagine that you are applying to an M.B.A. program. Using the expressions that are listed on pages 163 and 164 and that appear in the previous exercise, write seven sentences about your personal strengths that you hope would convince an admissions committee to accept you to the school.*

1. _____

2. _____

3. _____

4. _____

5. _____

6. _____

7. _____

4 *Complete the following essay with either the gerund or the infinitive of the verb provided.*

The Advantages and Disadvantages of Private Business Schools

INTRODUCTORY
PARAGRAPH

Students thinking of _____ business careers are required
                                  1. (pursue)

_____ four to five years of work experience in the business world
    2. (have)

before they embark on an M.B.A. program. When they are ready

_____ to school, it is important for them _____
    3. (return)   **4.** (do)

thorough research on each school that interests them. Because M.B.A. candidates

in the United States can choose between _____ at some excellent
                                 5. (study)

public and private institutions, part of the decision-making process involves

_____ whether to enroll in a private or public institution. M.B.A.
    6. (decide)

candidates who plan _____ at large multinational corporations
               7. (work)

should make every effort to attend a top private school. Despite the high tuition

costs of private business schools, they provide more competitive learning

environments and more job placement opportunities in the private sector.

BODY

The disadvantages of private institutions are easy _____.
                                    8. (identify)

Although private schools meet the needs of students who hope

_____ for large multinational corporations, what they offer comes
    9. (work)

at a great cost. The price of a two-year program at a top private business school

can cost more than $100,000, while an M.B.A. program in a public school costs

less than half that amount. There is no doubt that the very high costs of private

business schools discourage many M.B.A. candidates from _____.
                                    10. (apply)

Being faced with such a large new debt, when in most cases they have only started to pay back their college loans, is seen as a definite disadvantage despite the advantages of a competitive private school.

Competition attracts the best students, defined as those with the highest test scores and the most impressive portfolios. These students compete

_____ at the most expensive private business schools. Some of the
11. (enroll)

top private schools can review as many as 8,000 applications for admission in a given year, but no more than 15 percent of the applicants are usually admitted. Connected to this more competitive feature of the student profile is the diversity of the student population. Private institutions devote a lot of time and energy to

_____ a diverse representation of students from all geographic
12. (select)

areas of the United States and the world. This international "flavor" is also reflected in the fact that private school students have the opportunity

_____ in a great number of study abroad and internship programs
13. (participate)

with multinational corporations. Studying in a competitive atmosphere with the brightest students from many diverse backgrounds provides private business students with valuable insights and international experience.

These diverse insights and experience are appreciated by the multinational

corporations who favor _____ at the top private schools. In a
14. (recruit)

given year, hundreds of recruiters come to private school campuses

_____ students. Not only do private school students have superb
15. (interview)

job placement opportunities, but they often receive more lucrative job offers: The average starting salary for private school students can go as high as $150,000.

CONCLUSION   Studying for an M.B.A. degree at a top private school provides students with

definite advantages. Students who decide not _____ a private
16. (select)

institution because of the cost alone may be making a serious mistake because they may be able to earn back the initial investment quickly and have a higher-

paying job at the same time. After a few years of _____ for a large
17. (work)

multinational corporation, their loans will be paid back and the advantages of their choice of a private business school will become clear.

B STYLE: Writing Essays Showing Advantages and Disadvantages

1 *Reread the essay on pages 166–167, and discuss the questions below with a partner.*

1. What is the writer's purpose in this essay?

2. Underline the thesis statement. According to the thesis statement, will the writer's focus in the essay be on the advantages or on the disadvantages?

3. Which body paragraph(s) deals with the advantages, and which body paragraph(s) deals with the disadvantages?

4. In the body paragraphs, what kind of support does the writer provide?

5. How does the writer show the logical connection between one topic and another?

6. Is the message in the concluding paragraph expected or unexpected? Why?

Purpose of Essays Showing Advantages and Disadvantages

Essays about advantages and disadvantages are similar to comparison and contrast essays, but there are some special points to remember.

- The aim of this kind of essay is to persuade, not simply to inform. You should *not* merely list the positive and negative aspects of the subject in a neutral way. You should take a stand.

- Your thesis statement should therefore take a clear position: Do the advantages outweigh the disadvantages, or are the disadvantages more important than the advantages?

- If the thesis statement states that the advantages are more important, then the body of the essay will devote relatively more space to the advantages. Conversely, if the thesis is focused on the disadvantages, that aspect will take up relatively more space in the essay than the advantages.

- The essay must provide enough support for the thesis so that the main points will be clearly justified and explained. As in all essays, the use of good transitions between the points under discussion ensures this clarity.

Thesis Statement

As you learned in Unit 2, the thesis statement communicates the main idea of the essay. It reflects the writer's narrow focus and point of view, attitude, or opinion, and it also forecasts which aspects of the subject the writer will discuss to support the thesis in the body of the essay.

2 *Examine the thesis statement below from the essay on page 166. Answer the questions that follow.*

"Despite the high tuition costs of private business schools, they provide more competitive learning environments and more job placement opportunities in the private sector."

1. Is this an adequate thesis statement for an advantages and disadvantages

essay? Why or why not? _____

_____

2. The thesis tells the reader that the body paragraphs of the essay will deal with certain subjects. What are they?

a. _____

b. _____

c. _____

Transitional Sentences

Transitional sentences show the logical connection between topics under discussion. Transitions may be needed within a paragraph ("internal transitions") or between paragraphs. When a transitional sentence connects the ideas of one body paragraph to the ideas of another body paragraph, it can be placed at the beginning of a paragraph (as a topic sentence) or at the end of a paragraph (as a concluding sentence).

3 *Go back to the essay on pages 166–167. First underline the transitional sentences connecting the body paragraphs in the text. Then underline the internal transitional sentence in body paragraph 2.*

4 *In your notebook, write an outline for an essay showing the advantages and disadvantages of starting your own business rather than going to work for a company. Follow these steps:*

- Use the guidelines for point-by-point outline formation on page 120.

- Write your thesis statement.

- Write your transitional sentences from one paragraph to another.

C WRITING TOPICS

Choose one of the writing topics. Remember to provide a thesis statement and sufficient explanations, examples, and support to develop your main idea. Pay special attention to transitions. Wherever possible, use the vocabulary and grammar from the unit.

1. Using the outline you wrote in Exercise 4 on page 169, write an essay showing the advantages and disadvantages of starting your own business rather than going to work for a company. Remember to take a stand on the issue.

2. Imagine the perfect career pattern for yourself. Would it involve working for several different companies, or for only one company during the course of your career? Would it involve building your own company? If so, what business would you create? Explain the steps you would take to create it.

3. Why is business important for the life of a country? What sacrifices, if any, must a country make so that businesses can thrive? You can use the history of a country you know to answer this question.

4. Do successful businesses have any civic responsibility? Do they have a responsibility to "give back" to the community in terms of jobs, contributions to social causes such as homelessness, medical research, the arts, the environment, and education? Why or why not?

5. How do you balance the demands of career and family? Does one need to be sacrificed for the other?

D RESEARCH TOPICS

PREPARATION

You will create a questionnaire to use in interviewing several people at your school about what they think of business. For instance, you might want the students you interview to consider questions like the following:

- Do people in business have to be aggressive and ambitious?

- Is corruption a problem that is common to business?

- Would you be satisfied with your life if you had a career in business?

Work in groups. First discuss what you think of business. Then write at least five *Yes/No* opinion questions that you would like to have in your questionnaire.

RESEARCH ACTIVITY

When you conduct your survey, count the *Yes* and *No* responses to each question and take notes on the comments the interviewees (the students you interview) make. You can use the following grid to write your questions, tally responses, and record comments.

QUESTIONS	YES	NO	COMMENTS
Example: *Would your family be happy if you went into business?*	*✝✝✝ ///*	*✝✝✝*	• *Business brings financial security.* • *People in business have no time for family life.*
1.			
2.			
3.			
4.			
5.			

SHARING YOUR FINDINGS

Write a report on the results of your survey.

1. In the introduction, explain the purpose of the survey and share the questions you asked.

2. In the body, give a summary of the number of *yes* and *no* replies you received for each question and the comments the interviewees made.

3. In the conclusion, give your interpretation of the information you collected.

For step-by-step practice in the writing process, see the *Writing Activity Book, Advanced, Unit 7*.

Assignment	Analysis of Essay Showing Advantages and Disadvantages
Prewriting	Clustering
Organizing	Weighing Pros and Cons
Revising	Writing Effective Conclusions
	Using Infinitives and Gerunds
Editing	Using Transition Words

For Unit 7 Internet activities, visit the NorthStar Companion Website at
http://longman.com/northstar.

When the Soldier Is a Woman . . .

1 Focus on the Topic

What do you think women's lives are like in the military? Write a list of the problems you think women might face in the armed forces. Then make a list of the satisfactions you think they might find in military work. Compare your lists with those of a partner.

B SHARING INFORMATION

How do you feel about women in the military? First answer the survey individually. Then work in groups of four or five people. Tally the answers from your group, and discuss the reasons for each person's opinions.

Women in the Military: What Should Their Role Be?

	Your Answer (Circle One)	Group Tally
1. Women should be allowed to serve in the military.	Agree Disagree	Agree _____ Disagree _____
Explain your answer:_____		
2. Like men, women should be allowed to fight the enemy in direct combat situations.	Agree Disagree	Agree _____ Disagree _____
Explain your answer:_____		
3. Women with children should not be allowed to serve in the military.	Agree Disagree	Agree _____ Disagree _____
Explain your answer:_____		
4. Women officers should never command men.	Agree Disagree	Agree _____ Disagree _____
Explain your answer:_____		
5. Both women and men should have the right to refuse military service if it goes against their beliefs.	Agree Disagree	Agree _____ Disagree _____
Explain your answer:_____		

C PREPARING TO READ

BACKGROUND

Read this information, and do the exercise that follows.

Women have served in the American military throughout most of this century, but mostly in support roles: as nurses, supply workers, and transportation personnel. During World War II some women flew Air Force planes as test pilots, trainers, and transport auxiliaries, but they were not recognized for their contribution. After the war, women were forced out of their jobs in the armed forces and factories and were replaced by men returning from the war. Later, even during the Vietnam War in the 1960s and 1970s, one in seventy soldiers in the U.S. military was a woman.

In the 1990s, a new generation of American women participated in the Gulf War: repairing tanks, piloting supplies, doing intelligence work, flying helicopters, working computers, and training to save the wounded as women firefighters. In the new American military, which is an all-volunteer force, about one in nine soldiers is a woman. Part of the reason for this higher proportion is that technological advances have replaced purely physical strength in many military operations, allowing women to fill new roles. In addition, in an effort to attract the best candidates, the Army, Navy, and Air Force offer educational opportunities and significant financial incentives to all soldiers, making a soldier's life more attractive to women.

In some countries women soldiers can fight in combat missions with men, but not in the United States. Although women soldiers are now eligible for fighter pilot training (and will eventually be able to earn the flying hours required to later qualify as highly paid civilian airline pilots), they cannot volunteer for combat missions even though many may wish to do so.

Work in a small group. Compare the situation of American women in the military to the situation of women in the military in other countries. Discuss the following topics and any others your group may think of:

- the role of women soldiers, if there are any

- women's participation in war efforts of the past

- the role of women soldiers after the wars ended

- men soldiers' attitudes toward women soldiers

VOCABULARY FOR COMPREHENSION

Work in a small group. Study the military vocabulary and definitions below. Think about the relationship between these words and the concepts you will encounter in this unit's readings: ***danger, teamwork, suffering,*** *and* ***peace.*** *If a word relates to a concept, put a* **+** *sign in that column in the chart below. If the word does not relate to the concept, put in a* **–** *sign. If you are unsure, or if the word relates only partially to the concept, put a* **?** *in the column. Explain your choices. Try to reach a group consensus.*

ammunition	bullets, bombs, explosives; anything fired from a weapon
battalion	a group of 500 to 1,000 soldiers
bunker	a strongly built shelter for soldiers
casualties	military people lost through death, wounds, or illness
civilian	a person who is not in the armed forces
coalition	a union of political parties or countries for a purpose, usually for a limited time, often during wars
convoy	an armed group of ships or vehicles traveling together for protection
enlisted personnel	people in the military who are not officers
missing in action	soldiers lost in battle and not found
mission-capable status	a condition of being ready to go out for special duty
red alert	the most urgent warning to be ready for an emergency
survivors	people who continue to live after coming close to death or after others have died

	DANGER	TEAMWORK	SUFFERING	PEACE
1. ammunition	+	?	+	–
2. battalion				
3. bunker				
4. casualties				
5. civilian				
6. coalition				
7. convoy				
8. enlisted personnel				
9. missing in action				
10. mission-capable status				
11. red alert				
12. survivors				

2 Focus on Reading

A READING ONE: *Women at War*

List three topics that you would expect to read about in these letters written to Glamour magazine from American women soldiers who participated in the Gulf War. Compare notes with a partner. After you finish the reading, check to see if your predictions were correct.

1. _____
2. _____
3. _____

Women at War

from *Glamour*

Women at war—what was it like? Via an ad in the military newspaper *Stars and Stripes, Glamour* magazine asked American women serving in the Gulf to write and describe their day-to-day life. What did they think about, dream about, worry about? Here are some of the letters received.

Letter 1

1   I am a First Lieutenant serving with coalition forces in the Middle East. Most of all I am afraid my husband will find out that I am within range of Iraq's Scud missiles. I don't want him to worry about me. Of course, I worry about chemical attacks. You move as fast as you can, but if you get the shakes during a red alert, you can't put on your GCE [ground crew ensemble]. You can't let the fear get to you.

2   I am a weather forecaster in charge of two men, both staff sergeants. Our job is to bring accurate weather information to air crews. Sounds easy, yes? No! Sparse satellite data really hurts, and the weather during the late winter/early spring is subject to rapid change.

3   I dream of not having to walk 100 yards to the shower. I dream of taking a long, warm bath. And wearing a dress would be marvelous. Also, eating at certain favorite restaurants in Oregon, my home state.

4   I write home all that I want to remember. The collection will be my "Desert Diary" to read to my husband and children on cold winter nights.

Thyra A. Bishop

Letter 2

5   I am an E-6 [Petty Officer First Class] in the Navy and the mother of two: a three-year-old boy and an eleven-month-old girl. It breaks my heart to be here, so far away

from them. I put their pictures up on the wall in my room. I can barely look at them without crying, though. But I am fortunate because they are being very well cared for in the loving hands of their father. When all the death and destruction of this war starts to get me down, all I have to do is go to any of my fellow service members and see all the mail they have received from people they don't even know, the caring and concerned people of the U.S.A. When I think of all the yellow ribbons worn and all the American flags so proudly displayed, I get a great feeling in my heart.

Dawn Bell

Letter 3

6   I am a Second Lieutenant in the U.S. Army. I'm the executive officer [second in command] of a military intelligence headquarters company. I'm one of 17 females in a company of 127 personnel. My battalion flies aerial intelligence missions.

7   I keep myself busy by writing my fiancé, Jeff Devine, daily and planning our December seventh wedding.

8   My father is a Methodist minister in Appleton, Wisconsin. My parents are against the war and have marched for peace. They say that if the church doesn't stand up for peace, who will? That may seem strange to some people, as their only daughter is in Saudi Arabia. But the military paid for my college education, and I'm repaying that debt.

Jennifer Freese

Letter 4

9   Many people are curious to know how it is here for us females. Usually they ask the officers rather than the enlisted soldiers. Enlisted personnel are the backbone of the Army— we're the ones who get our hands dirty.

10   I am 24 years old, and I've been in the Army for almost two years. My biggest fear is being captured. We were told that if captured, we would be raped, tortured, and murdered. I could only say that they would have to murder me. I can't give up my ground to anyone.

11   I sometimes dream of shallow things like getting my hair and nails done or going shopping. When I see the natives and how poor they are, it hurts to see how I take some things for granted.

12   You do things here that you would never before dream of doing. If you're in a convoy that will not make many stops, you learn how to urinate in a Pringles or Planters can in a moving vehicle. It's really difficult, but you develop great balance.

Jillian Manderville

Letter 5

13   I am a 27-year-old soldier in the U.S. Army. Being in a Patriot [missile] unit, we have to move quite frequently. I saw torched bunkers, vehicles, shells from ammunition. It was truly unreal. The Iraqi soldiers were barely living from day to day on beans and rice. You could tell that they weren't expecting such an early ground war because they left their boots behind. You could also tell that an Allied tank not only shot at the bunker but ran right over the top of it. That is the price these soldiers had to pay. The thoughts that ran through me almost made me cry.

14   I honestly don't believe I'll continue my career in the Army, not because of the war but because the Army is tough and if you don't get tough with it and become strong, you are lost. I've learned to respect others, to survive in whatever conditions arise.

15   For those women who think that the service is for them, please think seriously about it. It's not a picnic. Getting up at 3 A.M. to move is scary, and deep down you know you have to go on and get it over with. I feel truly thankful to have made it through this war safely.

Carla Yvette Henry

Letter 6

16   I've been here for a month, and I really wish I were back home. I miss my daughters Kimberly and Candice. There are six of us on the midnight to 0800 shift. It's kind of lonely, but we always hope and pray that nothing happens because we're all working Casualties, which deals with personnel who are hurt, injured, or dead. We work eight hours a day, seven days a week. Before, it was twelve hours a day, but they worried about our getting burned out. The stress level in this place is very high.

17   They have just opened the sports complex so we can get a little recreation. The females can only go from 1300 to 1500 hours. We have to enter through the back door; the front door is for males. We're not allowed to drive civilian cars, only military vehicles, so to get anywhere they have public transportation for our use.

Barbara Ann Malone-Verduin

Letter 7

18   I am a sergeant in the Army. My job is equipment, records, and parts specialist. I make sure that equipment and parts are maintained properly and are at a fully mission-capable status.

19   My most dreadful moment was collecting two dead Iraqi soldiers and putting them in body bags. Normally, this wouldn't have been my mission. A crew who did this line of work was not available, so my unit asked for volunteers. I turned white as a ghost when I was asked to volunteer. But I felt someone should

care for them properly instead of just letting them rot away as soldiers missing in action. At least their families would know their whereabouts. If I had died in this war, I would have wanted people to take care of my body. Despite the fact that they were the enemy, they were still human beings fighting this crazy war, who were just as frightened as all of us.

Lisa Richards

Letter 8

20   When Iraq invaded Kuwait on August 2, my unit—the 11th Air Defense Artillery Brigade at Fort Bliss, Texas—was put on alert. I was scared, not of the war, but because I didn't want to leave my family behind. Now it's two o'clock in the morning, 60 miles from the Iraqi border, and all I think about is whether I'm going to get out of here alive and be with my family again.

21   This is one of the hardest things I'll ever have to face. Sometimes when I'm lying on my cot I find myself gazing up at the ceiling, and I start crying because my son is now walking and running on his own and I'm not there to see it. He's growing up without me. But at least he's safe with his dad. (My husband got out of the Army in June of 1990, so he started playing the role of house-husband while I worked, paid the bills, and was still a mom.) The only things my son and I have together right now are the few opportunities I get to talk to him on the phone and the letters my husband writes.

22   I know every mother over here feels just as I do about being away from her children. My friend has five children; her husband is also at home taking care of the kids, and she misses them dearly.

23   We try not to think about home too much, so we keep busy. Sometimes we don't even know what day it is. I just know it's been five months since I've been able to hold my baby and my husband—five months since someone told me he loved me—and

still we don't know how much longer we will be here. A few months, maybe a year.

24   But we are strong, we are survivors. We are here to fight if we have to, to keep the rest of the world, especially U.S. citizens, from harm. When I do get out of here, I'll be able to pass down war stories to my son and be proud of them. The fact that I am an American woman in a male-dominated country and am being given the chance to fight for what I believe in shows our women have come a long way.

Veronica Martin

Letter 9

25   I think if you talk to women in the military, we see ourselves as soldiers. We don't really see it as man versus woman. What I'm doing is no greater or less than the man who is flying next to me or in back of me.

Army Major Marie T. Rossi
Aviator and soldier, daughter and wife.
Killed in the Persian Gulf.

READING FOR MAIN IDEAS

*Read the following statements. Based on the reading, write a **T** (true) or **F** (false) next to each statement.*

__F__   1. None of the women were worried about appearing unfeminine.

__F__   2. All the women decided to remain in the military after the war.

__F__   3. The women were afraid of the enemy and wanted revenge.

__F__   4. The military separated the men and women soldiers in their work teams.

__T__   5. All the women were patriotic.

READING FOR DETAILS

Use the letter writers' exact words (with quotation marks) to explain their thoughts on the following subjects. Also, identify the letter writer by name.

1. Thinking about Fear

Choose direct quotes from letters 1, 4, 5, and 8 on this subject.

a. *"Of course, I worry about chemical attacks . . ." "You can't let the fear get to you." Thyra Bishop*

b. _____

c. _____

d. _____

2. Thinking about the Enemy

Choose direct quotes from letters 4, 5, and 7 on this subject.

a. _____

b. _____

c. _____

3. Discussing Their Jobs as Officers

Choose direct quotes from letters 1 and 3 on this subject.

a. _____

b. _____

4. Writing about Discrimination against Women

Choose direct quotes from letters 6, 8, and 9 on this subject.

a. _____

b. _____

c. _____

5. Thinking of Their Children Back Home

Choose direct quotes from letters 2, 6, and 8 on this subject.

a. _____

b. _____

c. _____

6. Thinking about Their Husbands

Choose direct quotes from letters 1, 2, and 8 on this subject.

a. _____

b. _____

c. _____

REACTING TO THE READING

1 *Work in a small group. Go back to the nine letters in Reading One, and evaluate how dedicated each woman is to military service. Rate each writer on a scale of 1 to 6, with **1** as not very dedicated to **6** as very dedicated. Some ratings may be very clear, but others may be open to considerable discussion and interpretation in the group. Try to convince each other by referring back to the letters. For each letter, circle the appropriate number on the scale.*

Letter 1	1	2	3	4	5	6
Letter 2	1	2	3	4	5	6
Letter 3	1	2	3	4	5	6
Letter 4	1	2	3	4	5	6
Letter 5	1	2	3	4	5	6
Letter 6	1	2	3	4	5	6
Letter 7	1	2	3	4	5	6
Letter 8	1	2	3	4	5	6
Letter 9	1	2	3	4	5	6

2 *Choose the one letter that affected you the most, and explain your choice in a small group.*

- Did you identify with the writer of the letter? In what way?
- Do you share the writer's opinions or reactions?
- Did anything surprise you in the letter?
- Were you shocked by anything in the letter?
- What other reasons did you have for choosing this letter?

B READING TWO: *In Peace, Women Warriors Rank Low*

In Reading Two, you will learn about the lives of women soldiers after they return home from a war in Eritrea, a country in East Africa. Before you read, discuss the following question with a partner.

How do you think women soldiers feel about their military experience after they return home?

Asmara Journal: In Peace, Women Warriors Rank Low

By James C. McKinley (from the *New York Times*)

1 Some days Nuria Mohammed Saleh says she actually finds herself missing the war—not the fear and horror, not even the adrenaline kick and camaraderie of soldiering. She misses being treated like a man. Like thousands of other Eritrean women, Mrs. Saleh fought side by side with the men in the rebel army that freed this rocky land from Ethiopian rule in 1991. Like most women who are veterans here, she has found it hard to return to the deeply traditional and patriarchal society[1] she left behind as a teenager.

2 A few years ago, she recalled, she was hammering the enemy with mortar fire. Now she sweeps floors for a dollar a day in an office building near the capital she helped liberate. The only hints of her past are the shrapnel[2] scars around her lips. Mrs. Saleh is one of about 20,000 women who have been discharged from the Eritrean Army in the last two years as part of a larger demobilization of nearly 52,000 troops. Though about 3,000 remain in the army, the vast majority of women were sent home. Some had spent their entire adult lives in the Eritrean People's Liberation Front. Most have little education, having quit school to join the guerrillas.

3 The front[3] changed their lives, they said. The rebel commanders were Marxists by training and treated women as equals. The front's soldiers were taught to ignore sexual, tribal, and religious differences. Women were trained to drive tanks, fight, and handle big guns. Though not many women had the education to become officers, a handful rose to command rebel battalions. Many married fighters from other religions and tribes.

4 Even outside the army in rebel-controlled regions, because the Liberation Front required most men to be in combat, women broke out of traditional molds, working as dentists, medical technicians, administrators, factory workers, mechanics, and teachers, a United Nations report said.

5 But if women who were guerrillas had hoped that fighting and dying in the war would change their status in Eritrean society, they have discovered instead that society's traditions die hard. Several said their families had rejected their mixed marriages and employers had been reluctant to hire them for skilled jobs. Even more galling[4] for some women is that once they put on civilian clothes, men started expecting them to play subservient roles again.

6 Aster Haile was 12 when she joined the rebels. While she fought and worked for the front as a teacher, her sister spent the war in Saudi Arabia. After liberation, Ms. Haile said, she could not find work teaching, so she borrowed from her sister and opened a dress shop on Victory Avenue. Despite her military service, she said many men she meets still resist treating her like a businesswoman.

[1] *patriarchal society:* a social system controlled only by men
[2] *shrapnel:* pieces of artillery, mortars, or hand grenades
[3] *the front:* the war zone
[4] *galling:* aggravating, frustrating

7   Other women who were veterans have banded together in cooperatives, pooling their savings and severance pay to start textile and honey-making businesses. Along with male veterans, they have been under-going retraining at government expense to work as truck drivers and carpenters.

8   Here in Asmara, the capital, one group of women who were fighters have opened a fish market, the Gejeret Fish Retail Shop, built with the help of grants from the United States and the United Nations. Nine women work there, having traded in their AK-47s for fillet knives. They share the profits with other female veterans who are partners. Each woman takes home about $72 a month. Ghenet Berhe, a 30-year-old mother, said she did not mind filleting fish, since the whole country is struggling to get back on its feet economically. But when she was asked if she missed her life in the rebel army, she smiled and said, "Of course." "We had equality," she said. "We had common goals and common ends."

1 *Examine the following incomplete statements. Then with a partner decide which choices could complete the sentences according to the point of view expressed in the reading. Circle your choices. There is always more than one correct answer.*

1. Women veterans of the Eritrean Army miss their army days because _____.
   a. many became officers
   b. they didn't want to get married
   c. they were treated as equals to men
   d. they did not face religious or tribal discrimination

2. A subservient position is when you _____.
   a. take orders, not give them
   b. do unskilled labor
   c. don't own your own land
   d. are partners in a cooperative

3. During the war, women made progress because they could _____.
   a. take jobs only men had before
   b. train for skilled jobs
   c. choose their husbands more freely
   d. go to school more easily

4. Former women soldiers find life in peacetime frustrating because _____.
   a. they can't find good jobs
   b. their marriages have become unacceptable
   c. they are no longer traditional women
   d. they thought their country would be more grateful to them

2 *On a separate piece of paper, write the answers to the following questions in your own words. Compare your answers to those of a partner.*

1. Why did the United Nations encourage the women to form cooperatives?

2. What, if anything, did the women gain by being soldiers?

C LINKING READINGS ONE AND TWO

In Readings One and Two you have read about the thoughts and feelings of several women soldiers. Choose one of the topics below, and write the letter indicated.

1. You are Veronica Martin. Write a letter to Nuria Mohammed Saleh discussing your family and your military service. Tell her about the similarities and differences between your life and hers. How do you see the future?

2. You are Ghenet Berhe. Write a letter to Dawn Bell telling her about how you felt being in the military and what your life is like now in the U.N. cooperative.

3. You are Aster Haile. Write to Carla Yvette Henry, who wants to leave the U.S. military. Tell her about your experiences and about your life after you left the army.

3 Focus on Vocabulary

> The suffixes **-al, -ial, -an, -ar,** and **-ary** mean "pertaining to," "related to," "connected with." When you add one of these suffixes to a noun, you create an adjective that means "pertaining to," "related to," or "connected with" the subject of the noun.
>
> **Example** education (noun)
> educational (adjective = "pertaining to education")

1 *Work with a partner. The noun forms of adjectives that appear in Readings One and Two are listed below. Add the correct suffixes to form adjectives. Make other necessary changes. Check your answers in the dictionary.*

1. medic _____

2. militia _____

3. tradition _____

4. patriarch _____

5. technique _____

6. sex _____

7. tribe _____

8. air _____

2 Work with a partner. The following nouns appear in Readings One and Two. Change them to adjectives by adding the correct suffixes and making other necessary changes. Usa a dictionary if you need to.

1. volunteer _____   3. vehicle _____

2. recreation _____   4. minister _____

3 There are many idioms in English that use **get.** The following are only a few of the many examples. Find the correct meaning for each idiom or expression according to the way the expression is used in the readings, and circle your choice. There is only one correct answer for each question.

1. "get the shakes" (Reading One, paragraph 1)
   a. become chilly
   b. become nervous
   c. become dizzy

2. "get to you" (Reading One, paragraph 1)
   a. approach you
   b. enter you
   c. bother you

3. "get me down" (Reading One, paragraph 5)
   a. depress me
   b. irritate me
   c. pull me under

4. "get our hands dirty" (Reading One, paragraph 9)
   a. become involved in illegal activity
   b. assume responsibility for all negotiations
   c. do all the heavy, physical work

5. "get it over with" (Reading One, paragraph 15)
   a. complete the task
   b. overcome all difficulties
   c. ignore all inconveniences

6. "getting burned out" (Reading One, paragraph 16)
   a. becoming exhausted or disinterested because of overwork
   b. becoming overly enthusiastic about work
   c. becoming inspired by too much work

7. "get back on its feet economically" (Reading Two, paragraph 8)
   a. assess its economic situation
   b. come to terms with its economic weaknesses
   c. recover its economic stability

*Working in a small group, write a list of any other expressions with **get** that you know.*

4 *Complete this dialogue between a young woman and her father. The young woman has joined the military, but her father is not happy about her choice. Use at least eight of the vocabulary words listed below in the dialogue. Continue the dialogue on a separate piece of paper.*

band together	~~enlist~~	get to you	missing in action	survivor
casualties	galling	grants	reject	traditional
civilian	get me down	handle	resist	~~volunteer~~

FATHER: *I can't believe that you are going to **volunteer** in the military. Why are you doing this? I don't understand.*

DAUGHTER: *Dad, I never meant to hurt you in any way. I just want to support my country, and that's why I **enlisted.***

FATHER: _____

_____

DAUGHTER: _____

_____

FATHER: _____

_____

4 Focus on Writing

A GRAMMAR: Direct and Indirect Speech

1 *Examine the two sentences below, and then discuss the questions with a partner.*

- "The military paid for my college education, and I'm repaying that debt." (Jennifer Freese)

- Jennifer Freese said that the military had paid for her college education and she was repaying that debt.

   1. Do these two sentences have different meanings?

   2. Why are they written in a different way?

   3. Why does the second sentence have no quotation marks?

   4. How have the pronouns and verb tenses been changed?

Direct and Indirect Speech

Direct speech is a quotation or recording of a person's exact words. Quotation marks are used to make this clear to the reader.

"The military paid for my college education, and I'm repaying that debt."
Jennifer Freese

Indirect speech paraphrases or reports what someone said without necessarily using the person's exact words. Quotation marks are not used. The verbs **agree, answer, believe, decide, explain, realize, say, tell,** and **think** are commonly used to introduce direct speech.

Jennifer Freese **said** that the military had paid for her college education and she was repaying that debt.

Changing Direct Speech to Indirect Speech

Verb forms and tenses and pronouns change when direct speech becomes indirect speech.

Direct Speech

Indirect Speech

1. Present tense changes to the past.

"I **am** an E-6 in the Navy."

She said she **was** an E-6 in the Navy.

2. Simple past changes to the past perfect.

"I **put** up pictures of my kids on the wall."

She said she **had put** up pictures of her kids on the wall.

3. Present perfect changes to the past perfect.

"I **have been** here for a month."

She explained that she **had been** here for a month.

4. The future **will** changes to **would.**

"I **will** read this diary to my children someday."

She thought that she **would** read this diary to her children someday.

5. The modal **can** changes to **could.** When **must** means **have to,** it changes to **had to. May, might,** and **should** remain the same.

"I **can** barely look at them without crying."

She realized that she **could** barely look at them without crying.

2 *Rewrite the following direct quotes in indirect speech. Compare your answers with a partner's.*

Lieutenant Veronica Martin is an Army Reserves Officer stationed at Fort Bliss, Texas. At her interview today, she said, "My unit, the 11th Air Defense Artillery Brigade, was put on alert last night."

Indirect Speech: (1) _____

_____

She said, "I am scared but not of the war."

Indirect Speech: (2) _____

_____

"I don't want to leave my family behind," she explained.

Indirect Speech: (3) _____

_____

It is two o'clock in the morning, and Veronica Martin is 60 miles from the Iraqi border.

"All I have been able to think about is my family," she said.

Indirect Speech: (4) _____

_____

"Will I ever see them again?" she wondered.

Indirect Speech: (5) _____

_____

"This is one of the hardest things I will ever have to face," she said.

Indirect Speech: (6) _____

_____

"But the soldiers are strong," she told us. "We are here to fight if we have to, to keep the rest of the world, especially U.S. citizens, safe from harm," she added.

Indirect Speech: (7) _____

_____

3 *Rewrite the following indirect speech statements in direct speech. Compare your answers with a partner's.*

Lieutenant Martin's husband was interviewed about his wife's service in the Gulf War. Mr. Martin told us that he had been in the Army until last June.

Direct Speech: (1) _____

_____

He explained he had started taking care of the children at that time.

Direct Speech: (2) _____

_____

He said his son was learning to walk and run and that he missed his mother.

Direct Speech: (3) _____

_____

He said they talked to her on the phone every two weeks.

Direct Speech: (4) _____

_____

4 *Go back to Reading One, and find Letter 2 by Dawn Bell. Rewrite the letter as indirect speech. Compare your letter with a partner's.*

B   STYLE: Paragraph Development—Writing a Summary

1 *Examine the following paragraph that summarizes three letters from Reading One. Discuss the questions that follow with a partner.*

Three letters, written by American women military officers during the Gulf War, dealt with the women's pride in their jobs, their thoughts of home, and the frustrations of life in the armed forces. In two of the letters, the women described commanding both men and women in weather forecasting units and aerial intelligence services. All three women expressed their concerns about home: leaving children in a husband's care, planning a wedding, hiding the dangers of war so that a husband wouldn't worry. The women also wrote of fear and sadness, but they were cheered by the support of their families and thoughts of home.

1. Look back at Reading One. Which three letters does this text summarize?

2. Is there a main idea sentence in the summary? Underline it.

3. Does the summary use the exact words from the letters, or new words?

4. Compared to the three letters, how long is the summary?

Preparing and Writing a Summary

A summary contains the essential information from a text or article. In a general way, writing a summary can help you check if you have understood or remembered the main ideas of any reading passage. More specifically, summarizing information from textbooks and course work is an essential tool in studying for examinations. Being able to write a summary is also a necessary skill when gathering information for research papers. Finally, summarizing facts and opinions is important for business presentations, work meetings, and conferences.

The list that follows outlines the steps for writing a summary.

1. Identify the main ideas.

2. Decide what you are going to leave out. Include only the essential details.

3. Reorganize the ideas in a way that makes your points clear. You do not have to follow the order of the original text.

4. At the beginning, include a sentence stating the subject of the summary, where the original text came from, and/or the original author's name.

5. Use your own words. Do not copy from the text unless you use direct quotes and quotation marks, or indirect speech.

6. State only the author's opinions and not your own.

7. Make sure your verb tenses are appropriate and consistent when you use reported speech.

8. Make the summary short, no more than 25 percent of the original text and, in many cases, much less.

9. Be sure to edit your work. Polish it to make the language flow smoothly.

2 *Summarize each paragraph that follows in one sentence. Remember to use your own words. Compare your sentences with those of a partner.*

1.   "The Iraqi soldiers were barely living from day to day on beans and rice. You could tell that they weren't expecting such an early ground war because they left their boots behind. You could also tell that an Allied tank not only shot at the bunker but ran right over the top of it. That is the price these soldiers had to pay. The thoughts that ran through me almost made me cry." (*Letter 5*)

_____

_____

2.   "My most dreadful moment was collecting two dead Iraqi soldiers and putting them in body bags. Normally, this wouldn't have been my mission. A crew who did this line of work was not available, so my unit asked for volunteers. I turned white as a ghost when I was asked to volunteer. But I felt someone should care for them properly instead of just letting them rot away as soldiers missing in action. At least their families would know their whereabouts. If I had died in this war, I would have wanted people to take care of my body. Despite the fact that they were the enemy, they were still human beings fighting this crazy war, who were just as frightened as all of us." (*Letter 7*)

_____

_____

3.   "They have just opened the sports complex so we can get a little recreation. The females can only go from 1300 to 1500 hours. We have to enter through the back door; the front door is for males. We're not allowed to drive civilian cars, only military vehicles, so to get anywhere they have public transportation for our use." (*Letter 6*)

_____

_____

4.   "I honestly don't believe I'll continue my career in the Army, not because of the war but because the Army is tough and if you don't get tough with it and become strong, you are lost. I've learned to respect others, to survive in whatever conditions arise.

"For those women who think that the service is for them, please think seriously about it. It's not a picnic. Getting up at 3 A.M. to move is scary, and deep down you know you have to go on and get it over with. I feel truly thankful to have made it through this war safely." (*Letter 5*)

"My biggest fear is being captured. We were told that if captured, we would be raped, tortured, and murdered. I could only say that they would have to murder me. I can't give up my ground to anyone." (*Letter 4*)

"It's kind of lonely. . . . We work eight hours a day, seven days a week. Before, it was twelve hours a day, but they worried about our getting burned out. The stress level in this place is very high." (*Letter 6*)

_____

_____

_____

3 *Look back at Letters 4–9 in Reading One. Write a summary of the information on one of the following themes from these letters: being female in the military, the attitude toward the enemy, patriotism.*

C WRITING TOPICS

Choose one of the writing topics below. For the essay questions (2–5), remember to provide a thesis statement and sufficient explanations, examples, and support to develop your main idea. When you write, use the vocabulary and grammar you have studied in this unit.

1. Find a magazine or newspaper article about women in the military in a country other than the United States; or find an article about the history of the military. (You can use an excerpt from the encyclopedia or other reference materials.) Write a summary of the article. Give a copy of the article to your teacher along with your finished summary.

2. Women of all ages are increasingly active in business, professional, and military life. Some people, both men and women, react to this trend by saying, "A woman's place is in the home." Do you agree or disagree? Explain your answer in a short essay.

3. Do you think letters from men who are soldiers would be similar to or different from the letters written by the women soldiers in this unit? Explain your answer in an essay, and refer to the readings.

4. Do you believe that military service should be required as a way to develop good citizens? If you believe that it should, would you require it for men only or for both men and women? Write an essay explaining your opinion, and refer to the experience of a country you know about.

5. Do you think a person has the right to refuse military service for religious or moral reasons? for political reasons? Write an essay to explain your view.

D RESEARCH TOPICS

PREPARATION

Choose a country not represented by any of the students in the class, and research the policies in that country toward women in the army. Before starting your research, brainstorm with a partner for questions that you believe would be worth investigating.

Here are some questions you may want to consider:

1. Are women allowed to serve in the military in this country? In what capacity? Can women do combat duty? What is the percentage of women soldiers?

2. Does this country have compulsory (required) military service, or do citizens volunteer for the military? Are women drafted?

3. Are there provisions for conscientious objectors—people who, because of religious or moral beliefs, refuse to engage in physical combat? Is some sort of alternative service to the country possible? Can women participate?

4. Does this country have professional military preparatory schools? Can women enroll?

5. Can women become officers? Can they command men as well as women?

6. Can women soldiers be married? Can they be mothers?

7. Does one's military service have an effect on one's future career in this country? Is there respect for the military in this country?

RESEARCH ACTIVITY

After you have prepared a list of questions, go to the library or do an Internet search. When you do your research, be sure to take detailed notes about the information you find and the sources you use.

SHARING YOUR FINDINGS

Write a summary of your findings to share with the class. Follow the guidelines for writing summaries in Section 4B of this unit.

For step-by-step practice in the writing process, see the *Writing Activity Book, Advanced,* Unit 8.

Assignment	Persuasive Essay
Prewriting	Focused Freewriting
Organizing	Using Persuasive Reasons to Support Your Point of View
Revising	Supporting Your Reasons with Examples
	Incorporating Direct and Indirect Speech
Editing	Punctuating Direct Quotes

For Unit 8 Internet activities, visit the NorthStar Companion Website at http://longman.com/northstar.

The Cellist of Sarajevo

1 Focus on the Topic

A PREDICTING

Look at the photo above and the title of this unit. What do you think this unit will be about? Write down your thoughts for a few minutes, and discuss your ideas with a partner.

B   SHARING INFORMATION

Work in a small group. Ask each other the following questions, and explain your answers.

1. What kind of music do you enjoy? Jazz? Rock'n'roll? Classical? Hip hop?

2. What creative things do you like to do? Play a musical instrument? Paint? Write? Dance? Design or decorate? Sew? Something else?

3. Do you enjoy going to the movies, the theater, concerts, museums?

C   PREPARING TO READ

BACKGROUND

Read this information, and then discuss the questions that follow with a partner.

Whether we are professional artists or not, the creative arts play an important role in our lives. Through the attention we pay to colors, materials, shapes, and sounds when we select our clothes and decorate our homes, our creative instincts are continually at work as we express our identity and make our mark in the world.

It is also through creativity—through the language of music, for example— that people reach out and connect with each other. Music allows people to share emotions and feelings that are common to all of us. It is also a comfort in or a refuge from a world that is sometimes cruel and hard to understand.

One of the most difficult realities that people must face is the destruction and cruelty of war. In recent years, the suffering of the city of Sarajevo in the former republic of Yugoslavia inspired artists and others to come to its aid. Sarajevo, once a prosperous, tolerant city where people of many backgrounds lived together in peace, became a city torn apart by war and ethnic rivalry. Sarajevo has come to represent the struggle of the human spirit to maintain its dignity in the face of hatred and destruction. The first reading in this unit, which combines the beauty of music with the sounds of war, grew out of this struggle.

1. What role does music play in your life?

2. Has it been a source of comfort or help through a difficult period?

3. In addition to comfort, what other emotions does music evoke?

VOCABULARY FOR COMPREHENSION

1 *Work in pairs, and help each other guess the meaning of the underlined words from the context of the sentences. Then write a synonym or your own definition of the word. Use your dictionaries if necessary.*

1. Despite his <u>unassuming</u> presence, the young composer was, in fact, a great musical genius.

   modest

2. The artist is often a <u>solitary</u> figure, unknown or misunderstood by a society that offers no help.

   _____

3. The children's <u>anticipation</u> was seen in their excited faces as they waited for the concert to begin.

   _____

4. The music had a <u>haunting</u> quality because its sad and wistful tones made the audience think of their unhappy past.

   _____

5. Handel's *Messiah*, Beethoven's Fifth Symphony, and Tchaikovsky's *1812 Overture* are all important parts of an orchestra's <u>repertoire</u> of Western music.

   _____

6. Much of the classical music of the nineteenth century reflected the <u>furor</u> and violence of revolutionary times.

   _____

7. The band played so loudly that the people held their hands to their ears, waiting for the sound to <u>subside</u>.

   _____

8. The folk music made the people feel so happy and <u>exuberant</u> that they became very hopeful about the future.

   _____

9. In the past, many composers have <u>defied</u> the standards of society to produce new music.

_____

10. Despite our poor, <u>croaking</u> voices, we filled the room with joyous song.

_____

11. Because of the joy and beauty it brings, this musical composition will be <u>cherished</u> by its listeners for years to come.

_____

12. When people are depressed, listening to music <u>soothes</u> their pain.

_____

2 *Match the words on the left with the synonyms on the right.*

_c_	1. unassuming	a. lonely
A	2. solitary	b. unforgettable
B	3. haunting	c. modest
F	4. repertoire	d. enthusiastic
i	5. furor	e. comfort
L	6. subside	f. pieces that an artist can perform
d	7. exuberant	g. hoarse
j	8. defy	h. expectation
g	9. croaking	i. angry disturbance
K	10. cherish	j. oppose
l	11. soothe	k. treasure
H	12. anticipation	l. decline

2 Focus on Reading

A READING ONE: *The Cellist of Sarajevo*

Read the following quotation from Georges Braque, and answer the question. Then read Paul Sullivan's article, and keep Braque's statement in mind as you read.

The French painter Georges Braque (1882–1963) said, "Art is a wound that becomes light." What do you think this statement means? Write a few sentences in response, and discuss your ideas with a partner.

_____

_____

_____

THE CELLIST OF SARAJEVO

By Paul Sullivan (from *Reader's Digest*)

1   As a pianist, I was invited to perform with cellist Eugene Friesen at the International Cello Festival in Manchester, England. Every two years a group of the world's greatest cellists and others devoted to that unassuming instrument—bow makers,[1] collectors, historians—gather for a week of workshops, master classes,[2] seminars, recitals, and parties. Each evening, the 600 or so participants assemble for a concert.

2   The opening-night performance at the Royal Northern College of Music consisted of works for unaccompanied cello. There on the stage in the magnificent concert hall was a solitary chair. No piano, no music stand, no conductor's podium.[3] This was to be music in its purest, most intense form. The atmosphere was supercharged with anticipation and concentration. The world-famous cellist Yo-Yo Ma was one of the performers that April night in 1994, and there was a moving story behind the musical composition he would play.

3   On May 27, 1992, in Sarajevo, one of the few bakeries that still had a supply of flour was making and distributing bread to the starving, war-shattered people. At 4 P.M. a long line stretched into the street. Suddenly,

---

[1] *bow makers:* people who make the flexible stick used to produce sound by players of the cello and other stringed instruments
[2] *master class:* form of teaching in which a celebrated musician instructs a group of pupils in front of other pupils or a paying audience
[3] *podium:* elevated platform

a mortar shell fell directly into the middle of the line, killing 22 people and splattering flesh, blood, bone, and rubble.

4   Not far away lived a 35-year-old musician named Vedran Smailovic. Before the war he had been a cellist with the Sarajevo Opera, a distinguished career to which he patiently longed to return. But when he saw the carnage from the massacre outside his window, he was pushed past his capacity to absorb and endure any more. Anguished, he resolved to do the thing he did best: make music. Public music, daring music, music on a battlefield.

5   For each of the next 22 days, at 4 P.M., Smailovic put on his full, formal concert attire,[4] took up his cello, and walked out of his apartment into the midst of the battle raging around him. Placing a plastic chair beside the crater that the shell had made, he played in memory of the dead Albinoni's *Adagio in G minor,* one of the most mournful and haunting pieces in the classical repertoire. He played to the abandoned streets, smashed trucks, and burning buildings, and to the terrified people who hid in the cellars while the bombs dropped and bullets flew. With masonry exploding around him, he made his unimaginably courageous stand for human dignity, for those lost to war, for civilization, for compassion, and for peace. Though the shellings went on, he was never hurt.

6   After newspapers picked up the story of this extraordinary man, an English composer, David Wilde, was so moved that he, too, decided to make music. He wrote a composition for unaccompanied cello, "The Cellist of Sarajevo," into which he poured his feelings of outrage, love, and brotherhood with Vedran Smailovic. It was "The Cellist of Sarajevo" that Yo-Yo Ma was to play that evening.

7   Ma came out on stage, bowed to the audience, and sat down quietly on the chair. The music began, stealing out into the hushed hall and creating a shadowy, empty universe, ominous and haunting. Slowly it grew into an agonized, screaming, slashing furor, gripping us all before subsiding at last into a hollow death rattle and, finally, back to silence.

8   When he had finished, Ma remained bent over his cello, his bow resting on the strings. No one in the hall moved or made a sound for a long time. It was as though we had just witnessed that horrifying massacre ourselves. Finally, Ma looked out across the audience and stretched out his hand, beckoning someone to come to the stage. An indescribable electric shock swept over us as we realized who it was: Vedran Smailovic, the cellist of Sarajevo!

9   Smailovic rose from his seat and walked down the aisle as Ma left the stage to meet him. They flung their arms around each other in an exuberant embrace. Everyone in the hall erupted in a chaotic, emotional frenzy-clapping, shouting and cheering. And in the center of it all stood these two men, hugging and crying unashamedly: Yo-Yo Ma, a suave, elegant prince of classical music, flawless in appearance and performance; and Vedran Smailovic, dressed in a stained and tattered leather motorcycle suit. His wild, long hair and huge mustache framed a face that looked old beyond his years, soaked with tears and creased with pain. We were all stripped down to our starkest, deepest humanity at encountering this man who shook his cello in the face of bombs, death, and ruin, defying them all. It was the sword of Joan of Arc—the mightiest weapon of all.

10   Back in Maine a week later, I sat one evening playing the piano for the residents of a local nursing home. I couldn't help contrasting this concert with the splendors I had witnessed at the festival. Then I was struck

---

[4] *concert attire:* a tuxedo or formal dark suit worn by musicians at a concert

by the profound similarities. With his music the cellist of Sarajevo had defied death and despair, and celebrated love and life. And here we were, a chorus of croaking voices accompanied by a shopworn[5] piano, doing the same thing. There were no bombs and bullets, but there was real pain—dimming sight, crushing loneliness, all the scars we accumulate in our lives—and only cherished memories for comfort. Yet still we sang and clapped.

11   It was then I realized that music is a gift we all share equally. Whether we create it or simply listen, it's a gift that can soothe, inspire, and unite us, often when we need it most—and expect it least.

[5] *shopworn:* not in the best condition after years of use

READING FOR MAIN IDEAS

Work with a partner. Read the statements, and decide which three represent the main ideas of Reading One. Then discuss the reasons for your choices.

1. Involving yourself in what you do best will always help you to emerge victorious from the most difficult situations.

2. Music can help solve political problems.

3. Music can give people the strength they need to soothe both physical and emotional pain.

4. Music can make people sympathize with the suffering of others.

5. Destroying things is not the only way to win a war.

6. Art creates a community of people.

READING FOR DETAILS

Work with a partner. Number the eight episodes in the order in which they appear in "The Cellist of Sarajevo."

_6_ Yo-Yo Ma plays a cello concert of David Wilde's work at the Royal Northern College of Music in Manchester, England.

_1_ Vedran Smailovic plays the cello with the Sarajevo Opera in the 1980s.

_8_ The author plays the piano in a nursing home.

_4_ David Wilde reads an article about Smailovic playing the cello in the midst of bombs; Wilde writes a cello composition in Smailovic's honor.

_3_ Smailovic plays the cello in the streets of Sarajevo.

_5_ The author is invited to perform at the International Cello Festival in Manchester, England.

_2_ On May 27, 1992, a breadline in Sarajevo is shelled.

_7_ Smailovic embraces Yo-Yo Ma in the concert hall.

REACTING TO THE READING

1 *Based on what you have read in "The Cellist of Sarajevo," answer the following questions about the motivations and feelings of the people in the story. When you are finished, compare your answers with those of another student.*

1. Why did Vedran Smailovic play the cello in the streets of Sarajevo for exactly 22 days and always at 4 P.M. every day?

   _____

   _____

2. Why did Yo-Yo Ma play the piece entitled "The Cellist of Sarajevo"?

   _____

   _____

3. Why did Vedran Smailovic agree to make an appearance at the festival?

   _____

   _____

4. Why did Yo-Yo Ma and Vedran Smailovic embrace each other and cry?

   _____

   _____

5. What was the author's purpose in describing exactly how Yo-Yo Ma and Vedran Smailovic were dressed?

   _____

   _____

6. What connection does the author make between the nursing home and the situation in Sarajevo?

   _____

   _____

2 *Discuss these questions in a small group.*

1. Have you ever acted bravely in your life? What were the circumstances?

2. Is music an international language? Do films use an international language? What do we mean by an international language of art?

3. Do artists have an obligation to society? What about very well-known performers, singers, or actors?

4. What current local war do you know something about? Does this war concern you? Why? What can citizens and politicians do about it?

B   READING TWO: *The Soloist*

You are going to read an excerpt from the novel The Soloist *by Mark Salzman. It is about a man who was a famous concert cellist when he was a child and a young man; he lost his "musical ear" because of the great nervous pressure of playing concerts. He became an unassuming music teacher for many years until, all of a sudden, his gift returned to him. Before you read, consider the following questions, and discuss them with a partner.*

1. Have you ever been able to do something very well (for example, a sports activity, playing an instrument, dancing) and then lost this ability because something happened to you or because you changed in some way?

2. How do you think people feel when they lose the ability to do something they really love doing?

3. What can they do about it, if anything?

THE SOLOIST

BY MARK SALZMAN

1   An idea came to me, and I turned off the lights in the studio. In the darkness, I put the cello's spike into a loose spot on the carpet, tightened the bow, and drew it across the open strings. I took off my shirt and tried it again; it was the first time in my life I'd felt the instrument against my bare chest. I could feel the vibration of the strings travel through the body of the instrument to my own body. I'd never thought about that; music scholars always talk about the resonating[1] properties of various instruments, but surely the performer's own body must have some effect on the sound. As I dug into the notes I imagined that my own chest and lungs were extensions of the sound box; I seemed to be able to alter the sound by the way I sat, and by varying the muscular tension in my upper body.

2   After improvising for a while, I started playing the D minor Bach suite, still in the darkness. Strangely freed of the task of finding the right phrasing,[2] the right intonation, the right bowing, I heard the

---

[1] *resonating:* making a deep sound that vibrates the material of the instrument or the body
[2] *phrasing:* a way of linking the notes in order to bring out the melody of the music

music through my skin. For the first time I didn't think about how it would sound to anyone else, and slowly, joyfully, gratefully, I started to hear again. The notes sang out, first like a trickle, then like a fountain of cool water bubbling up from a hole in the middle of a desert. After an hour or so I looked up, and in the darkness saw the outline of the cat sitting on the floor in front of me, cleaning her paws and purring loudly. I had an audience again, humble as it was.

3   So that's what I do now with my cello. At least once a day I find time to tune it, close my eyes, and listen. It's probably not going to lead to the kind of comeback[3] I'd fantasized about for so long—years of playing badly have left scars on my technique, and, practically speaking, classical musicians returning from obscurity are almost impossible to promote[4]—but I might eventually try giving a recital if I feel up to it. Or better yet, I may play for Dr. Polk if our date at the concert goes well. Occasionally I feel a stab of longing, and I wish I could give just one more concert on a great stage before my lights blink off,[5] but that longing passes more quickly now. I take solace in the fact that unlike the way I felt before, I can enjoy playing for myself now. I feel relaxed and expansive when I play, as if I could stretch out my arms and reach from one end of the apartment to the other. A feeling of completeness and dignity surrounds me and lifts me up.

---

[3] *comeback:* starting a career again and returning to the heights of fame or celebrity
[4] *promote:* to get bookings or jobs for a client
[5] *before my lights blink off:* before I die

Working with a partner, read the following situations, and decide how they may be similar to or different from the experience described in The Soloist. *Each situation may have both similarities and differences, or just similarities, or just differences. Explain your decisions in writing.*

1. The great composer Ludwig van Beethoven lost his hearing in mid-career. He was then unable to hear speech, music, or any sound, but he went on to write some of the greatest music in the Western classical repertoire.

   Similarities: Both of these men lost a part of themselves.

   They lost abilities that meant a lot to them.

   Differences: Unlike the cellist in The Soloist, Beethoven lost his ability to

   hear. Beethoven's total deafness was physical and not the

   result of nervous anxiety. Furthermore, Beethoven continued

   to compose great music, whereas the cellist was forced to

   give up playing concerts and become a teacher.

2. A successful painter becomes disillusioned with the rich people who buy his paintings but don't understand the meaning of his art. He goes off to a small town to teach and paint just for himself and his cherished friends.

Similarities: _STOP Play in Concerts_

Differences: _____

3. A famous novelist develops "writer's block" and can't write anymore. Every time she sits down at the computer, she gets hot and dizzy and can't continue. Many months later, she discovers that if she stops using the computer and holds a pencil until it seems to become an extension of her hand, her dizziness subsides and she can start to write novels again.

Similarities: _deppressing ✓ find solution_

Differences: _find solution_

4. A famous actor develops such severe nervousness before each performance that he has to abandon acting forever. He becomes an insurance salesman.

Similarities: _____

Differences: _Qual_

C   LINKING READINGS ONE AND TWO

Work in pairs. Each student should choose one of the interview situations below. Write three questions that you would like to ask the person you have chosen to interview. Interview your partner. Then have your partner interview you. Answer the questions in the way you think the person in the reading would answer them.

1. Interview Vedran Smailovic about his decision to play the cello in the midst of bombs and bullets.

2. Interview Mark Salzman's cellist in *The Soloist,* and ask him how he feels about the loss of his musical ability and its partial return after many years.

3. Interview Paul Sullivan, and ask him why he plays the piano for senior citizens in a nursing home.

3 Focus on Vocabulary

1 *Work in a small group. Decide whether each adjective listed in the chart below expresses the feeling of happiness, sadness, or anger. Some express more than one feeling. Put a check (✓) in the appropriate columns.*

	HAPPINESS	SADNESS	ANGER
1. agonized		✓	
2. cheering	✓		
3. emotional	✓	✓	✓
4. exuberant	✓		
5. haunting		✓	
6. mournful		✓	
7. moving	✓	✓	
8. ominous		✓	
9. raging			✓
10. screaming	✓	✓	✓
11. slashing		✓	✓
12. solitary		✓	

Participles as Adjectives

In the following sentences, both **moved** and **moving** are adjectives.

- The man was <u>moved</u> when he heard the cellist's story.

- The <u>moving</u> story brought tears to the man's eyes.

The adjective *moved* modifies the noun *man*. The **-ed** suffix shows that the noun it modifies has been <u>affected by something else</u>. In this case, the man was moved by the story. The **-ed** adjective reminds us of the <u>passive voice</u>. It reflects a reaction ("to be moved by").

The adjective *moving* modifies the noun *story*. The **-ing** suffix shows that the noun it modifies has an <u>effect on something else.</u> In this case, the story moves the man. The **-ing** adjective reminds us of the active voice. The **-ing** adjective reflects an action ("the moving story" = "the story that moves us").

2 *Complete the paragraph that follows by filling in the blanks with the correct adjective.*

The audience was settling into their seats, happy because the warm summer

evening in Boston had had a ___relaxing___ effect on them. But when the
         1. (relaxed/relaxing)

refugees came on stage to tell their stories of war and pain and suffering, the

audience was ___horrified___. The refugees told of ___terrifying___
              2. (horrified/horrifying)   3. (terrified/terrifying)

brutal soldiers and ___terrified___ panicked people running for their lives.
                    4. (terrified/terrifying)

The audience was ___inspired___ by tales of bravery and compassion, but
                 5. (inspired/inspiring)

this ___haunting___ story of senseless violence remained in their minds for
     6. (haunted/haunting)

a long time.

3 *Read the sentences that follow. Circle the antonym, or opposite, of the underlined word from the three choices given. Two of the choices are synonyms. Only one choice is an antonym. Check your answers with a partner.*

1. Vedran Smailovic had a <u>distinguished</u> career to which he patiently longed to return.

   a. respected   b. mediocre   c. remarkable

2. He was pushed beyond his capacity to <u>endure</u>.

   a. enjoy   b. survive   c. suffer

3. Smailovic <u>made his stand for</u> human dignity.

   a. supported   b. defended   c. opposed

4. He <u>witnessed</u> a senseless massacre in Sarajevo.

   a. participated in   b. scrutinized   c. viewed

5. A battle <u>raged</u> around him as he played the cello.

   a. roared   b. quieted down   c. exploded

6. Music is a <u>solace</u> to us when we need it most.

   a. consolation   b. comfort   c. injury

7. I contrasted the concert in the nursing home with the <u>splendors</u> of the concert in Manchester, England.

   a. luster   b. grimness   c. brilliance

8. I <u>improvised</u> on the cello for a while.

   a. played impromptu   b. ad-libbed a piece c. played a prepared
      melodies   piece

4 *Figurative language describes one kind of object in place of another to suggest a likeness. For example, in the sentence "The cello gave a sorrowful wail," the cello is making a human sound. The musical instrument symbolizes a human being.*

Explain these sentences from Reading Two. First identify the symbolism. Then write what you think the sentence as a whole means. Share your answers with a partner.

1. "I dug into the **notes**."

   (musical) **notes** = _____*earth*_____

   a. sky   **b.** ocean   **c.** earth

   The cellist compares his musical instrument, the cello, to a shovel and the musical composition to the earth. At this time in his life, playing music is as intensely physical as breaking ground with a shovel.

2. "I heard the music through my **skin**."

   skin = _____

   a. feet   **b.** ears   **c.** eyes

   _____

   _____

3. "The **notes** sang out, first like a trickle, then a fountain."

   (musical) **notes** = _____

   a. stars   **b.** water   **c.** fire

   _____

   _____

4. "Occasionally I felt a stab of **longing**."

   longing = _____

   a. pain   **b.** joy   **c.** itch

   _____

   _____

5. "I wish I could give just one more concert on a great stage before my **lights** blink off."

   lights = _____

   a. eyes   **b.** appetite   **c.** life

   _____

   _____

5 *Write a short paragraph summarizing what Vedran Smailovic did for 22 days in Sarajevo. Use at least ten of the words in the box.*

agonized	haunting	repertoire
defy	mourning	solace
emotional	moving	soothe
endure *suportar*	patiently	take a stand
furor	raging	witness

Vedran Smailovic **took a stand** for human dignity. *He used his ability to emotions the people and help than to endure the war and the death*

GIVE EMOTIONAL FEELINGS FOR THE PEOPLE WHO ENDURE THE WAR AND THE DEATH.

4 Focus on Writing

A   GRAMMAR: Reporting Ideas and Facts with Passives

1 *Working with a partner, examine the following sentences and discuss the questions that follow.*

- Many people say that music is an international language.

- Music is said to be an international language.

- It is said that music is an international language.

    1. Which sentences are in the active voice and which are in the passive voice?

    2. In the second and third sentences, who says music is an international language?

    3. Is there a difference in meaning among the three sentences?

Using the Passive Voice

To Shift Focus

Using the passive voice shifts the reader's focus to *the thing being done* or *the process being described,* rather than to the specific agent. For this reason, in academic writing and scientific description, the passive voice is often used.*

- *Active:* A **craftsman dried** and **varnished** the wood for the cello.

- *Passive:* The **wood** for the cello **was dried** and **varnished.**

Using the passive voice relieves the writer of a certain amount of direct responsibility for what is said. For this reason, it is often used in reporting the news when the source of the news is not clear or cannot be told.

- *Active:* An **observer said** that the soldiers came from Sarajevo.

- *Passive:* **It was said** that the soldiers came from Sarajevo.

To Report Ideas and Facts

The passive voice creates a distance between the writer and the idea being communicated. That *impersonal* distance is the reason why the passive is preferred for reporting the ideas of others. The writer is reporting on something without adding his or her personal views, creating a sense of objectivity and impartiality.

- *Impersonal distance:* **Music is said to be** an international language.

- *Greater impersonal distance:* **It is said** that music is an international language.

GRAMMAR TIP: Because the writer is not interested in identifying the specific agent responsible for this statement, he or she uses the passive voice without *by* or an agent. In this example, "music is said to be an international language" has become a universal truth, and it is not necessary to identify the agent ("by many people," or "by great musicians," or "by experts," and so on).

Structures Commonly Used

Two structures can be used to form the passive:

Subject + passive form of the verb + *to be*	**Music is said to be** an international language.
The agreement of the subject (noun) and verb must be carefully considered. If the subject of the sentence is plural, the verb must be plural.	**Musical *compositions are* said to be** included in the box found in the composer's attic.

* If there is no specific reason to use the passive, the active voice is preferred in English.

The second structure uses the impersonal pronoun *it* and ***that*** followed by an independent clause.

It + passive form of the verb + *that*	*It* **is said that** *music* is an international language.

Verbs Commonly Used

The verbs **think, consider, regard, say, allege, believe, claim, know,** and **suggest** are commonly used to report facts, ideas, and beliefs.

2 *The sentences below are in the active voice. First read each sentence, and rewrite it in the passive voice. Examine both versions of the sentence, and decide which is more effective. Then give a reason for your decision.*

1. Many people say that the arts are essential parts of a child's education.

   It is said that the arts are essential parts of a child's education.

   This sentence is more effective in the impersonal passive voice because the

   agent ("many people") is very vague.

2. The government decided to give money to the school creative arts program.

   Was decided by the government decided to give money to the school creative arts program

3. The orchestra will have to dismiss many musicians beginning next week.

4. Sigmund Freud, the father of psychoanalysis, claimed that the imagination is the link to our innermost feelings.

5. Many teachers believe that an education in the arts develops sensitivity.

_____

_____

_____

_____

3 *Work with a partner. Read the following passage about how the arts are being used to help children.*

Look at the underlined sentences. Decide whether or not these sentences would be more effective if they were changed into the impersonal passive. (Remember that the passive voice is preferred only in specific cases. Most lively writing will use the active voice.) Then, on a separate piece of paper, rewrite the sentences that you think should be changed.

(**1**) People say that the creative arts have a healing effect on children. (**2**) We know that administrators at the Illinois Department of Children's Services are active supporters of this method. Last year they offered classes in art, theater, dance, and music to help children deal with their inner feelings. (**3**) The program was so successful that it quickly expanded.

(**4**) Several hundred children participated in the arts program this year. Children in the Illinois program show an awareness of how the arts are related to feelings. According to their teachers, some children associate a specific color with a particular emotional state: red with anger, orange with happiness, and so on.

(**5**) Teachers, administrators, and others in the program say that many children are learning how to relieve their tensions by drawing pictures about fighting instead of actually fighting. (**6**) They also claim that some of the children, noting that Leonardo Da Vinci and Michelangelo expressed both exuberant and mournful feelings in their art, are convinced there is a definite connection between these great artists and themselves. These insights are wonderful moments in building a child's emotional world.

B   STYLE: Using Descriptive Language

1 *Working with a partner, examine this paragraph from Paul Sullivan's "The Cellist of Sarajevo," and discuss the questions that follow.*

"For each of the next 22 days, at 4 P.M., Smailovic put on his full, formal concert attire, took up his cello, and walked out of his apartment into the midst of the battle raging around him. Placing a plastic chair beside the crater that the shell had made, he played in memory of the dead Albinoni's *Adagio in G minor,* one of the most mournful and haunting pieces in the classical repertoire. He played to the abandoned streets, smashed trucks, and burning buildings, and to the terrified people who hid in the cellars while the bombs dropped and bullets flew. With masonry exploding around him, he made his unimaginably courageous stand for human dignity, for those lost to war, for civilization, for compassion, and for peace. Though the shellings went on, he was never hurt."

1. Why is the following brief summary less interesting and effective than the whole paragraph above?

   - Despite the bombs, a man named Smailovic played the cello in the streets of Sarajevo in memory of the dead.

2. Give examples of how the author makes a great effort to describe actions, places, and objects very carefully.

3. Do you see examples of repeating patterns in his language?

4. Study the sentence structure in the paragraph. How many sentences start in the same way?

The Use of Descriptive Language

Good writers use **descriptive language** when they want to give us the complete picture and to involve us fully in the story that they are telling. Writing without descriptive language just reports facts. This is good when the writer's primary goal is simply to communicate the facts of a situation. But if the goal is to go beyond the facts to move, inspire, and persuade the reader, the writer must use powerful descriptive language. Three ways the writer can create powerful descriptive language are to use well-chosen adjectives, to develop internal rhythms in the sentence by using parallel structure, and to vary sentence structure.

Adjectives

Adjectives can be used to describe feelings, to relate how any of the five senses—sight, smell, taste, hearing, and touch—were stimulated throughout an experience, and to report simple facts. They can also be used to reflect the writer's values and judgment.

Adjective phrases can also be used in descriptive writing. Adjective phrases begin with present participles ("-ing" forms of verbs) or with prepositions (*for, with, like,* and so on) and modify a noun just as adjectives do.

   - "[Smailovic walked] into the midst of the battle *raging* around him."

(continued)

Adjective clauses are also found in descriptive writing. They begin with *that, who, which* (adverb clauses beginning with *while, although, though*).

- "He played … to the terrified people *who* <u>hid in the cellars</u> …"

Parallel Structure

Powerful descriptive passages have a certain music-like quality that is achieved when paragraphs have good internal sentence structure. Musical sentence rhythms are created by using **parallel structure**—by repeating patterns or sequences of action verbs, adjectives, nouns, adverbs, prepositional phrases, or adjective-noun pairs in one sentence. By threading sequences of images together—as a film editor does with the frames of a film—the writer is able to paint a complete picture and draw the reader into the world he or she is describing.

- "… <u>for</u> human dignity, <u>for</u> those lost to war, <u>for</u> civilization …"

Varied Sentence Structure

Varied sentence structure also contributes to good descriptive writing. The repetition of word patterns can be effective within the sentences themselves, but the repetition of the same grammatical sentence structure is not effective. Good writing should never have all the sentences in a paragraph starting in the same way. When this happens, the writing is very boring. Sentences should be both long and short, both simple and complex.

2 *Look at the paragraph in Section B1 on pages 212–213, and do these activities.*

1. Circle all the adjectives, adjective phrases, and clauses, and identify each one's purpose. Do they make facts more precise; communicate sights, sounds, or smells; tell about feelings; or communicate the author's value judgments?

2. In that same paragraph, underline all the parallel structures that give a certain music-like quality to the language.

3. Which sentence is the only one in the paragraph that begins with a subject-verb pattern? Why do you think this is the only sentence that starts in this way?

3 *Work in a small group. Using the techniques you have just learned, analyze the descriptive language in the following paragraph from* The Soloist.

1. Underline the adjectives and adjective phrases.

2. Circle the repetitive patterns and parallel structures.

3. Discuss the variety of sentence structures in the passage.

After improvising for a while, I started playing the D minor Bach suite, still in the darkness. Strangely freed of the task of finding the right phrasing, the right intonation, the right bowing, I heard the music through my skin. For the first time I didn't think about how it would sound to anyone else, and slowly, joyfully, gratefully, I started to hear again. The notes sang out, first like a trickle, then like a fountain of cool water bubbling up from a hole in the middle of a desert. After an hour or so I looked up, and in the darkness saw the outline of the cat sitting on the floor in front of me, cleaning her paws and purring loudly. I had an audience again, humble as it was.

4 *Write a paragraph in which you describe your own feelings in response to a specific work of art. Do you feel like Paul Sullivan did when he heard the cello concert? Or like the narrator in Mark Salzman's book when he played the cello in the dark?*

1. Think of a particular piece of music, a poem, or a work of art that you love.

2. Introduce the work of art, and write a descriptive paragraph about your feelings, emotions, and reactions when you experience it.

3. Pay attention to the adjectives you use, to parallel structure, to sentence variety.

C WRITING TOPICS

Choose one of the following topics, and write a well-organized response. Use what you have learned about descriptive language to make your writing lively and effective. Use vocabulary from the readings and the passive voice when appropriate.

1. Choose a painting, a photograph, a piece of music, or any other nonverbal work of art (not a work of literature or poetry). Explain why you have chosen it, and write a paragraph describing your observations about it, your emotional and intellectual reactions to it, and your conclusions and recommendations to others who may want to see and/or hear it in the future.

2. Choose one of the quotes below, and write an essay explaining what it means to you. Use examples from your own life or your reading to explain your understanding. Say whether you agree or disagree with the quote.

"Art is a wound that becomes light."   —Georges Braque

"Art is a human activity having for its purpose the transmission to others of the highest and best feelings to which men have risen." —Count Leo Tolstoy

3. Do you think that art and music should be an important part of the academic program in elementary and secondary schools? Should every child be required to learn to play an instrument and work on studio art? Why or why not? Discuss the advantages and disadvantages of making music and art a part of the academic curriculum for each child.

4. Choose one of the traditional arts of your native culture: quilt-making; pottery-making; beadwork or weaving; making mosaics; practicing traditional dances, songs, or theater. Describe this traditional handiwork, craft, or art, and tell what kinds of material it used and what it meant in the culture. What is the meaning of this art for people today?

D   RESEARCH TOPICS

PREPARATION

The character in *The Soloist* was haunted by the loss of his musical ear and the exuberant feeling of accomplishment that he used to have when he gave concerts to audiences that cherished his flawless performances. We leave him on a positive note as he seems to have rediscovered his musical gift. He now anticipates the possibility of playing for new audiences, either on the concert stage or in the privacy of his own home.

Work with a partner. Interview a musician to find out how he or she feels about the instrument and when playing this instrument. Interview a professional musician, if possible. If not, you can interview someone for whom music is a serious hobby, or a rock guitarist who plays in a student band—someone who plays an instrument all the time even though he or she is not a professional.

Before conducting the interview, brainstorm with your partner to come up with questions you may want to use in the interview. In addition to your own questions, you may want to ask:

1. What was your first experience with the instrument?

2. At what age did you first take lessons?

3. How do you feel about the instrument?

4. What feelings do you have when you play for an audience and when you play for yourself?

5. Which do you enjoy more—playing with other musicians or playing alone?

RESEARCH ACTIVITY

To find a musician, you may want to consider the following possibilities:

1. Ask friends to introduce you to a professional musician or someone who plays an instrument.

2. Consult the orchestras or the music schools in your area.

3. Contact the host of a local radio program who interviews musicians on the air.

Talk with your partner, and consider what other resources may be available to you.

SHARING YOUR FINDINGS

After you have conducted the interview, work together and write a summary of your findings. Use descriptive language as you explain how the person you interviewed feels when he or she plays an instrument, either in public or at home.

For step-by-step practice in the writing process, see the *Writing Activity Book, Advanced,* Unit 9.

Assignment	Narrative Essay
Prewriting	Questioning Yourself
Organizing	Starting Narratives
Revising	Using Descriptive Language
	Using the Passive Voice
Editing	Using Parallel Structure

For Unit 9 Internet activities, visit the NorthStar Companion Website at http://longman.com/northstar.

The Right to Read

1 Focus on the Topic

A PREDICTING

Why is free speech important in a democracy? What would daily life be like without the freedom to speak your thoughts or read what you want? How important is freedom of speech? Discuss your views with a partner.

B   SHARING INFORMATION

Below are six free speech issues that have developed in the United States. In the space provided, write a sentence explaining whether you think this type of speech should be permitted or not. Then compare your answers in a small group. When you have finished your discussion, look at the information on page 251 to discover how these issues have been dealt with in the United States.

1. Should publishing a book that some people consider disrespectful or harmful to a particular religion be allowed?

   _____

   _____

2. Should burning the national flag because you disagree with your country's policies be allowed?

   _____

   _____

3. Should people be allowed to distribute pornography (disturbing sexual pictures and language)?

   _____

   _____

4. Should the U.S. government allow people who don't agree with war to encourage young men to refuse military service in wartime?

   _____

   _____

5. Should the press be allowed to make rude, mocking, or disrespectful comments about the U.S. president?

   _____

   _____

6. Should selling hip-hop music with obscene lyrics and lyrics that are disrespectful of the police be allowed?

   _____

   _____

C   PREPARING TO READ

BACKGROUND

Read this information, and then take the Class Poll that follows.

Because a free exchange of ideas is essential to preserving a democratic society, the First Amendment to the U.S. Constitution states that "Congress shall make no law . . . abridging [diminishing] the freedom of speech, or the press." But do Americans always respect this right?

Free speech has often been attacked in the United States by those who have opposed the expression of ideas they didn't like. Opposition to wars or military service, controversial political opinions including support for Communism or Nazism, and pornography or racism on the Internet are just some of the issues that challenge people's tolerance for dissent.

The fear of permitting the expression of unpopular ideas is reflected in some people's efforts to censor books in the local public library. The question of banning books in public libraries and school libraries is at the heart of the readings in this unit. School programs and public libraries can choose whatever books they want to use. These programs are under the financial and political control of the individual states and local communities. In some communities, there are bitter disputes about the kinds of books children read in school and the kinds of books they read in the free local library. Today these disputes represent free speech issues.

In a small group, discuss these questions. Then tally your answers. Compare your answers with those of the other groups in the class.

CLASS POLL

	YES	NO	UNDECIDED
1. If a racist wanted to make a speech in your neighborhood, should he or she be allowed to do so?	_____	_____	_____
2. Should this person be allowed to teach in the local college?	_____	_____	_____
3. If this person writes a book, should the book be permitted in the local public library?	_____	_____	_____

VOCABULARY FOR COMPREHENSION

Read the following sentences. Match the underlined word(s) with a synonym from the list on page 223. Write the appropriate letter in the blank next to each sentence. Compare your answers with those of a partner.

_____ 1. Some of the most <u>famous and well-known</u> lawyers in America specialize in constitutional law, the study of which laws are allowed by the Constitution.

_____ 2. In the first half of the twentieth century, many books, such as *Lady Chatterley's Lover* by D. H. Lawrence and *Ulysses* by James Joyce, were <u>banned</u> and couldn't be sold in bookstores.

_____ 3. These books were prohibited because they were <u>supposedly</u> too sexual and immoral. Attitudes have changed today, and these books have earned the respect of serious scholars.

_____ 4. Most parents and schools forbid young children to use <u>swear</u> words and other bad language.

_____ 5. <u>Hiding behind</u> the right to free expression, some people today sell pornographic material that makes many Americans angry.

_____ 6. In recent years, the courts have <u>supported</u> efforts to restrict or eliminate pornography and violence as it relates to children.

_____ 7. Some people are also concerned about language that is <u>treating the name of God with contempt</u>, because such language goes against their religious beliefs.

_____ 8. Some parents are afraid that their children are learning <u>rude and disrespectful speech and behavior</u> from American culture, which is too free.

_____ 9. In the 1950s, civil rights organizations, whose members were both black and white, <u>went to court</u> to obtain equal treatment under the law for all Americans.

_____ 10. When the Supreme Court ruled to end legal separation of the races in schools in the 1954 decision *Brown v. Board of Education,* it created a situation <u>favorable</u> to future struggles for racial equality in other areas of social life.

_____ 11. After <u>considerable</u> study of the question, most Americans would agree that the Bill of Rights is a necessary part of our fundamental liberties.

_____ 12. If we pass laws to <u>restrict</u> the public expression of opinions we disagree with, we are limiting our own freedom and hurting democracy.

a. censored

g. profane

b. conducive

h. purportedly

c. curse

i. renowned

d. extensive

j. under the guise of

e. filed suit

k. upheld

f. inhibit

l. vulgarity

2 Focus on Reading

A   READING ONE: *Book Banning Must Be Stopped*

You are going to read an essay by Marcia Cohen entitled "Book Banning Must Be Stopped." It was written when the author was 19 years old and a sophomore (second-year student) at Brown University, and it appeared in Seventeen *magazine. Before you read, do the activity that follows.*

Judging from the title, the author, and the information given above, write three questions that you think this essay might answer.

1. _____

_____

2. _____

_____

3. _____

_____

BOOK BANNING MUST BE STOPPED

By Marcia Cohen (from *Seventeen*)

1   "I can't wait to go home and relax," my friend Marianne declared as she stuffed assorted articles of clothing into her overnight bag. After taking three midterm exams that week, Marianne planned a quiet evening at home. "Marcia, you're an English major," she said, looking up from her bag. "Can you think of a good book for me to read?" "How about *Native Son* or *To Kill a Mockingbird*?" I said. "Or did you ever read *Flowers for Algernon* or *Ordinary People*?"[1] The four books I recommended have something in common. Although good by my standards, each has been attacked as dangerous by certain people or groups in communities across the United States. Along with other works by renowned authors, such as Alice Walker, John Steinbeck, Kurt Vonnegut, and Mark Twain,[2] these books—four of my all-time favorites—have been challenged, censored, banned, burned, or removed from American schools and libraries in recent years.

2   Censorship of textbooks and other books in school libraries appears to be increasing in all parts of the country. People for the American Way, a Washington-based lobby group that recently conducted its fourth annual study of censorship, reports that incidents of censorship have increased 35 percent in the past year. In the past four years these incidents have more than doubled. Last July, the American Library Association published a list of more than five hundred books that have been banned, challenged, or removed from schools and public libraries around the country, ranging from *Harriet the Spy,* by Louise Fitzhugh (considered "dangerous" because it "teaches children to lie, spy, back-talk,[3] and curse"), to *The Merchant of Venice,* by William Shakespeare (purportedly anti-Semitic).

3   Often under the guise of upholding community values, censors attack books for profane or obscene language or for scenes of sex and violence. Apparently they believe that by shielding us, they will discourage us from adopting undesirable attitudes, speech, and behavior. The censors may mean well; however, I don't think teenagers encounter many words or details in books that they have not already been exposed to in real life. Besides, I am no more apt to swear after reading *Go Ask Alice* than I am to speak in blank verse[4] after reading *Macbeth*.

---

[1] *Native Son* by Richard Wright: a book about growing up black in America; it contains violent scenes; *To Kill a Mockingbird* by Harper Lee: a coming-of-age story set in the American South; *Flowers for Algernon* by Daniel Keyes: a book about a mentally retarded man; *Ordinary People* by Judith Guest: the story of an unhappy family

[2] *Alice Walker:* contemporary African-American writer; wrote *The Color Purple; John Steinbeck:* American novelist; wrote *Grapes of Wrath* about very poor farmworkers in California in the 1930s who fight back against injustice; *Kurt Vonnegut:* contemporary American writer; wrote *Slaughterhouse-Five* about the senseless horrors of war and becoming a prisoner of war in World War II Germany; *Mark Twain:* nineteenth-century American writer; wrote *The Adventures of Huckleberry Finn*

[3] *back-talk:* to "talk back" to your parents means to be rude and disobedient

[4] *blank verse:* a type of poetry that doesn't rhyme

4   Instead of zeroing in on certain passages or words they find offensive, these censors should focus on understanding the value of the work as a whole. For example, J. D. Salinger's *Catcher in the Rye,* which contains numerous four-letter words,[5] has been a recent target of criticism. In recent years, the novel has been challenged, banned, or removed in school districts in states including Washington, Ohio, Florida, and Michigan. Perhaps by examining this work as a whole, the censors would realize its real literary value. Through his protagonist's use of strong language in a clearly unnatural "tough kid" style, Salinger depicts the struggles of a vulnerable boy who hides behind a facade as he grows up in a world that frightens and confuses him. In this work, vulgar language emphasizes Salinger's message and serves a definite purpose.

5   Even more disturbing to me than attacks on so-called dirty books are those against books that express *ideas* with which censors—who are often political, social, or religious extremists—disagree.

6   In Alabama, the state textbook committee rejected thirty-seven textbooks after various conservative groups had objected that the books failed to reflect certain "religious and social philosophies." In Oregon, environmentalists wanted to remove a social studies book because they believed it contained "pro-industry propaganda."[6] And last July a group of fundamentalist Christian parents in Church Hill, Tennessee, filed suit against the county's public schools. The group argued that a series of schoolbooks preached "secular humanism,"[7] a doctrine that they said places man above God. In a ruling conducive to still more censorship, the judge upheld the parents' right to keep their children out of the reading classes.

7   This kind of censorship alarms me because it resonates with intolerance. Why must our access to reading materials be denied simply because they violate some group's aesthetic, moral, religious, or political views? Why should one group be allowed to impose its views on an entire classroom, school, or state? By submitting to the demands of one group, don't we limit the freedom of another?

8   Education should teach us to be tolerant and respectful of differences. These virtues cannot be taught in a classroom that bans books with "unacceptable" ideas.

9   As students, we read for many reasons. We read to explore life in certain historical periods, cultures, and regions. We read to examine problems of human justice, to explore basic issues of race, class, sex, and age. By encountering many different and conflicting ideas and beliefs, we learn to think critically, to ask intelligent questions, and to form our own opinions.

10   Educators, I think, should not tell us what to think but should teach us how to think. Rather than flatly stating whether a certain book has value, instructors and school officials should encourage us to read extensively and to decide for ourselves. By encouraging lively debates in the classroom, teachers can help us to clarify what we believe and why.

11   Book censorship, by inhibiting a free and open exchange of ideas, squelches[8] the vitality of our classrooms and threatens our freedom to learn. In addition, I cannot help but wonder about its implications. When our right to read is restricted, how safe can our other rights be?

---

[5] *four-letter words:* words that deal with bodily functions and are not used in public

[6] *"pro-industry propaganda":* information from industrialists that is one-sided or that misrepresents the views of the opposite side, that is, the environmentalists

[7] *"secular humanism":* a philosophy that seeks to encourage moral behavior without religion; these ideas are opposed by many fundamentalist Christians because they believe that people must follow the literal meaning of the Bible

[8] *squelch:* to suppress or stamp on

READING FOR MAIN IDEAS

On the left are the ideas Marcia Cohen disagrees with. On the right are her own views. Use your own words to fill in the blanks on the right. Compare your answers with those of another student.

Pro-Censorship Views

1. Some books will influence teenagers to use bad words and to behave badly.

   (paragraphs 3, 4)

2. Censorship is necessary because without it children will be exposed to points of view that conflict with their communities' political, social, religious, and moral beliefs.

   (paragraphs 6–11)

Marcia Cohen's Answers

1a. Teenagers have already heard bad words and decided whether they wanted to use them or not.

1b. Censors do not consider the artistic value

_____

_____

_____

2a. When you give in to some people's demands, you (freedom) you Are livi in someone ideas,

_____

_____

2b. Through education, we should learn to be Toleronte, free interprete a book

_____

2c. Students need to learn how to choose the best things in Theirs life

_____

2d. Teachers should teach their students _____ How to think and interprut someone's opniony.

_____

2e. Book censorship not only threatens our freedom _____ but also puts our

_____ in danger.

READING FOR DETAILS

Read the following quotes from Marcia Cohen's essay. Then circle the correct response. Compare your answers with another student's.

1. "Besides, I am no more apt to swear after reading *Go Ask Alice* than I am to speak in blank verse after reading *Macbeth*."

   This sentence means that _____.
   a. the author is going to speak in blank verse now
   b. the author is going to use bad language now
   c. the author is not going to speak in blank verse or use bad language

2. "In a ruling conducive to still more censorship, the judge upheld the parents' right to keep their children out of the reading classes."

   This sentence means that _____.
   a. the judge decided to limit censorship
   b. the judge's ruling agreed with the parents
   c. Marcia Cohen agreed with the judge

3. "As students, we read for many reasons."

   What are *not* reasons mentioned in the reading?
   a. to explore other cultures and past civilizations
   b. to examine important social questions
   c. to find entertainment and a release for our imagination

4. "Even more disturbing to me . . . are [attacks] . . . against books that express *ideas* with which censors . . . disagree."

   Which example of people trying to get books banned was mentioned in the reading?
   a. a group of environmentalists who didn't like a book that took the business point of view
   b. a group of religious fundamentalists objecting to Darwin's theory of evolution
   c. a group of mothers objecting to dirty words found in a school library book

5. "Censorship . . . threatens our freedom to learn."

   What explanation of this statement was *not* provided in the reading?
   a. Censorship means that some authors would have to go to prison.
   b. Censorship makes it impossible to have a free exchange of ideas.
   c. Censorship means that someone else would have to do our thinking for us.

REACTING TO THE READING

1 *Decide how you think Marcia Cohen would respond to the following statements. Answer by writing in the spaces provided, and give the paragraph number from the reading to support your opinion. Then discuss your answers with a partner.*

1. "Reading the *Communist Manifesto* is too dangerous."

   Ms. Cohen _would disagree. She would say that young people must be_ _allowed to explore different ideas and beliefs, even if these ideas are_ _unpopular, and that teachers should help young people learn to think_ _critically and to ask questions._

   Paragraph: _9_

2. "Asking students to read books both for and against the Vietnam War is a good way to learn."

   Ms. Cohen _____

   _____

   _____

   Paragraph: _____

3. "I don't want my science class to read about Darwin's theory of evolution because it goes against my personal religious beliefs in God's creation."

   Ms. Cohen _Disagree_

   _____

   _____

   Paragraph: _____

4. "All these men exchanging pornographic stories on the Internet . . . it's just disgusting and it ought to be stopped."

   Ms. Cohen _____

   _____

   _____

   Paragraph: _____

5. "Films should not be cut [edited] to eliminate violent or sexual content."

   Ms. Cohen _Agree_

   _____

   _____

   Paragraph: _____

6. "If we tell our children the truth about how our country treated Native Americans and slaves, our children will be ashamed of their heritage."

Ms. Cohen _disagree_____

_____

_____

Paragraph: _____

7. "The university administrators should dismiss professors who have extreme political opinions."

Ms. Cohen _disagree_____

_____

_____

Paragraph: _____

2 *Read these statements, and check (✓) if you **Agree** or **Disagree** with them. Then discuss the reasons for your answers in a small group.*

	Agree	Disagree
1. Educators should not tell us what to think but how to think.	✓	❑
2. Books that offend other people's values or religion should not be published.	❑	✓
3. Children under the age of eighteen should not be permitted to read whatever they want.	❑	✓
4. Education should teach us to be tolerant and respectful of differences.	✓	❑

B   READING TWO: *Some Books That Have Been Banned from School Libraries*

1 *In Reading Two you will learn more about books currently banned from some libraries and school districts in the United States. Before you read, discuss the following question with a partner.*

Do you think certain books should be banned from local or school libraries, or do you think libraries should be free to choose the books they want?

SOME BOOKS THAT HAVE BEEN BANNED FROM SCHOOL LIBRARIES

1. To Kill a Mockingbird, by Harper Lee

Through the eyes of two white children, nine-year-old Scout and her brother Jem, the reader follows the story of their lawyer father's defense of a black man falsely accused of raping a white girl in a southern town in the 1950s. Scout's family is rejected by the other white people in the town even though her father is only doing his duty, and Scout learns the meaning of conscience and human dignity. Some people do not approve of this book because it is about segregation[1] and a period in history that Americans are not proud of, and because it deals with rape and shows some adults getting drunk and violent.

"What did her father say, Tom? You must tell the jury what he said."
Tom Robinson shut his eyes tight. "He says you goddam whore, I'll kill ya."
"Tom, did you rape Mayella Ewell?"
"I did not suh."[2]

2. Ordinary People, by Judith Guest

Ordinary People is the story of a family that doesn't communicate. One son accidentally drowns, and his brother, Conrad, tries to kill himself out of guilt. When he is released from a mental hospital, Conrad returns home to try to improve his relationship with his parents. His father reaches out to him but his mother cannot, and the family breaks up. In the end, Conrad finally meets a girl he likes who has recovered from the terrible life she led in the past. Some parents do not like the book's themes of suicide and breakdown of the family.

"I started hanging around. You know, with kids my parents were afraid of. They were wild, I guess. Only not really, they were just stupid. And I was stupid. And I started doing a lot of stupid things with them." She sighs, her voice tired and flat. "Nothing interesting. Nothing even unusual, just the same old stuff. We smoked, we took

---

[1] *segregation:* from the late nineteenth century to the 1950s and 1960s in the southern United States, the races were separated in all aspects of daily life: separate schools, separate cars on trains, taxis, water fountains, toilets, etc., giving inferior treatment to black Americans

[2] *suh:* sir

pills, we junked around. Sometimes we needed money and kids stole stuff. I had enough money. My dad felt so bad about me by then he was keeping me well supplied, but I would go with them and steal, just for kicks.[3] And then one time we got caught."

3. The Harry Potter Series, by J. K. Rowling

The *Harry Potter* stories are about a young, neglected orphan who discovers that he has magical powers. He is invited to attend the Hogwarts School of Witchcraft and Wizardry, a boarding school in a magical world that is hidden from ordinary humans known as "muggles." Harry makes friends and tries to protect the world from the return of the evil wizard Voldemort, who took his parents' lives. Critics of these exciting stories object to fantasy involving witchcraft and consider it an insult to religion. Although Harry always defends good against evil, some people feel that reading about witches and the supernatural will undermine traditional spiritual values.

"Never wondered how you got that mark on your forehead? That was no ordinary cut. That's what you get when a powerful, evil curse touches you—took care of your mum and dad and your house even, but it didn't work on you, and that's why you're famous, Harry. You're the boy who lived!"

4. The Catcher in the Rye, by J. D. Salinger

This is a book about Holden Caulfield. Ever since Holden's younger brother died, he has been having trouble doing what is expected of him. After getting thrown out of three private schools, sixteen-year-old Holden is deeply depressed and runs away to New York to try to find the meaning of life. He hates snobs and superficial people and calls them all "phony."[4] But since most people and most things in the world are phony to him, some parents are concerned about what they see as the antisocial message of this book as well as the four-letter words.

We horsed around a bit in the cab on the way over to the theatre. At first she didn't want to, because she had her lipstick on and all, but I was being seductive as hell and she didn't have any alternative. Twice, when the goddam cab stopped short in traffic, I damn near fell off the seat. Those damn drivers never even look where they're going, I swear they don't. Then, just to show you how crazy I am, when we were coming out of this big clinch, I told her I loved her and all. It was a lie, of course, but the thing is, I meant it when I said it. I'm crazy, I swear to God I am . . .

---

[3] *just for kicks:* just for fun
[4] *a phony:* an insincere person, a false person

Anyway, I'm sort of glad they've got the atomic bomb invented. If there's ever another war, I'm going to sit right the hell on top of it. I'll volunteer for it, I swear to God I will.

5. Heather Has Two Mommies, by Leslea Newman

This is a book about a lesbian couple who are raising a three-year-old daughter. The book explains that many children in America today are growing up in nontraditional families. According to this book, even though families do not always have a mother and a father, they can still be loving and caring. Some people do not want children to read this book because they fear it undermines their religious values and the traditional idea of the family.

A long time ago, before Heather was born, Mama Jane and Mama Kate were very good friends. After they were friends for a long long time, Kate and Jane realized that they were very much in love with each other. They decided they wanted to live together and be a family together.

6. The Grapes of Wrath, by John Steinbeck

The Grapes of Wrath was first published in 1939. It is the story of the Joad family, pushed off their land in Oklahoma by the banks and big agricultural interests. As unwilling migrants, they travel to California with many others and go from farm to farm, working for so little money that they can hardly eat. In a land of plenty, they are starving. Some people don't like this book because it shows American injustice to the poor, because it shows people so desperate that they do sad and terrible things, because much of the dialogue is written in a dialect of non-standard English, and because it shows how the have-nots fight back and try to form workers' unions.

Ma said, "How'm I gonna know 'bout you? They might kill ya an' I wouldn't know.". . .
"I'll be ever'where—wherever you look. Wherever they's a fight so hungry people can eat, I'll be there. Wherever they's a cop beatin' up a guy, I'll be there. If Casey knowed, why, I'll be in the way guys yell when they're mad an'—I'll be in the way kids laugh when they're hungry and they know supper's ready. An' when our folks eat the stuff they raise an' live in the houses they build—why, I'll be there."

2 *Work in pairs. Try to imagine what the six authors would say to defend the value of their works. Student A should write the authors' defenses of books 1, 2, and 3, and Student B should write the counterarguments. Then switch roles for books 4, 5, and 6.*

Student A	Student B

1.   **To Kill a Mockingbird**

Harper Lee

Author's Defense: *Counterargument:*

_____   _____

_____   _____

_____   _____

_____   _____

_____   _____

2.   **Ordinary People**

Judith Guest

Author's Defense: *Counterargument:*

_____   _____

_____   _____

_____   _____

_____   _____

_____   _____

3.   **Harry Potter**

J. K. Rowling

Author's Defense: *Counterargument:*

_____   _____

_____   _____

_____   _____

_____   _____

Student A	Student B

4.

The Catcher in the Rye
J. D. Salinger

Author's Defense: *Counterargument:*

_____   _____

_____   _____

_____   _____

_____   _____

_____   _____

5.

Heather Has Two Mommies
Leslea Newman

Author's Defense: *Counterargument:*

_____   _____

_____   _____

_____   _____

_____   _____

_____   _____

6.

The Grapes of Wrath
John Steinbeck

Author's Defense: *Counterargument:*

_____   _____

_____   _____

_____   _____

_____   _____

_____   _____

C LINKING READINGS ONE AND TWO

It is your turn to write what you think about banning books in schools and libraries. On a separate sheet of paper, write your opinion about the issues raised in Readings One and Two. Then form small groups, and take turns reading your opinions to each other. Discuss your agreements and disagreements, and answer the following questions.

1. How many people in the group agreed with you? _____

2. How many disagreed? _____

3. Among those who agreed with you, were there any arguments and ideas you hadn't thought of? Summarize them.

4. Among those who disagreed, were there any arguments that convinced you to change your mind? Summarize them.

3 Focus on Vocabulary

1 *Working in groups, fill in the chart below with other forms of the words from the readings. Use the dictionary if necessary. (An **X** indicates that no word belongs in that space either because no such word exists or because it is not commonly used.)*

	Noun	Verb	Adjective	Adverb
1.	access			X
2.	X		conducive	X
3.		confuse		
4.		expose		X
5.		inhibit		
6.			offensive	
7.			profane	
8.		remove		X
9.		shield	X	X
10.		X	vulnerable	

2 *The letter that follows was written by a parent to the principal of the high school her children are attending. Complete the letter by placing the correct words from this box in the blanks.*

access	confused	inhibiting	profanities	shield
conducive	exposed	offensive	remove	vulnerable

Dear Mr. Anderson:

I have decided to write to you today because I have learned that the novel *Ordinary People* is going to be read this year in all tenth-grade English classes. I am very upset about this decision and would like you to (1) _____ this book from the proposed curriculum. Let me explain why I believe this should be done.

First of all, *Ordinary People* is (2) _____ to me because it gives teenagers the message that it is normal or "ordinary" these days to have sex with one another. Moreover, the teenagers in the book use language that is full of (3) _____.

In my opinion, there is no reason why children should have (4) _____ to such reading material. I say this because vulgar language is definitely bad for children. My children, like all children their age, are too young and (5) _____ to be (6) _____ to such obscene language and behavior. Without the proper guidance, they may end up speaking and behaving that way.

Another reason why I object to the book is that *Ordinary People* also communicates the message that "ordinary" families are falling apart these days. I find this viewpoint to be particularly alarming because it is totally contrary to the image that I want my children to have of the family. I am trying to teach my children family values so that they will have the greatest respect for family life and the kind of security it provides. If they learn things in school that conflict with what they see in their life at home, they will be very (7) _____.

I can only say that as a parent, I am very much aware of the fact that parents need to (8) _____ their children from any references to the ugly realities of life. It is for this reason that I do not want to send my children to school to learn about the difficulties only a minority of people experience. Instead, I want their school lessons to reflect the morally healthy lifestyles that the majority of the people in their community lead. I uphold this view because I truly believe that a certain unity needs to exist between the home and the school. And if this kind of unity is not achieved, our schools will be guilty of (9) _____ rather than encouraging our children's growth. Furthermore, once this happens, the potential value of their education will be undermined, and we will have no hope of ever producing good and loyal citizens for American democracy.

I do hope you will consider my request. Deep in my heart, I know that the inclusion of *Ordinary People* in the school's curriculum is not (10) _____ to the kind of education my children deserve to receive.

Thank you for your kind attention to this matter.

Sincerely,

Elizabeth Jones

Elizabeth Jones

3 *Explain the meaning of the underlined words from Reading Two. Choose the best possible answer. Compare your answers with those of a partner.*

1. "Scout learns the meaning of <u>conscience</u> . . ."
   a. ethics
   b. consciousness
   c. thought

2. "His father <u>reaches out to him</u> . . ."
   a. tries to hold on to him
   b. tries to scold him
   c. tries to communicate with him

3. "She has <u>recovered from</u> the life she led in the past."
   a. a better life than
   b. a worse life than
   c. a life similar to

4. Some people feel that reading about witches in *Harry Potter* will <u>undermine</u> traditional spiritual values.
   a. weaken
   b. support
   c. dramatize

5. Holden Caulfield was "<u>thrown out of</u> three private schools . . ."
   a. accepted to
   b. expelled from
   c. suspended from

6. "In a land of <u>plenty</u> . . ."
   a. prosperity
   b. scarcity
   c. poverty

4 *Write the school principal's letter of response to the parent's complaint in Exercise 2 on pages 236 to 237. Use eight of the following vocabulary words from this unit in your letter.*

access	confused	extensive	profane	shield
censor	conscience	inhibit	remove	~~vulnerable~~
conducive	exposed	~~offensive~~	renowned	undermine

Dear Ms. Jones,

   I received your letter today, and I understand that you are worried about how **vulnerable** young people of 15 and 16 years of age will react to a work of literature that may be **offensive** to the values of their family. Let me explain our thinking on this matter. _____

_____

_____

_____

_____

_____

_____

_____

Sincerely,

Laurence Anderson

Laurence Anderson, Principal

4 Focus on Writing

A   GRAMMAR: Review of Verb Tenses

1 *Examine the following sentences with a partner. Indicate whether the underlined verbs refer to the past, present, or future. Then identify any words that are used to indicate the need for each tense, for example, **since**.*

1. The Constitution <u>has been functioning</u> as the supreme law of the United States since April 30, 1789, when George Washington became the first president.

2. Although the Constitution <u>was</u> officially <u>approved</u> on June 21, 1788, it <u>had been written</u> by the Founding Fathers almost a year before, in the summer of 1787, at the Constitutional Convention.

3. The people were afraid that the rights they <u>had enjoyed</u> up to then would be taken away by the new Constitution, which <u>spoke</u> only of the branches of government and <u>said</u> nothing about the rights of the individual.

4. People <u>were</u> therefore <u>protesting</u> quite angrily about the lack of guarantees for individual liberties when the Constitution <u>was</u> finally <u>approved</u> on June 21, 1788.

5. With the support of James Madison, the first ten amendments to the Constitution <u>were approved</u> in 1791.

6. These amendments—which <u>guarantee</u> freedom of worship, of speech, of the press, of assembly, and other rights such as the right to live safely within the privacy of one's home without fear of the police—<u>are known</u> as the Bill of Rights.

7. The Bill of Rights <u>has been</u> the basis of American democracy for more than 200 years now.

8. By the year 2091, when a great celebration will undoubtedly take place, the Bill of Rights <u>will have existed</u> for 300 years as the protector of our freedom.

Verb Tenses

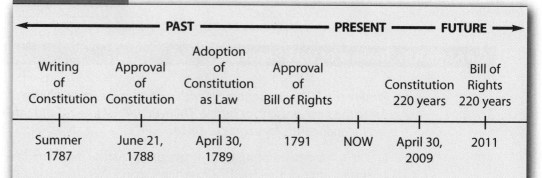

Simple Past Tense

Use the **simple past tense** to refer to an action or state of being that happened only once on a specific date in the past, or to refer to a series of actions or states of being that occurred over a period of time in the past:

Specific Date in the Past

- The Constitution **was approved** on June 21, 1788.

- George Washington **became** the first president on April 30, 1789.

- The first ten amendments to the Constitution **were approved** in 1791.

Series of Actions That Occurred over a Period of Time in the Past

- It **took** about four years for the Bill of Rights to become a reality.

- During that period, people **argued** that the Constitution did not guarantee their individual rights.

- People **were** afraid that their individual liberties would be taken away.

Past Perfect Tense and Simple Past Tense

Use the **past perfect tense** when referring to two related past events, where one occurred before the other. Because we know that the Constitution "had been written by the Founding Fathers almost a year before" it was approved, we need to use the past perfect tense for the action that occurred first and the simple past for the second event:

- Although the Constitution ⌐— simple past —⌐ **was** officially **approved** on June 21, 1788,

  it ⌐— past perfect —⌐ **had been written** by the Founding Fathers almost a year before in the summer of 1787, at the Constitutional Convention.

Past Progressive Tense and Simple Past Tense

Use the **past progressive tense** in conjunction with the simple past tense when referring to an action that was taking place at the same time ("when") another action took place:

- People **were** therefore **protesting** quite angrily about the lack of guarantees for individual liberties when the Constitution **was** finally **approved** on June 21, 1788.

Past Perfect Progressive Tense and Simple Past Tense

Use the **past perfect progressive** tense in conjunction with the simple past tense when referring to an action that had already been taking place for a period of time when another action took place:

- People **had** already **been protesting** quite angrily *for almost a year* about the lack of guarantees for individual liberties *when* the Constitution **was** finally **approved** on June 21, 1788.

Present Perfect Tense and Present Perfect Progressive Tense

The **present perfect tense** and the **present perfect progressive tense** are both a combination of the past tense and the present tense. We know that the Constitution began to function on April 30, 1789, in the past and that it still functions/is still functioning in the present. Use these tenses to show that an action or state of being that started in the past continues/is continuing in the present:

- The Constitution **has functioned** officially as the supreme law of the United States since April 30, 1789.
- The Bill of Rights **has been** the basis of American democracy for more than 200 years now.
- The Constitution **has been functioning** officially as the supreme law of the United States since April 30, 1789.

For the present perfect and past perfect progressive tenses, the operative words are *since* (followed by the specific date: *since April 30, 1789*) or *for* (followed by the length of the period of time: *for 200 years*).

(continued)

Future Perfect Tense and Future Perfect Progressive Tense

The future tense is used when we refer to how things will be in the future. Use the **future perfect tense** and the **future perfect progressive tense** to say "definite" things about the completion of events in the future. For instance, because the Constitution will have functioned/will have been functioning as the official law of the land for 300 years by the specific date, April 30, 2009, we are making a statement about a "definite" fact of the future:

- The Constitution **will have functioned** (future perfect) officially as the supreme law of the United States for 220 years by April 30, 2009.

- *By* 2011, when a great celebration will undoubtedly take place, the Bill of Rights **will have existed** (future perfect) *for* 220 years as the protector of our freedom.

- The Constitution **will have been functioning** (future perfect progressive) officially as the supreme law of the United States for 220 years *by* April 30, 2009.

For the future perfect and future perfect progressive tenses, the operative words are *by* (followed by the specific date or *then*: *by April 30, 2009* or *by then*) and *for* (followed by the length of the period of time: *for 220 years*).

2 *Work in pairs. Read the time line about Mark Twain and his masterpiece,* The Adventures of Huckleberry Finn. *Then complete the sentences with the correct verb tenses.*

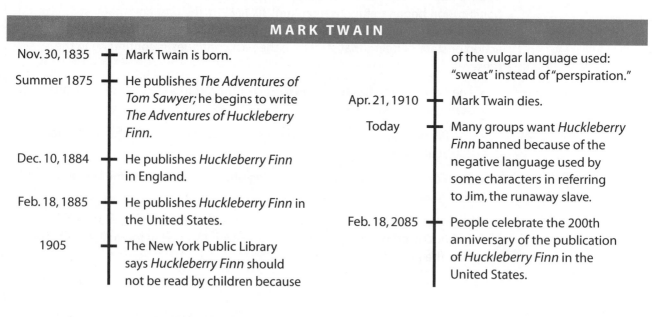

MARK TWAIN	
Nov. 30, 1835	Mark Twain is born.
Summer 1875	He publishes *The Adventures of Tom Sawyer;* he begins to write *The Adventures of Huckleberry Finn.*
Dec. 10, 1884	He publishes *Huckleberry Finn* in England.
Feb. 18, 1885	He publishes *Huckleberry Finn* in the United States.
1905	The New York Public Library says *Huckleberry Finn* should not be read by children because of the vulgar language used: "sweat" instead of "perspiration."
Apr. 21, 1910	Mark Twain dies.
Today	Many groups want *Huckleberry Finn* banned because of the negative language used by some characters in referring to Jim, the runaway slave.
Feb. 18, 2085	People celebrate the 200th anniversary of the publication of *Huckleberry Finn* in the United States.

1. Since 1905, there _____ a controversy about the
   (has been/is/had been)
   appropriateness of *The Adventures of Huckleberry Finn* for young readers.

2. Mark Twain _____ *Huckleberry Finn* when he
   (had published/published/publishes)
   _____ 49 years old.
   (had been/is/was)

3. When *Huckleberry Finn* _____ in the United States
   (were published/published/was published)
   on February 18, 1885, *The Adventures of Tom Sawyer*

   _____ already _____ a
   (have/has/had)   (became/becomes/become)
   favorite of American readers.

4. When *Huckleberry Finn* _____ in the United States,
   (is published/had published/was published)
   it _____ already _____ in
   (had/has/will have)   (be/been/is)
   print in England for more than two months.

5. Readers _____ the book for at least 20 years when,
   (enjoyed/had enjoyed/were enjoying)
   in 1905, the New York Public Library upheld the view that it was not

   appropriate for children because of the vulgar language used.

6. When Mark Twain _____ , people
   (dies/is dying/died)
   _____ still _____ the
   (was/were/had)   (questioned/questioning/questions)
   literary value of *Huckleberry Finn*.

7. When many groups try to ban the book today, they do so because they

   _____ concerned about the ugly words used by
   (had been/were/are)
   some characters in the book to describe Jim, the runaway slave.

8. By the year 2085, *Huckleberry Finn* _____ by
   (will be read/will have been read/had been read)
   young readers for two centuries.

3 *Work with a partner. The following text is about the U.S. Supreme Court, the highest court in the United States, which decides how to interpret the Constitution. Complete these paragraphs about free speech for students by filling in the blanks with the correct tense of the verbs provided. The verbs can be in the active or passive voice.*

How the Supreme Court Has Changed

In 1969, when school administrators _____ it difficult for
1. (make)
students to demonstrate against the Vietnam War, the nine Justices of the

Supreme Court _____ that "students do not shed their rights to
            2. (rule)

freedom of speech or expression at the schoolhouse gate." In other words,

students have the same right to free speech that adults have. But by 1988, the

Supreme Court _____ much more conservative. The new Justices
            3. (become)

_____ restrictions on students' First Amendment rights when they
  4. (put)

_____ a high school principal who _____ student
  5. (support)   6. (remove)

articles on teen pregnancy and divorce from a school newspaper. When this

decision _____ , some people were very shocked because students
       7. (make)

_____ their right to free speech for nineteen years!
  8. (enjoy)

Since 1988, there _____ a growing debate in the United States
             9. (be)

about the free speech rights of students under eighteen years of age. Some people

are happy that the more conservative Supreme Court of recent years has

changed the 1969 ruling. They insist that high school students

_____ not mature enough to deal with such sensitive issues as
    10. (be)

pregnancy, drug addiction, and divorce. But others maintain that if students are

not allowed to present their views on sensitive issues in school newspapers, they

_____ to participate fully in a democratic society's free exchange
  11. (prepare—use "not")

of ideas when they are no longer in school. For these people, the 1988 ruling

_____ a form of censorship. After all, "If you can't write it, you
    12. (legalize)

can't read it." Looking to the future, they wonder by what point in time they

_____ in convincing people that students have rights, too.
  13. (succeed)

B   STYLE: Argumentative Essays

1 *Reread "Book Banning Must Be Stopped" by Marcia Cohen. Think about why her essay is successful in presenting its arguments. How does she organize her arguments to make them clear and forceful? What language does she use to argue for her point of view? Discuss these questions with a partner, and find examples from her essay that contribute to making it a strong one.*

Argumentative Essays

Introduction and Thesis Statement

The aim of an **argumentative essay** is to convince the reader to agree with the author's point of view or opinion. An argumentative essay tries to be very persuasive by appealing to *reason* and *logic*.

An argumentative essay must introduce and explain the background to the issue or problem. But, in the thesis statement, the author must take a stand and present his or her point of view *strongly* and *clearly*. In addition, an argumentative essay usually suggests a course of action for the future, such as "we must stop banning books."

Supporting Your Views

In most good argumentative essays, the writer's point of view is obvious in the first paragraph. However, an essay is not a mere opinion. The body of the essay should provide support or reasons for the author's point of view: factual details, explanations, examples, and even, in appropriate cases, anecdotes from personal experience.

Refuting Opposing Points of View

Writing an argumentative essay is like taking one side in a debate, either for or against. The writer must not only show that his or her ideas are correct; he must also show that his opponent's views are wrong. Refuting an opponent's views involves showing why the opponent's arguments are incorrect. To be effective, an argumentative essay must contain a point-by-point **refutation** of the main arguments of the opposing view.

Concession

If an opponent has a valid point or expresses an idea that is true, the writer must, in honesty, concede it. It is very rare that the arguments on one side are *all* bad and on the other *all* good. After admitting that the opposition may have a good point, the writer can go on to show that overall, his or her reasons are superior to the opponents' views. For example, supporters of book banning say that children must be guided and protected by their parents. Even someone who is against book banning can realize that parents do have a duty to guide their children. An opponent to book banning could write a **concession** like this:

- Although it is true that parents must guide their children's development, censorship is not the best way to accomplish this because it does not allow for the development of critical thinking skills.

(continued)

Every argumentative essay should have at least one concession to show some understanding of the ideas of the opposite side. The concession should not appear in the conclusion, and it cannot be allowed to change the main idea or divert attention from the thesis statement of the essay.

Conclusion

The **conclusion** should follow logically from the arguments in the essay. It summarizes the main ideas and reaffirms the thesis. It may also offer suggestions.

2 *Go back to Marcia Cohen's essay. In which paragraphs does she provide the reasons, explanations, and examples that support her views? Underline the passage that refutes the specific ideas of her opponents about a book. Do you find any concession in her essay?*

3 *Work in a small group. First reread the letter on pages 236–237, in which a supporter of censorship gives reasons in favor of banning books. Come up with counterarguments to refute this point of view. Use the vocabulary from the readings.*

Then write an outline for an essay defending the need for book banning. Go through Marcia Cohen's anticensorship essay, and think of ways that you could refute each of her main arguments, which are outlined in the chart below. List your refutations in the space provided, and make at least one concession.

Anticensorship (Marcia Cohen's view)

Refutation

1. Censors do not consider the artistic merit of the book as a whole but only focus on specific parts out of context.

2. Censorship represents intolerance toward other people's ideas.

3. When some people don't like a book, they want to ban it and take it away from all of us. Censorship will take away our freedom to decide for ourselves.

4. Teenagers should be allowed to make up their own minds about important issues. That is the best training for the citizens of a democracy.

Concession

C   WRITING TOPICS

Choose one of the following topics, and write a well-organized response agreeing or disagreeing with the opinion expressed. Be sure to support your point of view with explanations and examples. Include a refutation of the main ideas of your opponents and one concession. Use the vocabulary you studied in this unit, and make sure the verb tenses are appropriate.

1. "We all know that books burn—yet we have the greater knowledge that books cannot be killed by fire. People die but books never die. No man and no force can abolish memory."

   —Franklin Delano Roosevelt, 1942

   Explain the meaning of this quote. Do you agree or disagree with this statement?

2. *Opinion:* Citizens should love and respect their country whatever happens. This is especially true of the national flag. Burning the flag because you disagree with a government policy or a war effort is unpatriotic and disrespectful to soldiers and fellow citizens. Flag burning should be forbidden.

   Write an essay agreeing or disagreeing with this opinion statement.

3. The museum director in a small town has been arrested because the museum has shown an exhibit of photographs, some of which are considered pornographic. Conservatives in the town feel that a museum which families attend together is no place for "dirty pictures." The director claims that the photos are only one part of a larger exhibit by a renowned artist. He has placed the erotic pictures in a special section of the museum where only adults over eighteen years of age may enter.

   What do you think? Should the museum director be arrested for promoting obscenity or not? Argue your case.

4. *Opinion:* Freedom only for the supporters of the government, only for the members of one party—however numerous they may be—is no freedom at all. Freedom is always and only freedom for the one who thinks differently.

   Explain the meaning of this statement. Do you agree or disagree with this definition of freedom of expression?

5. "We hold these truths to be self evident, that all men are created equal, endowed [given] by their Creator with certain inalienable rights, that among these are life, liberty and the pursuit of happiness. That to secure these rights, governments are instituted among men, deriving their just powers from the consent of the governed. Whenever any form of government becomes destructive of these ends, it is the right of the people to alter or abolish it. . . . When a long train of abuses . . . evinces [shows] a design to reduce them to absolute despotism, it is their right, it is their duty, to throw off such government."

—*The Declaration of Independence*, 1776

This passage from the Declaration of Independence defends the need for revolution if a government destroys its people's natural rights. Do you agree or disagree? What are these natural rights, according to the Declaration? Does this passage offer a good basis for government? Can you give other examples of people demanding their rights?

D RESEARCH TOPICS

PREPARATION

We have seen how important the issues of free speech are in American life. You are going to do research on an important free speech issue of your choice. You may choose any issue that is currently being debated anywhere in the world, such as freedom to criticize the government, publishing pornography, prayer in public schools, or creating Web sites that promote discrimination against people because of their religion, ethnicity, or sexual orientation. Before you begin:

1. Form a small group, and discuss with the members of your group which free speech issues are most important to you. Identify the one free speech issue that you would like to research.

2. You will need to consider the kinds of questions that will guide you in your research. You may want to consider the following:

   • the existence of a formal document guaranteeing free speech rights in the area in question

   • the reasons for the current struggle

   • the background of the groups fighting for free speech rights

   • the background of the groups resisting their demands

   • other significant historical details

3. Brainstorm with the group to consider other aspects of the problem that might be important.

RESEARCH ACTIVITY

If you were not able to identify a free-speech issue of interest to you during your group discussion, you will need to read newspapers, "surf" the Internet, or consult a local librarian for help. You may also want to write to the following international human rights organizations for information:

Amnesty International
322 Eighth Avenue
New York, New York 10001
U.S.A.
www.amnesty.org

The International Committee of the Red Cross
19 Avenue de la Paix
CH-1202 Geneva, Switzerland
www.icrc.org

The United Nations Human Rights Commission
Center for Human Rights Office at Geneva
CH-1211 Geneva 10, Switzerland
www.unhchr.ch

Once you identify an issue that you would like to study, use all of the above resources—newspapers, the Internet, the library, international organizations, and so on—to help complete your research.

SHARING YOUR FINDINGS

Write a report. Explain to your group all aspects of the issue you studied. Be sure to focus on the opposing views and to give your own viewpoint as well.

For step-by-step practice in the writing process, see the *Writing Activity Book, Advanced,* Unit 10.

Assignment	Argumentative Essay
Prewriting	Choosing a Technique
Organizing	Including Counterarguments and Refutations
Revising	Writing Persuasive Introductions
	Using Tenses Correctly
Editing	Proofreading

For Unit 10 Internet activities, visit the NorthStar Companion Website at http://longman.com/northstar.

Student Information

1B. Sharing Information, page 220

The question is not whether most Americans agree or disagree with flag burning, pornography, and so on, but whether such expression is protected under the Constitution's guarantee of free speech. Examples of speech that are not protected by the First Amendment include libel (destroying a private person's reputation in writing), slander (destroying such a reputation in speech), and inciting to riot. Even in these cases, however, there is no "prior restraint," meaning that the government cannot forbid the publication of a book or article. Authors assume the responsibility and suffer the consequences if their work is prosecuted in the courts after the fact.

1. In the United States, there are no laws against blasphemy (insulting a religion), and, according to the separation of religion and the state written into the First Amendment, people can think and write what they choose about God.

2. Citizens have burned the American flag as a protest against war—for example, during the Vietnam War and the Gulf War. The Supreme Court ruled that flag burning is allowed as free-speech protest.

3. In 1996 a federal court ruled that the Internet, "the never-ending, world-wide conversation" and "the most participatory form of mass speech yet developed," deserves "the highest protection from government intrusion." In other words, there should be no censorship on the Internet. There is not even any government regulation of the Internet, as there is for television. However, any kind of pornography involving children on the Internet and everywhere else is illegal and is prosecuted.

4. Threats to free speech have existed in America in times of war (during the Civil War, President Lincoln barred mail and newspapers sympathetic to the enemy; Socialists were jailed for encouraging resistance to World War I). During the cold war (a period of political tension between the United States and the Soviet Union, 1945–1990), people were jailed or lost their jobs if they were accused of being Communists. During the Vietnam War, however, many people encouraged opposition to the war and were not arrested.

5. The press and public in the United States are free to criticize the president.

6. In the 1973 case *Miller v. California,* the Supreme Court declared that a work must be "patently offensive" (obviously disgusting) and lack all artistic, literary, political, or scientific value to be declared legally obscene. Because a definition of obscenity is difficult to arrive at, it is hard to get juries to prosecute such a crime. In addition, many Americans dislike the idea of censorship. However, in the 1980s many parent groups began encouraging the use of warning labels on musical recordings containing material that they considered inappropriate for children under age 18.

Grammar Book References

NorthStar: Reading and Writing, Advanced, Second Edition	Focus on Grammar 5, Third Edition	Azar's Understanding and Using English Grammar, Third Edition
Unit 1 Past Unreal Conditionals	**Unit 23** Conditionals; Other ways to Express Unreality	**Chapter 20** Conditional Sentences and Wishes: 20-4
Unit 2 Noun Clauses	**Unit 21** Noun Clauses: Subjects, Objects and Complements	**Chapter 12** Noun Clauses: 12-1, 12-2, 12-3, 12-4, 12-5
Unit 3 Identifying and Nonidentifying Adjective Clauses	**Unit 11** Adjective Clauses: Review and Expansion **Unit 12** Adjective Clauses with Prepositions: Adjective Phrases	**Chapter 13** Adjective Clauses
Unit 4 Adverb Clauses and Discourse Connectors	**Unit 18** Adverbs Clauses **Unit 20** Connectors	**Chapter 17** Adverb Clauses: 17-2 **Chapter 19** Connectives that Express Cause and Effect, Contrast, and Condition: 19-1, 19-2, 19-3, 19-4
Unit 5 Adverb Clauses of Comparison and Contrast	**Unit 18** Adverb Clauses **Unit 20** Connectors	**Chapter 17** Adverb Clauses: 17-3, 17-4 **Chapter 19** Connectives that Express Cause and Effect, Contrast, and Condition: 19-6

NorthStar: Reading and Writing, Advanced, Second Edition	Focus on Grammar, Advanced, Second Edition	Azar's Understanding and Using English Grammar, Third Edition
Unit 6 Definite and Indefinite Articles with Count and Non-Count Nouns	**Unit 7** Count and Non-Count Nouns **Unit 8** Definite and Indefinite Articles	**Chapter 7** Nouns: 7-7, 7-8
Unit 7 Specific Uses of Gerunds and Infinitives	**Unit 16** Infinitives **Unit 15** Gerunds	**Chapter 14** Gerunds and Infinitives, Part 1 **Chapter 15** Gerunds and Infinitives, Part 2
Unit 8 Direct and Indirect Speech	**Unit 22** Direct and Indirect Speech	**Chapter 12** Noun Clauses: 12-6, 12-7
Unit 9 Reporting Ideas and Facts with Passives	**Unit 13** The Passive: Review and Expansion **Unit 14** The Passive to Describe Situations and to Report Opinions	**Chapter 11** The Passive: 11-1, 11-2, 11-3
Unit 10 Review of Verb Tenses	**Unit 1** Present and Future Time **Unit 2** Past Time **Unit 3** Simple and Progressive: Action and Non-Action Verbs	**Chapter 1** Overview of Verb Tenses